T0066986

1001
HUNTING TIPS

THE ULTIMATE GUIDE TO TAKING DEER, BIG AND SMALL GAME, UPLAND BIRDS, AND WATERFOWL

LAMAR UNDERWOOD
and
NATE MATTHEWS

Illustrations by John Rice

Photographs by Tim Irwin

Skyhorse Publishing

Copyright © 2010, 2022 by Lamar Underwood and Nate Matthews

Illustrations copyright © 2010 by John Rice

Photographs copyright © 2010 by Tim Irwin, except on pages 86, 130, 240, 249, 266, 332, and 350.

All Rights Reserved. No part of this book may be reproduced in any manner without the express written consent of the publisher, except in the case of brief excerpts in critical reviews or articles. All inquiries should be addressed to Skyhorse Publishing, 555 Eighth Avenue, Suite 903, New York, NY 10018.

Skyhorse Publishing books may be purchased in bulk at special discounts for sales promotion, corporate gifts, fund-raising, or educational purposes. Special editions can also be created to specifications. For details, contact the Special Sales Department, Skyhorse Publishing, 555 Eighth Avenue, Suite 903, New York, NY 10018 or info@skyhorsepublishing.com.

www.skyhorsepublishing.com

10 9 8 7 6 5 4 3 2 1

Library of Congress Cataloging-in-Publication Data

Underwood, Lamar.
  1001 hunting tips : the ultimate guide-deer, upland game and birds, waterfowl, big game / Lamar Underwood.
    p. cm.
  ISBN 978-1-5107-6678-5 (pbk. : alk. paper)
  1. Hunting--Handbooks, manuals, etc. 2. Deer hunting--Handbooks, manuals, etc. 3. Fowling--Handbooks, manuals, etc. I. Title.
  SK33.U53 2010
  799.2--dc22
                          2010032538

Cover Design by Kai Texel

Printed in the United States of America

Contents

Acknowledgments

Nate Matthews and I would like to express our deepest appreciation to the following folks, without whose efforts this book would not have been possible: Tony Lyons, creator of Skyhorse Publishing and the man who drives the wagon there; Jay Cassell, for his stewardship and editing prowess; John Rice, whose superb artwork brings the pages alive with feeling; writers Nick Sisley and John E. Phillips for special contributions.

—Lamar Underwood

About the Photographer

Most of the photographs in this book (and some of the tips) are by the very talented Tim Irwin, whose Madison Agency in Montana is a prime source for photographs, handling advertising accounts, and creating brochures. You can see Tim's entire photo gallery on his Web site, www.TimIrwinImages.com. The word "multitasker" should have a picture of Tim beside it in the dictionary. For his clients, he not only takes the photographs, but he also writes the copy and does all the layout and production work himself. Contact Tim at The Madison Agency, 135 Little Bear Rd. West, Gallatin Gateway, Montana 59730. 406-763-4900. His email is tim@madisonadz.com.

Introduction

The other evening, after I had spent the day going over material for this book, my wife made a remark that brought doubt and fear crashing into my thoughts like lightning bolts. She simply said, "The newspaper had a section today called '101 Grilling Tips.' I looked at them all and didn't find a single one to be useful."

Suddenly, I felt almost ill. I thought about picking up the phone and calling Nate Matthews, my co-editor and writer on this book. Was a fate similar to "101 Grilling Tips" in store for our book—multiplied ten times? Were our tips destined to be ignored, cast aside with shrugs and expressions of disappointment? It didn't seem possible, yet there it was: the possibility that we would not connect with our audience.

Instead of allowing my anguish to continue unabated, I decided to look at "101 Grilling Tips" myself. I only liked a couple of the tips. The others were bland, without any juice to make me want to whip the cover off the Weber. My confidence in the work Nate and I were finishing began to rise again. Later, over the next few days as I gave our tips a final reading, that confidence level peaked out again. Today, ready to commit our tips to print, I guarantee our readers that they are going to find many, many useful tips. And I shall go even further by saying that many of the tips are so important that they mean the difference between success and failure on your hunt.

Yes, a single tip on hunting can carry that kind of importance behind it. If followed, it can mean you're literally bringing home the bacon. Ignored or forgotten, it can mean you're coming home only with that tired old expression, "Sure was nice being in the woods today." Yea . . . sure . . . it *was* nice. There's no disputing *that*. But you have nothing new to put into the freezer.

Allow me, if you will, to try to press my point about tips home with an example.

My personal deer hunting education was slow in evolving. I'm an Army brat, who grew up mostly in the south where my hunting was focused on smoothbore opportunities. Using dogs to drive deer to standers was still in vogue back then and never appealed to me, especially with the great hunting we had for quail, doves, ducks, squirrels, and rabbits.

There came a long-awaited morning, however, when as a young man I became a serious player in the great game known as whitetail deer hunting. I was settled against the trunk of an enormous white oak in the heart of classic whitetail country among the folded hills and ridges of Pennsylvania. Under a flashlight's glow, with my friend Larry's direction, I had swept aside leaves and sticks to make my nest as quiet as possible. I had a pack with a thermos and sandwiches, and in my hands rested a Winchester lever-action .30-30 with iron sights. The rifle triggered memories of the Daisy Red Ryder I had grown up using. When I was all set, Larry moved away to work another part of the ridge.

At first light, the horizon was cut from steel—black lumps of white pines, the knife-like rim of a distant ridge looming above the forest. Without wind, the stillness seemed almost electric as I shivered in the cold, nervous to the raw edge at the thought of a buck coming my way.

When the crows began to patrol, their raucous cries announcing that it was time for things to get moving, I detected the rustle of squirrels in the branches overhead. As the light came on, I began to hear occasional gunshots, echoing from the distant ridge.

The gunfire made me nervous. For some time, I had been hearing about reckless deer hunters, shooting at anything that moved. "Oh, I had a couple of brush shots." That often-repeated comment wasn't funny to me.

Suddenly, the sound of a limb breaking jerked my attention toward the trees to my left. I strained to see. Nothing! The sound came again, louder still, and followed this time by the dry rustle of leaves beings shuffled. I could only think of one thing that could make that much noise in the deer woods: another hunter! I was suddenly very, very afraid. I stood up, waving and shouting, "Hi there!"

There was a moment of total silence. Then, in an explosion of crashing brush, the buck of my dreams bounced into the full light in a clearing between the pines, white tail flagging, then was instantly gone before I could even think of raising my rifle.

I stood there, stunned, hurt to the core. I was thinking terrible thoughts about myself. About being stupid, fumbling the ball, blowing my big chance. I was sure I would never have such an opportunity again.

I felt like heading for our car, going home. But I sat back down instead, trying to get a grip on myself. I had no faith that another chance would come my way, but I knew the game would not be over until sundown. I would play it out, give Lady Luck a chance to shine on me again.

Gradually, the forest worked its therapy on my beleaguered spirit. Bird activity was plentiful—crows, blue jays, chickadees, woodpeckers, juncos were on the move and calling. As always when I'm on a stand, they furnished a interesting sideshow during the hours of waiting for game to show. Then, about noontime, I noticed that the squirrels were moving as industriously as they had been at dawn. Strange, I thought, there must be some dirty weather around. I can't see it coming, but they can feel it coming.

I knew I was getting back into the groove then, focused on nature instead of myself. I dug into my pack for the sandwiches and coffee. They were very satisfying. I felt my confidence rising, and I realized now I owned something precious: the image of that buck in the clearing between the pines, the light full on what William Faulkner in a hunting tale called ". . . that rocking chair he carried."

I did not get my "rocking chair" buck that day. That night, it snowed, and two days later I shot a fork-horn buck. For the first time in my life—though certainly not the last—I found myself saying to the other fellows, "Well, boys, you can't eat horns."

As for the buck of my dreams . . . he would have to wait. And I could not help but think, rather bitterly: Why didn't Larry tell me: Bucks can make considerable noise when they're out for a morning stroll and haven't been disturbed. One single tip . . . that's all it would have taken. A tip I did not have.

If you've ever used the expression "I'd rather be lucky than good," then you just might be a whitetail deer hunter. You're a card-carrying dreamer out to beat the odds, your heart set on a rack for the wall and a freezer where packets of venison take up most of the room. You're not discouraged by the possibility that this may not be your year to bag a buck, for the pull of the deer woods and deer camp are strong. You've just got to be out there, watching the weather, checking for sign, enjoying the company of good buddies.

That the task of bagging a whitetail buck—any buck!—requires skills is obvious to the brethren of Hunter Orange. While they are animals of fairly rigid habit, whitetail deer are interesting and complex creatures prone to a witch's brew—for hunters anyway—of contradictory behavioral patterns that are sometimes hard to understand and impossible to predict. When you think you have a lock on where they're feeding, they move to some other dining halls in another part of the forest or croplands. The white oak patch where you scouted a buck feeding a week before turns out to be empty on opening day—except for its colony of squirrels. This list of failed game plans could go on and on.

You think you know what the deer will be doing. Perhaps you do. But all too often it seems like they're doing it somewhere else—somewhere you don't know about! And don't think for a minute that your quarry doesn't know you're coming.

Opening Day. The pre-dawn explodes with noise, like a bomb going off. A deer, especially a veteran "survivor" buck, would have to be deaf not to know what's going on. The cacophony includes the sounds of engines being revved up, wheels spinning in the mud, truck and SUV doors slamming, the *snick-snick* of gun actions being worked, and a myriad of shouts, "Hey, Joe, you goin' to the Oak Tree stand?" "I'll meet you at noon by the apple orchard." "Oh no, I forgot my shells!"

Well, perhaps we *can* get lucky. Happens all the time. Just drop by any check-in station, and you'll see people there who wouldn't know a scrape from a hog wallow. Nevertheless, they will have tags on bucks.

The goal Nate Matthews and I have set for ourselves is to give you something to cut the odds on your next hunt, for whatever game interests you—whitetail deer, mallards, pheasants, moose, you name it.

Nate and I come your way from a background of working with some of the most highly respected magazines in the outdoor field—*Field & Stream, Sports Afield,* and *Outdoor Life.* We do not present ourselves as experts in the various hunts we cover. But we know the people who *are*—and you will find them in the pages ahead.

If you feel lucky, I'm sure you will carry that on your next hunt. As I have suggested, Lady Luck makes a fine companion. Nate and I hope, however, that you will be taking some of these tips along to supplement the Lady's efforts. You might be on a deer stand at dawn and hear something shuffling your way, breaking sticks, making noise. Sounds like another hunter, except . . . oh yes . . . there was this tip you heard somewhere. About bucks sometimes making noise instead of sneaking in. You keep watching . . . and then raise your gun. Yes!

Sometimes, just the right tip is all you need to have a great day.

Good luck!

—Lamar Underwood

CHAPTER 1

White-tailed Deer Hunting

1. Don't Shoot Bucks That Look Insecure

When you first see a buck, take a moment to check its posture. Dominant bucks hold their heads high and walk loosely with their tails held straight out. A subordinate buck walks with stiff legs and a hunched back, and keeps its tail between its legs. If you see a good buck in a subordinate posture, consider holding your shot. It could mean there's a real monster in the area.

2. Find Small Bucks Near Big Scrapes

If you're looking to shoot a buck quickly during the rut and aren't much concerned about the size of its antlers, look for a large scrape that's torn up, irregularly shaped, and looks like it's being used by more than one deer. Younger, more submissive bucks frequent such scrapes. Since these bucks are less wary and more numerous than trophy animals, you'll stand a good chance of filling your tag faster than you would when hunting scrapes made by solitary (and often bigger) deer.

3. The Surefire Spot for Big Bucks

Don't give up on a hunting spot when you learn a big whitetail has been taken there. If it was a dominant buck, a host of suitors for this vacated territory will soon move in. The sudden void may dramatically increase other bucks' activity. If you can hunt where another hunter has already bagged a big buck, do it!

4. See More Deer by Scanning an Area Twice

Immediately after stopping at a vantage point, allow your eyes to relax and move them slowly back and forth over the surrounding terrain without focusing on any specific feature. Relaxed eyes automatically focus on any movement within their field of vision. If no deer are moving in your immediate vicinity, shift to a tightly focused analysis of every piece of cover you can see. Peer into the shadows, looking for pieces of deer—bits of antler, the curve of an ear, or the horizontal line of a back. Move to your next vantage point once you're satisfied that you've probed all the places a deer might be hiding.

5. Don't Store Your Gear Directly beneath Your Stand

Always pile equipment you're not bringing up into your tree stand (or are bringing up by rope after you climb up yourself, such as your gun or bow) on the opposite side of the tree from where you're climbing. You won't land on it if you're unlucky enough to fall during your climb.

6. Blood Drops: It's Direction that Counts

When a blood trail begins to peter out, mark the locations of blood drops—however sparse—as you find them. Eventually, the tape will point to the general direction the wounded critter is heading, useful information when the blood stops.

7. Don't Use Too Much Freshly Collected Scent

If you plan to use scent collected from the glands of a freshly-killed deer, make sure to use less of it than you would of the bottled stuff. The fresh gland scent will be much more potent than what you can buy commercially.

8. Deer Stand Alertness

Don't be fooled by loud noises coming your way when you're on the deer stand—sticks breaking, leaves being shuffled. What you think sounds like another hunter coming your way may, in fact, be a buck. They don't always sneak through the woods.

9. Avoid Startling Squirrels, Jays, and Other Animals That Have Loud Alarm Calls

The smart hunter doesn't concern himself solely with how or what nearby deer may hear, but does go to great pains to make sure he does not alert or spook other creatures as well, which may turn on their own warning sirens.

—John Weiss,
Advanced Deer Hunting, 1987

10. Three Steps to Proper Still-hunting

Proper still-hunting can be described as a three-step process. Step one is to stand motionless behind an object that will break up your outline while searching the surrounding area thoroughly for any sign that deer are present. Step two is to remain still and use your eyes to pick out a way forward that lets you place your feet on the quietest ground cover possible, such as bare rock, moss, wet leaves, or soft snow. Step three is to scan the woods for deer one more time, then slowly and silently navigate the route you've picked out. Repeat steps one through three until you find your buck. Do not rush. A good still-hunter will sometimes take an hour to traverse 100 yards of heavy cover.

11. Catch Wary Peak-season Bucks Off Guard during Lunch

Because of increased pressure during the rut, mature bucks will often change their patterns to avoid hunter activity. Many will become nocturnal, but a significant number instead spend more time searching for does during the middle of the day, when most hunters are back at camp taking naps and eating lunch. Try sitting your stand during the hours before and after noon to catch these deer off guard.

12. Use Different Routes to Your Deer Stand at Sunrise and Sunset

Never walk through a crop field in the early morning when approaching a deer stand set up near its edge. Deer are likely feeding in this field under cover of darkness—you will startle them if you don't take a back route to your stand. The opposite is true when you're approaching the same stand during the afternoon or evening hours. Deer are likely bedded in the cover you used to hide your approach in the morning, waiting for the sun to go down before moving out to feed. You should approach your stand through the field at this time of the day.

13. The Last Thing to Do before Giving Up on a Wounded Deer

There are too many stories about wounded big game animals returning to where they were first hit to ignore it as an occasional occurrence. Perhaps because deer and elk are herd animals and feel safe in numbers, the wounded animal often comes back to the location where it was first shot to find its companions. Whatever the reason, if you fail to recover the animal, go back and search the area where it was shot.

—The Hearst Corporation, *Deer Hunter's Almanac: A Complete Guide to Finding, Taking, and Preparing America's Premier Game Animal,* 1996

14. Hunt over Dew during Drought

A great place to hunt during dry, hot, early season conditions is on the edge of a meadow where there's lots of bright, green grass. Deer don't just drink water from ponds and rivers. They'll also lick dew off vegetation, especially when there's been a drought in your area, so these meadows will attract lots of thirsty animals.

15. Hunt Standing Corn on Windy Days

Fields of standing corn make fantastic habitat for whitetails, but they can be difficult to hunt by yourself. The noise you make while pushing through the dry stalks will startle deer long before you're close enough to see them in the thick cover. The secret is to wait for a windy day, then still-hunt upwind through the dry stalks, letting the sound of the wind in the corn mask the noise of your passage. Do this and you'll stand a good chance of catching your quarry unaware at close range.

16. When Shots Are Fired

The sound of a single shot, followed by silence, is awesome in the deer woods. There's a wonderful old Indian expression about it that goes: One shot . . . meat! Two shots . . . maybe. Three shots . . . heap shit!

17. Drive Deer on Opening Day

If you're going to use deer drives, the best time to hold them is on opening day, when you know where bucks are holding based on the information you learned while scouting before the season opened. If you wait until later in the season, other hunters will likely have disrupted the patterns you worked so hard to identify.

18. Set up Multiple Deer Decoys at Once

If you're planning to hunt over a deer decoy, consider using more than one at a time. Bucks often view single decoys with caution and may not approach them quickly, but will be much less likely to grow suspicious if you've set up a group of two or three.

19. Clearing out Your Ground Stand

Before taking a simple stand at the base of a tree or stump, clear the area where you'll be sitting of leaves and debris that would otherwise give you away every time you move.

20. Call Startled Bucks by Rattling Your Antlers

Rattling can be a good way to pique the curiosity of bucks that you've inadvertently startled while still-hunting. If you see a white flag or hear a deer snort, pull out your antlers and clack them together for a few seconds. If the deer you've startled did not smell or otherwise recognize you, it may assume that the motion that startled it was made by another deer, and could return to investigate. Be ready.

21. Guess a Deer's Sex by Analyzing Its Gait

You can tell buck tracks from doe tracks more easily when tracking deer through the snow. Does place their feet with precision; bucks sway from side to side while walking, a rolling gait that often leaves drag marks in powder. Longer drag marks may mean you've found the trail of an older or heavier buck.

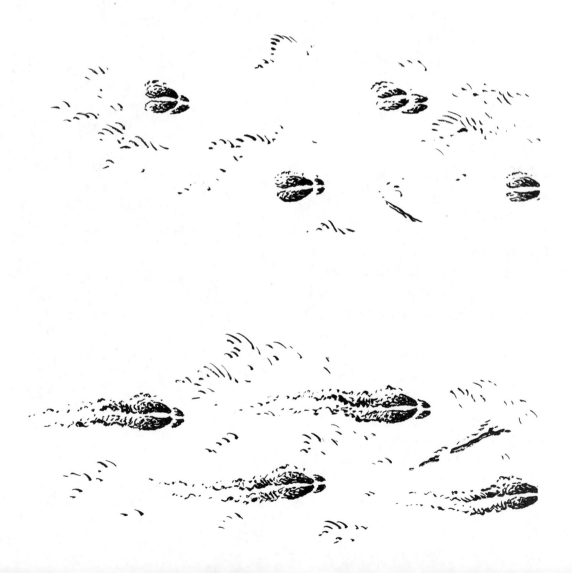

22. Let a Doe's Ears Tell You When a Buck is Nearby

When you encounter a single doe near your stand or while still-hunting during the rut, watch her ears. If she's walking, unalarmed, and has one ear cupped backward and the other pointing forward, chances are good that she's keeping tabs on a buck following her back trail. Get ready.

23. Never Wrap a Deer Carcass in Plastic

Do not use plastic when transporting your deer from where you hunt to where you plan to butcher it. The material will prevent heat and moisture from escaping the carcass, which could lead to poor flavor and even spoiled meat.

24. Size a Buck's Rack by Following His Trail on Snowy Days

One way to tell if you're following the track of a big buck is to see how much snow the buck's antlers knock off when he walks under tree branches or through low brush. The rack will knock snow off a two-foot or wider space if he's a big one.

—The Hearst Corporation,
Deer Hunter's Almanac: A Complete Guide to Finding, Taking, and Preparing America's Premier Game Animal, 1996

25. Hunt Near Food Sources When the Barometer Starts Dropping

White-tailed deer feed heavily in the days and hours leading up to the arrival of violent low-pressure systems. Watch your barometer. When the pressure starts dropping, head to the edges of crop fields and alfalfa meadows, or to stands of mature oak where the ground is covered with acorns. As the front gets closer, start hunting from stands set up along trails that lead from these food sources to heavy cover where you know deer go to hunker down during nasty weather.

26. Flush Big Bucks from beneath Downed Trees

When still-hunting through mature forest during hot weather, keep your eyes peeled for large trees that have been uprooted recently by storms. The maze of shade and cover offered by the fallen limbs and branches provides one of the best hiding places in the forest, and big bucks will often bed down deep within their embrace to escape the heat of the day. Experienced animals feel very secure in such cover and may not flush unless you get extremely close to them. Approach every such tree you can find.

27. Identify Active Scrapes by Looking for Overhead Branches

If you're looking to tag a buck, don't bother hunting over scrapes that don't have branches hanging overhead. Bucks rub their foreheads on such branches in order to leave their scent behind. If none are present, the scrape is not being actively used.

28. Learn How to Hang Your Stand Quickly and Quietly

It's a good idea to practice putting up and taking down your portable tree stand quickly and quietly before the season starts. Carrying your stand with you while you hunt is a great tactic that lets you adapt to changing wind, weather, and deer behavior patterns throughout the day, but not if it takes you a noisy hour to hang one. You should be able to pick out a tree, hang your stand, and start hunting from it in less than twenty minutes.

29. Your "As Needed" Bore Cover

A leftover balloon from your child's last birthday party will make a good bore cover if you're hunting in the rain or snow.

30. Don't Rattle When . . . (Part I)

Don't waste your time rattling on warm, sunny days. Bucks will be bedded down and less likely to move to respond to your calling.

31. Don't Rattle When . . . (Part II)

Don't waste your time rattling in gusty wind. Bucks must hear the sounds of your antlers in order to respond to them, and heavy wind will prevent your calls from traveling far enough to attract your quarry.

32. A Heart Attack Will Definitely Ruin Your Hunt

If you're carrying a lot of extra flab and are not used to exercise and physical exertion, you ought to take it easy in your deer hunting. Climbing hills, slogging through mud and rough terrain, and climbing to a tree stand can put you at serious risk if you're not accustomed to such activity. If you have any doubts at all, have your doc check you out. Perhaps you should even consider a stress test. It's better to know the truth about your condition than go down with a heart attack in the deer woods.

33. Don't Get Too Hot to Sit Still in Cold Weather

When hiking out to your tree stand in cold weather, do not wear all the layers you'll need to stay warm while sitting still. Doing so will cause you to sweat heavily on the way in, and this sweat will cool quickly once you stop moving, leaving you too chilled to remain quiet for long. Dress lightly and carry your outer layers in a backpack. Pull on warmer clothing only after you've climbed up into your stand and sat long enough for your heart rate to slow down.

34. Keep Your Cartridges Clean to Avoid a Jammed Action

Cleaning and oiling your gun is vital to its smooth operation, but won't prevent it from jamming if you don't also clean your cartridges. Do so regularly with a well-oiled cloth, and you'll prevent this frustrating malfunction.

35. Pop a Cap to Prevent Muzzleloader Misfires

Always fire off a blank cap or two before loading your muzzleloader in preparation for a hunt. The small explosion produced by the cap will clean your rifle's nipple of any residue that could result in a misfire at a critical moment when you're out in the field.

36. Read Rub Lines to Anticipate a Buck's Movements at Different Times of the Day

Rubs can show you to where, at what time of the day, and in what direction a buck normally travels. When you first find a rub, get down on your knees so that your field of vision is similar to that of the buck that made the rub. Scan for additional rubs in the area—chances are good you'll find another from thirty to fifty yards away. Repeat this process until you've identified a series of rubs, called a rub line. Rub lines often mark the routes a buck uses to travel to and from his preferred feeding and bedding areas. Most rubs in a line will be made on the same side of each tree; this tells you the direction the buck travels when using the route. If the line leads from a feeding area to thick bedding cover, set up a stand nearby and hunt there in the morning. If the line leads away from bedding cover, hunt it in the evening.

37. Hunt All Three Phases of the Rut

A good deer hunter knows that there is not just one rut, but three. The first, called the pre-rut, occurs in early October, when mature, four- and five-year-old does first come into estrus. The second, known as the peak or primary rut, runs from late October to the last week of November, and is when the majority of female deer come into heat. The third, called the post-rut or late rut, takes place twenty-eight days after the end of the primary rut, as does that were not bred during October and November come back into estrus. These pre- and post-rut phases do not last long. Look for a sudden explosion of fresh buck sign, then hunt hard for several days using techniques, such as rattling, that take advantage of the increased aggression triggered by competition for a limited number of willing does.

38. Hitch a Ride to Spook Fewer Deer

You can avoid spooking deer on your way to your stand if you hitch a ride on a truck, tractor, or ATV if you hunt on farmland or other property where the owners regularly use motorized vehicles to get around. The deer in such habitat become used to the sounds of engines and will be less likely to flee than they will from the sounds you make sneaking to your stand on foot.

39. Fill Doe Tags Early

Fill your doe tags early in the season. With meat in the freezer, you'll be far less tempted to shoot a small buck or attempt a marginal shot.

40. Baby Steps Mean Quiet Steps

When you're still-hunting at a snail's pace, you can't use your regular walking stride or you'll fall off balance. Each step forward should be no longer than your boot length.

—John Weiss,
The Whitetail Deer Hunter's Almanac, 2000

41. Don't Rely on Early Season Scouting Later in the Year

Do the bulk of your deer scouting two or three weeks before the season. If you scout much earlier, foods, the stage of the rut, and deer movement patterns may change before opening day, invalidating your findings.

—The Hearst Corporation, *Deer Hunter's Almanac: A Complete Guide to Finding,
Taking, and Preparing America's Premier Game Animal*, 1996

42. Use a Sled to Haul Your Buck

A cheap plastic sled makes short work of dragging deer out of the woods in snowy conditions. You can buy these sleds for less than $10 at most big-box department stores.

43. Stay Focused on Your Stand by Baiting Squirrels and Birds

Here's a great tip from Jerome B. Robinson of *Field & Stream*. To help pass the time when you're spending long hours in a deer stand, take along a few ounces of birdseed, he says. Scatter the seed on a nearby log or other bare area within a few yards of your stand. Birds, chipmunks, and squirrels are sure to discover the horde and will give you hours of entertainment, and their presence will keep you alert and remind you to remain still.

44. Gain Extra Seconds to Shoot When Rattling in a Buck

Bucks will often appear at the most inopportune moments, especially when you're rattling antlers to call them in. If you spot one while holding a rack in your hands, don't be afraid to put it down and pick up your gun. The buck you've called will be expecting to see some motion and will be less likely to startle immediately when he sees you, which gives you a few extra moments to shoot him. Using one smooth, unhurried motion, pick up your rifle, shoulder it, and fire. Make sure that you do not move too fast or jerk your arms, rifle, or body. Such sudden movements signal your excitement and may alarm the animal.

45. Never Put Scent Too Close to Your Tree Stand

Avoid placing a scent attractant too near your tree stand or ground blind. Doing so may cause a deer to focus its attention close to where you are trying to hide, which increases the risk that it will spot you before you're ready to take a shot.

46. Scout Hunting Land during Early Spring

The best time to scout and map out an area is during the spring before foliage develops. Rubs, scrapes, trails, and bedding areas are highly visible, and the intrusion will be long forgotten by next fall's season.

—Hearst Communications, Inc. and Cowles Creative Publishing, Inc.,
Hunting Today's Whitetail: Strategies for Success, 1998

47. Tie Back Branches When Hanging Your Tree Stand

While a good pair of pruning shears can be a bowhunter's best friend, there are many situations in which you should refrain from overclipping. For example, when setting up your tree stand, it is a good idea to try tying back any branches that obstruct your view, using a length of rope or wire. This method is quieter than clipping, will cause less damage to the tree you're using, and the branches can often be more easily positioned behind your stand in order to break up your silhouette.

48. Act like You're Grazing during Open-country Stalks

Open spaces are the toughest places to stalk. One proven strategy is to approach on all fours from downwind in a meandering fashion, as if you were a grazing animal. Use tall grass, shrubs, or whatever cover is available to hide your profile, and stop frequently, as if feeding.

—Len McDougall, *Tracking and Reading Sign: A Guide to Mastering the Original Forensic Science*, 2010

49. Let Blood Color Tell You How Fast to Follow a Wounded Buck

Blood trails don't just tell you the direction a wounded deer is moving. They can also provide good information about where on its body you shot the animal, and how quickly you should follow its trail. Bright red blood is full of oxygen and often means you've hit your deer in the lungs. Deer hit this way don't go far, so you can pursue them quickly. Dark red or purple blood may indicate a gut shot. If you find such blood, particularly in conjunction with bits of intestinal fat, and there's no precipitation forecast that could wash away or obscure the trail, consider giving the animal time to bed down and stiffen up before looking for a follow-up shot. Gut-shot deer often run long distances if they're chased immediately after being wounded.

50. Buy a Good Scope to Hunt Longer during Low Light

One of the best investments a hunter can make is a good-quality scope. Not only will one allow you to shoot with more confidence and accuracy at long distances, but the best scopes also collect enough light during the early morning and late evening hours to give you nearly thirty minutes of extra shooting time at either end of the day, a critical advantage considering that these hours are the ones when bucks are most likely to be on the move. Do not buy a cheap scope—the lower-quality glass will not collect the light you need.

51. Find Big Bucks by Locating Thrashed-up Brush

If you find a rub on a big tree, do not assume it was left by a buck with a big rack. Smaller-racked deer often rub on large-diameter trunks (although a big-racked buck will generally not waste his time rubbing on a small tree). Big bucks will, however, destroy a bush. If you're looking for a true trophy, locate a patch of brush that's been torn up and dislodged from the ground. Dominant deer use these to demonstrate their power and to leave more scent behind.

52. Trying out Your High-Tech Stuff

Practice with all the technical gear in your arsenal. Deer season is the wrong time to learn how to use your laser rangefinder and GPS unit. As you do with your hunting rifle, practice with those units until their operation becomes second nature.

53. Don't Be Too Lazy to Hunt Downwind

Still-hunting can be hard work when you're stalking through steep terrain. Don't be lazy. If you spot thick cover where you think a buck might be holed up, make sure to approach it from downwind, even if that means circling down, around, and back up steep slopes and ledges. Make sure you move slowly enough to avoid getting winded—it's very difficult to shoot accurately when you can't catch your breath.

54. The Most Important Decision

Making sure of your target is the most important decision in whitetail hunting. Depending on seeing blaze orange isn't good enough. You've got to be damn sure of what you're aiming at. Is it a deer? Is it a buck? Or is it something that sort of looks like a deer? If there's any doubt whatsoever, don't touch that trigger! Being too quick on the trigger has caused countless tragedies in deer hunting.

55. Leave Treetops to Feed Your Herd

When felling trees and bucking up logs for winter firewood, never haul the crowns of the trees out of the lot. Deer will browse on the tender branch tips all through the cold winter months.

56. Use Binoculars in Close Quarters

Get in the habit of bringing and regularly using a good pair of binoculars, even in close terrain where you'd normally not think to do so. Their magnification power and ability to pick up extra light will let you penetrate shadows in thick cover and locate animals there that you'd never have been able see with your naked eyes.

57. Find Deer in Transition Zones

During the end of October and in early November, before the peak of the rut, deer switch from grazing in fields to browsing on twigs, branches, and buds. These foods are most easily found in wide transition zones of thick understory that grow up between mature forests and more open fields and meadows, where the shade cast by tall trees is not deep enough to inhibit the growth of younger saplings. The thick growth also serves as cover for the animals after leaves have fallen from the branches of more mature timber. Set your stand near deer trails close to rubs or scrapes in these transition zones, and you'll have a good chance of filling your tag.

58. Still-hunt Uphill in the Early Morning

On calm days when there's little wind, air will flow downhill as it cools in the evening, and uphill as it heats up during the day. Deer use these currents to keep track of their surroundings. To keep them off your scent, hunt your way uphill in the late evening and early morning hours, and down during the rest of the day.

59. Store Emergency Equipment in Inner Layers

Always keep vital survival gear (whistle, matches, compass, med kit, etc.) in a pocket of one of your inner layers—something you know you won't remove, even if you warm up while sitting in your stand. Do not store it in your pack or in anything else that's easy to take off and hang on a limb next to where you're sitting. You'll be in a bad spot if you fall from your stand and are too injured to climb up to retrieve the tools you need to call for help and keep yourself alive until it arrives.

60. Hunt in Three Places at Once

One of the best locations to hunt is the intersection of three different types of vegetation. Look for a field corner bounded by timber on one side and a swamp, slough, or bottomland on the other, then hang your stand in a tree with a good view of any trails that lead from one to the other.

61. Don't Hang Your Stand Too High in Steep Terrain

While hanging your stand high in a tree will better hide your presence in level terrain, doing so in steep, hilly country may actually put you at eye level with deer working down the ridges you're hunting. Try lowering your stand to camouflage your silhouette in such conditions. A deer looking downhill will have a more difficult time spotting you against a backdrop of leaf litter than it will spotting you against the sky.

62. Use Hunting Pressure on Public Land to Your Advantage

If you hunt public land that gets lots of pressure during the prime shotgun or rifle season, you're going to run into other hunters in the woods. Instead of letting them ruin your hunt, figure out how to use them to your advantage. Set your stand up on trails leading to thick cover near routes you know other hunters are using. Deer will flee to these areas when spooked by all the unusual sights, sounds, and smells in the woods, so you'll be in a good position to catch them as they sneak through.

63. Get Your Decoy's Antler Size Just Right

Whitetail buck decoys work well during all three phases of the rut. Since most bucks in an area can recognize each other by sight and smell, any interloper represents a challenge that will often be met with curious and even violent behavior. Make sure, however, that your decoy's antlers are neither too large nor too small for the area you're hunting. Too small, and dominant animals may not consider the decoy worthy of their attention. Too large, and it may intimidate the buck you're hunting.

64. Guess a Deer's Sex by Following Its Trail

If you are following tracks that meander through the woods, you can bet you are on the trail of a doe. Bucks walk with purpose. Their tracks will often move from point A to point B while taking the path of least resistance.

—Hearst Communications, Inc. and Cowles Creative Publishing, Inc., *Hunting Today's Whitetail: Strategies for Success*, 1998

65. A Very Necessary Extra

Carry a blunt or judo point in your quiver on high-country bowhunts. They're perfect for thumping a grouse or two for dinner. However, make certain your blunt-equipped arrow is distinctively different from your regular shafts; otherwise you could nock it by mistake when a critter with antlers shows up. He'd end up with a bruised shoulder, and you with an equally damaged ego.

66. The Deer Are Watching You!

When you're hunting whitetails on small woodlots, deer can pattern you as much as you try to pattern them. So change stand locations frequently. Even change where you park from time to time.

67. A Basic Rule for Knowing When to Move and When to Sit Still

When you know deer are on the move, such as in the morning and evening hours, you should sit still in a good stand or other ambush point and wait for the animals to come to you. It is only during conditions in which deer stop moving that you should move to find them.

68. Still-hunt Heavy Cover on Windy Days

Many deer hunters don't like to go out on windy days, but such days can be good for stalking. When the wind is blowing hard, deer lie up in heavy cover and won't move. You can stalk brushy draws and other tangles and often get extremely close to the deer.

—Hearst Communications, Inc. and Cowles Creative Publishing, Inc.,
Hunting Today's Whitetail: Strategies for Success, 1998

69. Don't Eat Breakfast at a Diner on Opening Morning

If you're planning to meet your hunting buddies before heading out into the woods on opening day, don't meet in a roadside diner. Food and tobacco odors are very strong in restaurants, and these can quickly contaminate your clothing, making it much easier for deer to scent you.

70. Develop a Quiet Stride for Still-hunting

Maintaining proper balance is the key to walking quietly across the forest floor. A long stride combined with little forward momentum will often leave you tipping to one side or the other, which can force you to place your feet awkwardly as you catch your balance. To reduce the noise you make, learn to take smaller steps, and to place your feet heel or toe first. Shift your weight slowly onto your forward leg while rolling your foot from heel to toe (or toe to heel). When performed properly, this movement—called the rolling compression step—will allow you to feel any twigs, branches, or other objects that might make noise before you place your full weight on them. This lets you shift your weight to your back leg before the object snaps, then place your front foot in a new, less noisy spot.

71. Analyze Stomach Contents to Pattern Feeding Behavior

It's a good idea to examine the stomach contents of a deer you've shot. Less-digested food is what the deer ate last; well-digested food was eaten earlier in the day. You can use this information to guess where the deer was feeding in the hours before you killed it, and then apply what you've learned toward filling any open tags you or your buddies still have.

72. Set up Multiple Stands to Beat the Wind

A good way to compensate for changing wind directions is to have multiple stands set up over a single site. If the wind shifts while you're sitting in one of them, simply change stands so that you're sitting downwind of where you think deer will appear.

73. Walk More Quietly by Staying on Established Trails

Try to stay on game trails and logging roads whenever possible while still-hunting through the woods. It is much easier to walk quietly on ground packed by other feet or hooves than it is to cut silently through loose litter on a forest floor, and chances are good that deer are using these trails for the same reason.

74. Moon Up, Whitetails Moving

Living, as I do, adjacent to a sizable stretch of forest many whitetails call home, I have been able to observe a particular whitetail habit you can count on with absolute assurance: An early-rising moon in the late afternoon sky triggers early whitetail movement. They do not bother waiting until dark to begin their foraging. And, of course, the early full moon is the best of all.

75. Let Biting Flies Show You Where Your Buck is Hiding

When the weather is hot during the early season, bucks will hole up deep in cool, well-shaded swamps and bottomlands. Unfortunately for the deer, such places are often infested with biting flies. Stalk slowly through this cover and look for the motion of a buck shaking his head or flicking his ears to dislodge them.

76. Find Bucks in a Startled Herd by Counting Raised Tails

If you spook a group of deer while hunting in heavy cover, look to see if all of them have raised their tails. Does use this white flag to signal danger more often than bucks do when startled. If you see a deer running with its tail down, chances are good you've found a buck.

77. Follow Tracks in Low Light by Using Their Shadows

Deer tracks become difficult to detect and even seem to disappear in certain light conditions. When faced with this frustrating situation, use the old Indian trick of moving from side to side to get the light in the most favorable position. When the light is at the right angle, the hoof impressions or disturbed leaves will become apparent because of the shadows they cast.

—The Hearst Corporation, *Deer Hunter's Almanac: A Complete Guide to Finding, Taking, and Preparing America's Premier Game Animal*, 1996

78. Easy Way to Check the Wind

Save a few of the black neck feathers from your next ruffed grouse—or the lightest feathers you can pick off doves, pheasants, or quail if they're your favorite birds. Hung from a bow limb with a piece of dental floss, a light feather is a great wind direction indicator.

79. Don't Scare Big Bucks out of Bedding Sites

If you've located a good buck before the season, resist the urge to hunt him in his bedding site. This is almost certain to drive a wary trophy animal out of the area. Instead, hunt the travel zones between his bedding and feeding spots.

—The Hearst Corporation, *Deer Hunter's Almanac: A Complete Guide to Finding, Taking, and Preparing America's Premier Game Animal*, 1996

80. Tweak Your Climbing Stand to Make Less Noise

Climbing stands are great tools to use for hunting through unfamiliar territory. They let you combine the mobility of still-hunting with the concealment and view of a stand. Their biggest drawback is that they tend to be noisy. You can reduce the noise your stand makes by modifying it slightly. Use bungee cords to secure the two pieces of your stand so that they don't bang together as you walk. Replace wingnuts with plastic knobs, which make less noise when bumped against the metal frame, are quieter when being tightened, and are easier to turn when you're wearing gloves.

81. Throw in a Pullover Cap

Watch caps, ski caps, or beanies. Call them what you like, but a simple pullover cap will capture more body heat than just about any garment. There are many choices today besides the traditional knit type. Some are made large enough to pull over the top of a regular, baseball-type cap. Tuck one in your gear bag. It weighs next to nothing and could save your hunt—or even your life.

82. Big Rub, Big Buck

When the rub you spot has been made on a tree of considerable diameter, instead of a sticklike sapling, it probably looks as if it was made by a big buck. And it was! Small, fork-horn bucks don't make those big rubs.

83. Gauge How Well Your Stand Is Hidden Using Black-and-White Images

A good way to tell if your stand or blind is well concealed is to photograph yourself sitting in it during the exact hours of the day you think you'll be hunting from it. Use a digital camera, and convert your images from color to black-and-white using the image-processing program on your computer. Deer are colorblind, so these black-and-white images will give you a good idea of the patterns, shapes, and tones that seem out of place. If you and your stand are easily recognizable, reconfigure its position and make sure that it is not too bright or too dark compared to its surroundings.

84. Keep Your Rattling Antlers Fresh

Keep your favorite pair of rattling antlers sounding as if they're attached to a live buck with regular applications of linseed oil. The antlers should make sharp clicks and clacks when rattled, not dull clunks.

85. Practice with Your Bow in Hunting Situations

Always practice shooting your bow under the same conditions in which you expect to shoot your deer. You may be able to stick five arrows into a circle the size of your fist at fifty yards when you're standing on flat ground and wearing a T-shirt, but that won't help you much if you don't know how to do the same thing while wearing a heavy jacket. Spend time during the preseason simulating live hunting situations. Use broadheads rather than field points, wear your hunting clothes, and practice shooting from awkward positions and elevated angles.

86. Hunt Sleepy Bucks on Beds during a Full Moon

When the moon is full and the sky is clear, white-tailed deer will feed heavily during the evening hours and move less often during the day than they will when the sky stays dark all night. Run drives through heavy cover or still-hunt other likely bedding areas after a well-lit night to increase your chances of filling your tag in such conditions.

87. Don't Hang Your Stand Where You Find the Most Sign

Areas chock-full of deer trails, droppings, rubs, and beds are not always the best places to hang your stand. The abundance of sign could mean that the area is being used as a sanctuary—a place where deer congregate before heading out to feed, or where they bed down during the middle of the day. Since deer spend a great deal of time in such places, they become very familiar with them and will be sensitive to unusual sounds, smells, and sights. It can be extremely difficult to camouflage your presence under such conditions.

88. Identify Places Where Deer Go to Drink

White-tailed deer do not require watering holes in the true sense of the term, but they will drink at specific spots along their normal travel routes. If you can find a watering area that's secluded and near heavy cover, you will increase your deer sightings immensely.

—Hearst Communications, Inc. and Cowles Creative Publishing, Inc.,
Hunting Today's Whitetail: Strategies for Success, 1998

89. Don't Wait to Cut Shooting Lanes

When setting up your tree stand, it's always a good idea to clear a few shooting lanes into brush where you think deer will be moving. But make sure you do this well in advance of opening day. Clear too late, and the deer you want moving unconcerned through the area you're hunting will get spooked by the freshly cut brush.

90. Clippers Aren't Just for Shooting Lanes

You can reduce the noise you make while still-hunting through heavy cover by using a pair of pruning shears to clip awkward branches and brambles that are blocking your path.

91. Sit Your Stand in the Morning When Hunting Hot Weather

Whitetails are more active than normal during the night when the weather is unseasonably warm, and will stay bedded down in well-shaded cover that's close to a water source during the heat of the day. They may start moving again as the temperature starts dropping early in the evening, but when it's really hot the air won't begin to cool until well after darkness. The best time of the day to hunt deer during hot weather is during the first two hours of shooting light in the morning, when the air is coolest and you can catch your quarry moving from where they've been feeding to where they'll bed during daylight.

92. Hunt over Acorns to Catch Trophy Bucks Off Guard

Acorn-producing stands of red and white oak trees in forested terrain are great places to find big deer that are too wary to enter open fields before dark. Such terrain offers more cover and lower light conditions; shy animals will tarry as they feed toward their bedding sites, giving you a longer window in which to ambush them.

93. Practice with Your Bow for at Least a Month

No matter how well you shoot, you should always practice regularly for at least a month before opening day of bow season. A bow will often shoot differently after it's been hung up for the off season. You too become familiar with any quirks it's picked up from the effects of long storage, and even the best archer will grow rusty without practice.

94. Watch a Feeding Deer's Tail

Feeding deer always twitch their tails immediately before raising their heads to look around. If you immediately freeze when you see this motion, you'll be much less likely to alert the animal to your presence. Continue your stalk when the animal puts its head back down to feed.

95. Bagging a Lunchtime Buck

Since most whitetail hunters are on their stands at first light, they tend to get restless from midmorning to noon. Many head back to camp, or their vehicles, seeking a sandwich and a chat with their buddies. That's when they inadvertently spook whatever deer are around, sending them sneaking away or bolting through the countryside. And that's exactly when hunters who have stayed on their stands, quiet and alert, reap the rewards of the biggest bucks.

96. Hunt Late Season Deer during the Warmest Time of the Day

As daylight grows short and the weather grows colder, most white-tailed deer stop feeding during the twilight hours of early morning and late evening, as they do earlier in the season. Instead, they conserve energy by searching out the twigs and branches that make up their winter forage mostly during the warmest hours of the day. Try sleeping in and sitting your stand when the sun is high to catch them on the move.

97. Learn to Make Less Noise by Analyzing Your Trail

Here's a good way to improve your ability to walk quietly. First, practice your technique for about fifteen minutes while walking through noisy terrain. Remember the places where you felt you did well, and the places where you made mistakes. When your time is up, reverse course and analyze the trail you left. Your tracks can give you valuable clues about the best ways to place your feet.

98. Look for a Body When the Blood Trial Disappears

If you're tracking a wounded deer that you thought you hit well, but the blood trail you're following suddenly dries up, don't give up hope. Animals often stop bleeding just before they fall down dead. Search the area thoroughly, and you'll often find your deer nearby.

99. Look for Deer When the Wind Blows Late

Wind normally dies down late in the day. If it does not, or if it picks up in the late afternoon or around sunset on a calm day, there's likely a weather system about to move through your area. Deer are generally more active ahead of bad weather, so keep your eyes peeled for movement, and make sure you're downwind of where you expect them to work through your stand site.

100. Any Buck Is a Good Buck!

In my personal opinion, the concept of hunting only trophy deer seems misguided for most hunters. If you get a kick out of it, fine. Have at it. Most hunters, however, simply want to get out to the deer woods with the idea of bringing home a buck, any buck. The bigger the buck, the more thrills we might feel. But in the end, the old deer-hunting bromide is so, so true: You can't eat horns. My advice is to relax, enjoy your hunting, and stick to the premise that any buck is a good buck.

101. Biggest-bodied Whitetail of All Time

The heaviest white-tailed deer ever recorded was shot in Minnesota in 1926 by Carl Lenander, Jr. The animal weighed 402 pounds, dressed; its live weight was estimated at 511 pounds.

102. Clean Your Muzzleloader after Every Shot

Always swab out your barrel with a clean, moist patch after every shot you take at the range with your muzzleloader. Blackpowder guns foul quickly. The buildup will hurt your accuracy and make loading difficult if you do not remove it right away.

103. Keep Your Buck's Hair off the Meat to Improve Its Taste

When gutting, skinning, quartering, and butchering a buck, take care to keep its hair off the meat, especially if you shot your deer during any phase of the rut. This will help prevent it from taking on that strong, gamy flavor that most people find distasteful.

104. Bang on a Root to Call in Deer

Deer are curious animals, and you can use this characteristic to call them out of thick cover or within shooting range. One simple way to do so is to tap a tree root with a metal object such as a spent cartridge or a knife handle. If you're well hidden and the woods are quiet, this unusual sound may cause any deer close enough to hear it to move. If you're watching closely, you can spot this movement, then plan your shot or stalk accordingly.

105. Age a Buck by Looking at His Droppings

Adult buck droppings are generally thicker, longer, and more clumped together in a single mass than are doe droppings. A good rule of thumb to determine the approximate age of a buck is that a single pellet measuring about ¾ inch is from a buck about 2½ to 3½ years old. Larger pellets up to 1 ⅜ inches long are usually from the truly trophy-size animals.

—Hearst Communications, Inc. and Cowles Creative Publishing, Inc., *Hunting Today's Whitetail: Strategies for Success*, 1998

106. The Best Layer to Keep Warm

A light jacket or shirt that has a wind-stopping membrane can keep you warmer than a couple of layers of standard fabric. These are perfect garments for creating layers.

107. Only Stalk Fresh Tracks Early in the Morning

The best time to follow fresh deer tracks through snow when still-hunting is during the early morning hours. At this time of the day, deer are on their feet but moving slowly toward their beds, which means you stand a decent chance of catching up to them before they settle down in thick cover. Follow a parallel course as far from the tracks as you can without losing the trail. Use trees, brush, and other obstructions to hide your movements. Remember that tracks only show you where an animal has been; maintain most of your focus not on the tracks themselves, but on the area to which they seem to lead.

108. Make a Deer Decoy that Fits in Your Pocket

You can use the tail of a deer you've killed as an effective decoy by simply hanging it from a tree near your stand and sprinkling it with scent. Tie a length of string to it that's long enough to reach where you're sitting, and use it to twitch the tail every half hour or so. Deer notice twitching tails from great distances and will often come from far away to investigate the movement.

109. Play a Bleat Call like a Musical Instrument

You won't have much success if you simply rely on the basic sound a bleat call makes to attract white-tailed deer. Bleat calls are like musical instruments. It's easy to use them to create simple sounds, but nobody wants to listen unless you put some feeling behind the notes. Convince yourself that you're a fawn in true distress; be plaintive, frightened, hungry, and disoriented, and make sure your call expresses how you feel. Then sit back and watch the does come running.

110. Look Downhill When Still-hunting during Bad Weather

The best places to still-hunt during violent weather are found on elevated terrain. Benches crossing the sides of ridges make excellent routes to follow because they give you top-down looks into the kinds of thick cover where deer like to hole up. That extra field of view means you'll have more shots than you would if you were stalking through level ground, where the cover you're hunting will usually obstruct your line of sight.

111. Fletching Waterproof: Quick and Easy

A little hair spray will put a nice waterproof finish on your natural feather fletching.

112. Locate Bedding Areas for Great Ambush Sites

One reliable way to determine a buck's bedding area is to look for lots of rubs within a small area of fifty yards or less. These bedding areas are great ambush sites. Look for a heavily used trail nearby, set up downwind of it, and wait.

113. Use a Stick to Track Wounded Game over Sandy Soil

Some soil types can absorb both tracks and blood, making trailing wounded deer difficult. If the trail you're following becomes indistinct, break off a straight stick that's the same length as the stride of the animal you're tracking. Place one end of the stick on the last clear track you can identify so that it's pointing in the direction you think the animal was traveling. Look for new tracks or flecks of blood at the other end.

114. Give Deer Time to Respond to Your Rattling

Most bucks do not immediately charge toward the sound of two intruders battling in their territory. When rattling for whitetails, always wait, motionless, for at least thirty minutes after finishing an imitated fight sequence. Many hunters make the mistake of leaving the area in which they were calling too soon, before deer who may have heard the commotion have had time to respond.

115. Make Your Steps Sound like a Deer's to Spook Fewer Bucks

There are some situations in which it is impossible for you to walk silently through the woods. Dry leaves, for example, will crunch loudly no matter how carefully you place your feet. If you find it necessary to cover ground in such conditions (and there are no convenient game trails to follow that offer quieter places to walk), you will get closer to your quarry without spooking it if you learn how to pattern your steps so that they sound like the steps of a deer. Instead of a regular crunch, crunch, crunch, crunch, crunch (the standard human cadence), randomize the rhythm of your footsteps so that they form an erratic series of steps and pauses. Step, step, pause. Step. Pause. Wait. Step. Step. Step. Pause. And so on. You'll be much more likely to surprise bucks within shooting range if you use this pattern.

116. The Best Clothing for Still-hunting

Soft fabrics such as wool or fleece are far better still-hunting garments than noisy, hard fabrics such as canvas, denim, or nylon.

— John Weiss,
The Whitetail Deer Hunter's Almanac, 2000

117. Use the Five-second Rule to Creep into Shooting Range

Feeding herbivores generally keep their heads down, vision obscured by grasses, for about five seconds before rising up to look about. A stalker can use those seconds to crawl a few feet closer before freezing.

— Len McDougall, *Tracking and Reading Sign: A Guide to Mastering the Original Forensic Science*, 2010

118. Age Buck Tracks by Comparing Them to Your Own

An easy way to estimate the age of a track is to make a fresh mark alongside it. Use your boot heel, fingers, or even a carry-along deer hoof. Press down hard and compare the marks. The closer they match in texture, sheen, and definition, the fresher the original track.

—*Deer Hunter's Almanac: A Complete Guide to Finding, Taking, and Preparing America's Premier Game Animal,* copyright © 1996 by the Hearst Corporation

119. Find Unpressured Bucks on Smaller Public Lands

The next time you look at a map of a national or state forest you're interested in hunting, search for small parcels of land disconnected from the main tract. These loose pieces of public land are often less well advertised and more difficult to access. Since most hunters won't be aware that they are also open to public hunting, you'll often find less pressure and more deer.

120. Try Hip Boots for Whitetail Hunting

Simply wearing hip waders on your whitetail hunt can provide a number of tactical options. The ability to wade allows you to access areas—like islands—most others won't bother with. You can also approach some stands from the water, much of your noise masked by the sound of moving water in a small stream.

121. Still-hunt First on Unfamiliar Property

Still-hunting is a good tactic to use when you're hunting in unfamiliar territory that you haven't had the opportunity to scout. It makes little sense to hang a stand when you don't have a good idea of how deer use the property. By hunting along the ground, you'll be able to find more sign and gain a mental picture of the landscape that tells you where to best find deer.

122. When Stand Sites Dictate Your Hunting

There's a whitetail hunting fantasy fun to think about. In it, you see yourself roaming through the woods and fields, hunting wherever you please. The hard reality is that for most hunters, stand site choices where they have permission to hunt are few and far between. Picking the best stand site usually isn't an option. You must hunt where you have permission, and your tactics must center on getting the best hunt possible from what you have.

123. Don't Judge the Quality of Your Shot by the Amount of Hair Left Behind

When starting to trail a wounded deer, do not assume you've missed the animal if you can't find clumps of hair at the site of your shot. Hard-hit deer often lose surprisingly little of their coats. Conversely, do not assume that you've hit your animal well if you find a great deal of hair scattered about. Grazing shots often leave the most hair behind.

124. Hold Still for Five Minutes after Snapping a Branch

A white-tailed deer's short-term memory is limited to about three minutes. If you snap a branch or make any similar noise while approaching a deer on the ground, you can salvage your stalk by stopping immediately and holding completely still for at least five minutes. By the time you start moving again, any animal in the area will have forgotten your mistake.

125. Get in Your Stand Early on Opening Day

"If there's one day of the year to be on stand earlier than usual, opening day of firearms season is it. Try to arrive at your chosen hunting location at least a full hour before daylight, well before other hunters begin stirring in the woods."

—John Weiss,
The Whitetail Deer Hunter's Almanac, 2000

126. Don't Scout Too Early on Private Hunting Land

"In regions not subjected to intense hunting pressure, try to scout for sign as close to opening day as possible. If you scout too early, the sign you find may no longer be relevant when the season opens."

—John Weiss,
The Whitetail Deer Hunter's Almanac, 2000

127. Have a Stand Ready for Every Wind Direction

"A savvy hunter has several stands in place for opening day but doesn't decide which one to occupy until he checks the wind direction before leaving camp in the morning."

—John Weiss,
The Whitetail Deer Hunter's Almanac, 2000

128. Use Crowded Hunting Lands to Your Advantage

One of the best places to hunt on opening morning is near a heavily-used access to public hunting land. If you can sneak in quietly enough to avoid disturbing any deer using the area and early enough to beat the crowd of hunters who will enter the woods at first light, you'll have a good chance of seeing bucks pushed by the late risers.

129. Don't Give Up if You Miss

Shooting at and missing a buck does not necessarily mean you've burnt your tree stand or ground blind for the day, especially if that day is opening day. If you've spent the time to locate a good spot, especially one overlooking trails leading to security cover, other bucks will be heading your way after encountering other hunters.

130. Dress for All-day Hunting

"The longer you can remain afield on opening day of the firearms season, the better your chances of success. The best advice on this that I've ever heard is: 'Dress like you're going to spend the day sitting in a duck blind in December in northern Minnesota.'"

—John Weiss,
The Whitetail Deer Hunter's Almanac, 2000

131. The Ultimate Local Food

If you're into organic, local health food, killing a deer yourself is the way to eat. Venison is one of the best-tasting and healthiest meats you can find. It's higher in protein, lower in fat and cholesterol, and doesn't contain the hormones, antibiotics, and other chemicals you get from most farm-raised beef, pork, or other domestic meat.

132. Donate Your Hides to Fly Tiers

Deer body hair is hollow and helps insulate the animals during the winter. Because of this, it floats very well, making it an excellent material to use in dry flies that imitate high-floating bugs to catch trout, bass, and other surface-feeding fish. The hairs on a whitetail's tail also take dyes well and are used as "wings" on fly patterns that imitate baitfish. The next time you shoot a deer, make sure none of your friends are fly tiers before you discard the hide. They'll appreciate the free source of materials to work with.

133. Spot Bucks Down Low

The horizontal line of a whitetail's back is one of the best things to look for when still-hunting through thick brush. Most lines in the woods are vertical, and while you'll eyeball a great many fallen logs by keying in on the horizontal lines, you'll have a better chance of locating a hidden deer this way than you would by looking for a whole animal. Remember, though, that even mature bucks stand only three feet at the shoulder, so don't raise your eyes any higher than this when scanning the area ahead of you.

134. Measure Your Draw Length before Buying a Bow

"The most important thing you can do when choosing a compound bow is to select one with exactly the right draw length for you. . . . The best way [to gauge draw length] is to pull a light-draw-weight bow to full draw with a long arrow on the bowstring, anchor it using the same anchor point you'll use when shooting, and have a friend mark the shaft at the back of the bow handle. Measure the shaft from that mark to the string groove on the arrow's nock, and that's your draw length."

—Bob Robb,
The Field & Stream Bowhunting Handbook, 2000

135. The Proper Draw Weight for Hunting Situations

According to outdoor writer and bowhunting expert Bob Robb, you can determine the best draw weight to use on your bow by taking the following three tests. First, "standing flat-footed, hold the bow at arm's length and pull it back. If you have to 'cheat'—lifting the bow up above your head—to achieve full draw, it's too heavy." Next, do this while seated, and last, while from a kneeling position. "Being able to draw your bow with a minimum of movement, even from weird angles, is important while bowhunting," writes Robb. "Extra body movement can spook an animal, so the less the better."

—Bob Robb,
The Field & Stream Bowhunting Handbook, 2000

136. You Shoot a Bow Better When Relaxed

"If there is one key word in accurately shooting a bow, it's this—*relax*. Don't be taut and tense. Instead, relax both your muscles and your mind as you shoot. The best bow shots keep their muscles working naturally for them, not tensely against them."

—Bob Robb,
The Field & Stream Bowhunting Handbook, 2000

137. Avoid Overtraining with Your Bow

Make sure you practice with your bow regularly during the off season, but don't practice too much. If you shoot while your muscles are sore, you'll see reductions in accuracy that could cause you to lose confidence in your form. If you start getting tired during a practice session, take a break, then pick up your bow once you feel rested.

138. Practice with Your Bow at Close Range First

"The best way to improve your shooting skills is to begin practice sessions at relatively short distances. Somewhere between 10 and 15 yards is good. After your shooting form improves, move out to 20 yards. . . . As you become more skilled in your shooting, move farther away from the target. Soon you'll be able to consistently make good shots at 40 yards or more. "

—Bob Robb,
The Field & Stream Bowhunting Handbook, 2000

139. Learn How Far Deer Travel to Feed in Your Area

"Once you've located deer trails, look for tracks in the trails. If all the tracks are going in the same direction, follow the trail to determine where it goes. Depending on where the food source is, you may have found the main trail heading for the food source. It's helpful to know how far deer are traveling from the bedding are to the food source."

—Jackie Bushman,
Jackie Bushman's Top 50 Whitetail Tactics, 2002

140. Find Bottleneck Bucks

"Whenever I'm studying aerial photos or scouting the woods, I look for bottlenecks. A bottleneck acts like a funnel, and is a natural or man-made contour that the deer like to follow. A perfect example is a point of woods that extends across an open field. Whitetails like to stay in the cover as much as possible. Rather than cross the wide-open field, they'll stick to the woods where it narrows down. And that is a perfect place for a deer stand."

—Jackie Bushman,
Jackie Bushman's Top 50 Whitetail Tactics, 2002

141. Look for High Rubs on Big Trees

"I've seen some mighty big bucks tear up bushes, but if I see a big tree that's torn up, I'll roll the dice and say that's a big deer. I'm more likely to pay attention to the height of scar marks left on a tree than the size of the tree itself, as it takes a big buck with a big rack to scar way up on a tree."

—Jackie Bushman,
Jackie Bushman's Top 50 Whitetail Tactics, 2002

142. Don't Face Your Stand at the Sun

When placing your tree stand, avoid setting it up so that it faces a rising or falling sun. The rays beaming directly into your eyes will make it harder for you to see into shadows during critical low-light hours, and will glance off glasses, gun barrels, and reflective items, spooking deer that would otherwise be unlikely to spot you.

143. Don't Hunt from Your Stand in an Unfavorable Wind

Never hunt from a stand over a site you know a big buck is frequenting if the wind is blowing from you toward where you think the animal will approach. If you're already in your stand when the wind changes to an unfavorable direction, leave the area immediately.

144. Stop Bucks in Small Shooting Lanes

It can be difficult to find a clear shooting lane when you're hunting deer in heavy cover, especially if the animal you're aiming at is moving quickly through the forest. A good tactic to use in this situation is to grunt or whistle at a buck just as he enters a gap in the brush. He'll likely stop briefly to identify the source of the sound, giving you a chance to release your arrow. Do not hesitate; he'll be moving again in seconds, especially if he spots you as the source.

145. Rattle for Bucks with a Partner

It's always a good idea to hunt with a partner if you're planning to rattle for whitetail bucks. Bucks will usually approach the sound of rivals fighting by circling downwind. The rattler should set up in heavy cover with open ground directly downwind, and the shooter with clear shooting lanes into this open ground. The buck should pass the shooter's downwind stand as it circles, and will be less likely to detect this threat because it's focused on the sound of the rattling.

146. Find Free Fresh Tarsal Glands at Check Stations

Tarsal glands are excellent sources of scent you can use to attract big bucks during the rut. If you're looking for fresh glands to use, simply head to the nearest check station and ask the hunters who've brought in their deer if you can remove them from their bucks.

147. Always Wear Orange during Deer Drives

This tip is should be obvious to all hunters, but bears repeating nonetheless. If you're planning to participate in a drive, make sure you and every other hunter on the drive wears an adequate amount of hunter orange.

148. Start Your Scope on Low Power

"One tip for using a variable scope is to always leave it set on the lowest power. . . . If you see a deer in the distance, you'll have time to change the scope to a higher power setting. At close range, you won't [always] have time to adjust."

—Jackie Bushman,
Jackie Bushman's Top 50 Whitetail Tactics, 2002

149. Commit to Your Trophy

If you're looking for a truly huge buck, you need to commit to hunting solely for a trophy. Set the bar high, then pass up any deer below it. You might end the season with nothing to show for your efforts, but if you keep at it year after year, chances are good you'll eventually fill your tag with that big buck of your dreams.

150. Make Good Snap Judgments to Size Bucks in Cover

"When you're hunting in tight cover, you have to be able to assess a deer quickly to determine if he's a shooter. You may only have a few seconds to make a shot as the buck crosses an opening, and there's not much time to study the buck before making a decision."

—Jackie Bushman,
Jackie Bushman's Big Buck Strategies, 2002

151. Scout Well to Get Close

"Scouting is time well spent. Especially when you're bowhunting, just being able to see the deer is not good enough. You've got to set up where you'll have a 30-yard or closer shot when a buck comes by."

—Jackie Bushman,
Jackie Bushman's Big Buck Strategies, 2002

152. Bring a Spare Gun

When traveling to an expensive hunting destination, always bring a backup rifle that you've spent time shooting and have properly sighted in. If your primary gun is damaged during your trip, or even in the field, you'll be able to continue hunting without wasting any of the hours you've saved so long to use.

153. Roll Rocks to Move Bucks

According to Jackie Bushman in his book *Jackie Bushman's Big Buck Strategies*, one good tactic to use when the hunting is slow in canyon country is to roll a rock or two down a steep slope to startle a buck into leaving cover. You'll generally have a good view of the surrounding landscape and should be able to take a shot at the animal when it stops running to take stock of the situation. Most shots will be long, so make sure you've got a solid rest prepared before you start rolling.

154. Don't Shoot the First Buck You See

The biggest bucks are often the last animals to appear when a herd of deer files into a feeding area. If you're hunting in the late afternoon, hold your fire until the last minutes of shooting light before selecting an animal to take. Your patience could pay off with a trophy.

155. Hunt the Odd Corners

One of the best places to find feeding deer is in clearings or small fields just barely large enough to let in the sunlight crops need to grow. You'll often find these in the corners of larger, irregularly sized fields, where corners come together in odd, narrow shapes. Deer like these clearings because they can feed there without being completely exposed. If you find one, place a stand overlooking it, and hunt there in the early morning or late afternoon.

156. Beat Buck Fever

Buck fever can strike even a seasoned whitetail hunter, especially when the buck is a true trophy. If you see a big deer like this and find yourself tensing up too much to make an accurate shot, look away for a moment and take a few deep breaths to calm yourself. Then look back, identify your target, and focus on where to place your shot. Do not look at the animal's antlers again until you've put him on the ground.

157. Draw When You Can't See Eyes

One of the most challenging parts of bowhunting is knowing how and when to draw your bow without your quarry spotting the movement. Draw too soon, and you'll have to hold the weight too long; draw too late, and you might never get a shot at all. If you've got a clear sense of the route the deer you're planning to shoot is taking, wait until its eyes are completely obscured by the closest stump, rock, or tree trunk.

158. Concentrate through Your Shot

"When you shoot a muzzleloader, you have to concentrate to stay on target until the powder ignites. I aim behind the shoulder at the lower one-third of the deer's body because I'm more likely to shoot high with a muzzleloader."

—Jackie Bushman,
Jackie Bushman's Big Buck Strategies, 2002

159. Practice Shooting from a Blind

"When you're hunting from a box blind, practice getting a solid rest for your rifle and for your elbow. When the time comes to make the shot, you'll know how to do it. I sometimes cut a piece of 2x4 and prop it between the front and back window to use as an elbow rest."

—Jackie Bushman,
Jackie Bushman's Big Buck Strategies, 2002

CHAPTER 2

Elk Hunting

160. How to Field-judge a Bull Elk

If you're looking for a trophy elk, you need to be able to quickly judge the quality of its antlers before taking a shot at the animal. You can do this in three steps. First, try to count the points. A true trophy will have no fewer than six points on each side. Second, gauge the length of each antler's beam. A good bull should look as if it can tip back its head to scratch its rear end with the tips of his beams. Third, make sure that the bull's brow tines reach out over its muzzle, and that the other points have good length.

161. Don't Scout for Elk like You Scout for Deer

Unless you're hunting on private land, patterning an elk herd's activities before hunting season can be a waste of time. Elk react quickly to hunting pressure, and such pressure can be enormous on public lands, especially during the days leading up to the first of the season, when other hunters are out in force. Instead of scouting to identify a herd's normal, unstressed behaviors, focus your efforts on identifying where they go when spooked by the presence of other hunters. Look for heavy blowdown cover on steep slopes that are relatively close to meadows surrounded by thick timber. Elk feeding in these meadows will head toward such escape areas when startled. Identify good ambush sites along the likely routes they take, and you stand a good chance of shooting an animal pushed out by another hunter.

162. Don't Let Elk Spot You Twice in the Same Spot

If you notice an elk in the herd you're hunting suddenly stop chewing its cud to stare at your position, the ideal response is to immediately stop all movement, no matter how awkward the position you're in, and remain motionless until it turns its head away. There will be times, however, when it will be impossible to stay still long enough for the animal that's spotted you to lose interest. If you must move to a more comfortable position, your best option is to lower yourself as slowly as possible to the ground. Lie there as long as necessary, then crawl to a new position before raising your head to take stock of the situation. Even if the elk did not spook, it will still be monitoring the spot where it saw you move.

163. There's Only One Place to Shoot an Elk with a Bow

If you're hunting elk with a bow, the best shot to take is easy to remember, because there's only one ethical target to choose. Neck shots, shoulder shots, or shots at any other part of an elk's body are not recommended; to kill an elk quickly with a bow, you must shoot it directly behind its shoulder, piercing its heart and/or lungs.

164. Dressing Out Your Kill in Grizzly Country

If the red gods smile when you're hunting in the Rocky Mountain West, be aware that grizzly bears have learned to equate the sound of a rifle shot to a pile of meat. Take a buddy with you when you go in to recover your prize. Make lots of noise during the process. Your friend can keep an eye out for trouble while you're dressing the kill and can help you pack meat out once you head out.

165. Don't Use Your Rifle Scope to Spot for Elk

When hunting elk in big country where long shots are necessary, always use your binoculars or a spotting scope to identify movement in faraway brush. Hunters who use their rifle scopes to search for their targets run the risk of pointing their muzzles at things they should not, such as other hunters walking through the area.

166. Save the Cheers!

It can be hard to resist, but don't launch into a loud celebration immediately after you've placed an arrow perfectly in the chest of a bull elk. Bulls get rooted and poked by other elk during the rut, so he may not know he's been shot. Stay quiet. He might just walk less than 100 yards, lie down, and bleed out.

167. Hunt ahead of the Storm Fronts

Elk and deer have an uncanny sense for knowing when the weather is turning bad, and often feed more heavily in advance of a major storm. So track weather conditions and plan to be on your hunting ground in the days before a big storm.

168. Practice for Elk Season by Varmint Hunting

Long-range shooting is common when hunting elk in the wide open country of the American West. Hunters should be comfortable taking shots of 300 yards and longer. A great way to practice at these distances is to use the rifle you'll be carrying during your elk hunt to shoot small varmints. If you can consistently hit a target the size of a woodchuck at 300 yards, you should have little problem hitting an elk's vital organs at the same distance.

169. Secure Your Elk's Carcass on Steep Slopes

If an elk you've shot falls on the side of a steep slope, your first action after making sure the animal is dead should always be to secure the carcass to a solid anchor, such as a tree trunk, using a stout length of rope. The last thing you want is for the animal's body to slide downhill, which could damage the meat and/or put it at the bottom of a ravine where you'll have to work twice as hard to pack it out.

170. Catch Elk Moving from Their Food to Their Beds

The worst time to still-hunt for elk is at midday, when they will be bedded down in thick cover that they've chosen because it is impossible to approach without them seeing or smelling you. You'll have more luck spotting them before they spot you if you still-hunt during the early morning and late afternoon, when elk are moving from the meadows and clearings where they feed to the heavy evergreen cover where they often prefer to bed, and vice versa.

171. What You Can Learn from Elk Trails

It is impossible to sex an elk from a single track, but you can often make an educated guess by looking at one's trail. If you find the track of a lone elk, and the trail dodges low-hanging branches, it is likely a bull keeping his antlers clear of obstructions. Follow trails made by two large elk (big bulls often travel in pairs), but avoid trails in which a large track is accompanied by a small one, which will always mean a cow and a calf. It's also useful to identify how many animals may be in a herd. Small bands of five or six elk rarely hold mature bulls, but larger groups of ten or more likely contain an elk worth tracking.

172. Set up an Afternoon Ambush

If you spot elk feeding in a clearing early in the day but they are too far away for you to shoot with your rifle, don't give up on the herd. Elk leave the meadows where they feed in the morning to bed down in cover during the day, and will often return to the same place to feed in the late afternoon. Use the middle of the day to set up an ambush. Position yourself behind an obstruction at the edge of the clearing downwind of where you expect them to approach it, then wait. Avoid using or crossing the route they took when they left, as they will often use the same route to return.

173. Bark like a Cow to Stop Startled Elk

You can briefly stop a spooked herd of elk by imitating the sound of a barking cow. A cow barks when she is alarmed. Other elk in the area will instinctively stop and look at her until she's identified the danger and run off, and then will follow her lead in exiting the area. If you're within range and have identified your target, use the moment when they stop and stare to take your shot.

174. Skin Your Elk Quickly to Preserve Its Flavor

Always quarter and remove the hide as soon as possible after you shoot a large animal, such as an elk. Otherwise its massive body will not lose heat quickly enough to prevent the meat from spoiling in all but the coldest weather.

175. Spot Late Season Bulls at High Elevation

Late in the season, you'll often find small groups of older bulls at higher elevations, where the snow is deep and the terrain is open. These bulls may be quite far from the rest of the herd, as much as a mile or more. Glass for them from below. When you spot such a group, try to pattern where the bulls feed and bed. Then set up a stalk to fit what you've observed. When planning your stalk, remember that if you spook the animals they will likely run to the nearest trees for shelter. If you're hunting in a group, post hunters along the tree line to intercept them.

176. Which Slopes to Hunt, and When

According to T. R. Michels, author of *Elk Addicts Manual,* northeast slopes are heavily used in summer and early fall because they retain more moisture and provide succulent forage for the animals to eat. South-facing slopes are used twice as heavily in winter as north-facing slopes, probably because of solar radiation, which causes snow to melt and exposes available forage.

177. How to Recognize Elk Tracks

Elk tracks look like very large deer tracks, and a mature bull's prints will be much larger than those left by female or juvenile elk. Make sure that you do not confuse elk tracks with those left by moose or cows. Cow tracks are rounded and do not look much like those of a deer, and moose tracks are longer and narrower than those left by elk. Study a guidebook (or this illustration) before you hunt to avoid this problem.

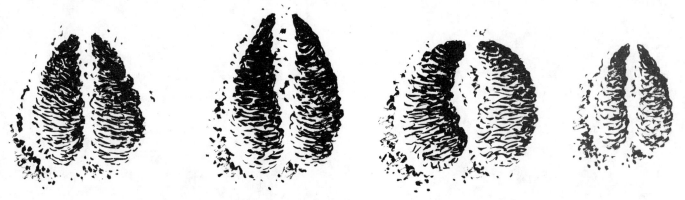

From left to right: bull elk, bull moose, cow elk, and juvenile elk tracks

178. Charge a Bull Elk to Rile His Temper

If you're bugling for an elk you've spotted and the animal refuses to answer, try provoking his temper. Start running toward him, bugling and breaking branches off trees in your path as you go. The sound of such a challenge could be the stimulus he needs to break from his position. Make sure, of course, that you're both downwind of him and completely screened from view.

179. Set Up Your Stand on Northern Slopes

North slopes are great places to locate a tree stand for elk. Since north slopes hold more trees than south slopes, elk will retreat to them both when it's hot (because they like the shade) and when it's cold (because the trees trap heat). These slopes also tend to hold green grass later in the season. Look for trails that lead from these slopes toward open parks and meadows where you think the animals are feeding. Sit your stand at sunrise and sunset, when the elk will be returning from (or leaving for) these feeding areas.

180. The Top Ten Elk States (by Elk Population)

Colorado: 200,000
Montana: 150,000
Idaho: 140,000
Oregon: 106,000
Wyoming: 85,000
Washington: 60,000
Arizona: 55,000
Utah: 50,000
New Mexico: 45,000
California: 7,500

181. Look for Moving Elk in Hot Weather after It Rains

Early season elk hunting often takes place in very warm weather. Elk move less often during the day when it is hot, preferring instead to feed at night. The best time to glass them will be very early in the morning, but you can also catch them on the move for a quick snack just after a rain.

182. Wallowing around in the High Country

Rutting bulls love to roll in muddy wallows to bathe themselves in a rather foul, musky odor. They'll return to a favorite wallow quite often, so put up a tree stand nearby to ambush them.

183. Keep Predators Away from Your Kill with a Smoky Fire

If you are hunting elk on foot and shoot one far from the road, you will have to make more than one trip to pack out the meat, leaving the remaining meat alone in the backcountry. One way to keep bears, wolves, coyotes, and other predators from stealing your kill while you are away is to build a small, smoky fire from damp, pitchy wood near the quarters you had to leave behind. The smoke will help scare away predators, and you can use the plume to locate your kill quickly when you return to collect the rest of the animal. Make sure to do this only where it's both legal and safe, and never leave a fire untended in dry conditions where there is any possible risk that it might spread.

184. Don't Bugle Too Often

A bugling bull makes an impressive sound, and one that's not hard to reproduce using today's commercial calls. Because of this, and because many hunters have the unrealistic expectation that bulls often charge headlong toward the sound of a challenge, the bugle is the most over-used call in an elk hunter's repertoire. Instead of relying on bugling to draw in a rutting bull, it's a better idea to use the call just to locate one, especially if you're hunting an area that gets lots of pressure. Once you've found a responsive bull, try to close with him by using other means. Call him in using cow calls, imitate the sounds of raking antlers, or even stalk silently downwind into shooting range.

185. Roaded vs. Roadless Areas

"Roadless areas may harbor twice the number of bulls than roaded terrain holds. Where roads are open, few bulls live to maturity and hardly any past five years. But when roads are closed, 15 percent may live to maturity. Roadless areas are even better, often boasting a population of 30 percent mature bulls. Hunt a mile from open roads; half a mile from closed roads."

—Sam Curtis, www.fieldandstream.com

186. Critical Advice to Elk Hunters

Calling elk in areas of heavy hunting pressure may be counterproductive. Bugling will draw other hunters, and bulls that have been called in and spooked wise up quickly. It is better to simply spot the bulls, then stalk them.

187. Three Common Elk Decoy Mistakes

Elk decoys will often bring bulls into shooting range that may otherwise hang up at a distance, looking for the source of your calling, but they can also warn away elk if used improperly. Wear gloves when handling them in the field, and consider spraying them with a cover scent after you set them up. When a bull approaches, he will be looking closely at the decoy, so make sure you're well camouflaged and are not hidden directly behind the decoy. Never place a bedded elk decoy in the middle of a trail.

188. Watch Out for Brand New Boots

Never wear brand new boots on a backcountry elk hunt; you're guaranteed to get sore feet, hot spots, and blisters if you do. Always break them in well in advance of hunting season by wearing them while doing outdoor chores such as chopping wood, mowing the lawn, or working in your garden.

189. Approach Bedded Elk from Above

Elk like to bed in flat spots on side ridges where they can see well to the left, right, and downhill, and are high enough to feel comfortable that nothing will be approaching from behind. If you're following one's track and it suddenly turns upslope, it could mean the elk is ready to bed. Avoid following its tracks any longer, as the animal will be paying close attention to its back trail. Instead, circle uphill, staying downwind of the trail, and try to approach where you think the elk has lain down from above.

190. Hunting Camp Manners

This may seem rather obvious, but I've seen hunting camp manners violated so many times I can't help bringing it up. In hunting camp, there's usually one chap who takes over the cooking. He'll need help. Not everybody can sit in front of the fire telling stories all evening. The cook needs a couple of "cookies," as helpers are sometimes called. And when supper's over, the cook doesn't do the dishes!

191. Aggressive vs. Timid Bulls

Once a bull responds to your calling, you'll need to figure out if he's a timid or an aggressive animal. If he's timid, you'll need to move toward him quickly, getting as close as you can so that he doesn't have to travel very far to meet you. If he's aggressive, you'll need to set up very quickly, because he could appear at any moment. Note that even aggressive bulls will often approach a caller very quietly— do not assume you'll hear him before he's too close for you to draw your bow.

192. Let the Birds Show the Way

In the West, scavengers such as magpies, crows, and even eagles can help pinpoint lost game. If you've lost an elk or deer you've wounded, glass terrain where you think the critter may have gone, looking for concentrations of the birds. They will often flock to a carcass with just a couple of hours after it hits the turf.

193. Change Vantage Points to Fully Scope an Area

Don't dismiss an area as empty of game if you don't see any elk from a particular vantage point. You should always scope out an area from at least two positions so that you can view pockets and basins where elk may be feeding that are not easily identified from the beaten path. Changing vantage points takes work, and that's one reason why it can be such a successful tactic; most hunters won't be willing to make the effort and allow their desire for an easy hunt to let them dismiss an area before they've covered it fully. Use this to your advantage when hunting on public land.

194. Use Spotting Scopes in Antler Management Units

Always bring a good spotting scope with you when you're hunting in management areas that limit your targets to bulls with specific point configurations. Also bring binoculars; they will help you scan more quickly to initially find a bull. But it will be much easier to analyze the animal's antlers when it's standing behind a brush pile if you have high-power magnification.

195. Look in Wet Meadows for Feeding Elk

Always pay close attention to wet meadows when looking for feeding elk. These small, moist clearings are rich in forbs and sedges, forage elk prefer. Wet meadows surrounded by thick timber are best; elk feeding in them will feel more secure when such cover is available, and will often feed later in the morning than they might in less accommodating terrain.

196. Leave Clearings Alone during the Day

Don't bother watching meadows or clearings for elk during the daytime. Elk almost always stay bedded in thick cover near a water source when the sun is high, and move out to feed in such areas only late in the evening. You'll have better luck during the daylight hours if you hunt in places where you think elk will be pushed by the activities of other hunters in the area.

197. Don't Call Elk from Too Close to the Road

It's become a commonly held belief that bull elk have grown more skilled over the past ten years at identifying the difference between the calls made by other elk and those made by hunters imitating them. But elk make many different noises, and each animal has its own unique sound. It is therefore unlikely that they are distinguishing hunters from elk based on the sounds hunters are making; it's actually rather hard to use modern elk calls to make sounds that will scare away an elk. Instead, elk may be keying in on unnatural factors related to the sound, such as the proximity of a call to heavily used trails or roads, sounds, scents, or other human sign. If you're hunting in an area that receives heavy pressure, it's a good idea to start calling only once you're far off the beaten path.

198. Use Shooting Sticks Instead of Bipods When Hunting Elk

A bipod that mounts on your rifle makes a great accessory for varmint and predator hunters but can be cumbersome when used in elk hunting situations. Bipods snag brush easily and affect the balance of your rifle if you must shoot while kneeling or while leaning against a tree. A better option is to carry a pair of shooting sticks, which can be set up quickly for long shots for which you need a stable rest, but placed to one side if an offhand shot is necessary.

199. Set Up a Drive as a Last Resort

Never attempt to drive elk if you've established a pattern to their behavior, such as when and where they feed in the morning and in the evening. Your drive will disrupt the herd so much that this knowledge will become nearly useless, and you'll have a much more difficult hunt. Driving should only ever be used as a method of last resort, when you've got no more time left or know that the elk in the area you're hunting have gone completely nocturnal. If you do decide to attempt a drive, make sure you account for the direction the wind is blowing, and set up any standers downwind of where you expect to first encounter any elk.

200. Campfire Smoke on Your Hunting Clothes

Clothing will quickly absorb the smells of a campfire and cooking food. So when you're in elk camp, have a set of clothing you wear around camp. Wear hunting garments only when hunting.

201. Slow Down When You Find a Temporary Bed

Bull elk often lie down multiple times on their way to a favorite bedding site. If you've been following a fresh trail and find a recently vacated bed, don't get discouraged. Look first at the tracks leaving the area. If they don't indicate a startled animal, it's likely that the bull is simply looking for a better place to settle down for the day. It's also likely that this location is not far away, so move slowly and be prepared to shoot.

202. The Best Place to Cut a Fresh Track

If you're hoping to tag a bull by following its tracks through the snow, start your search for his trail in the early morning. Find an open clearing where a herd has been feeding at night. The tracks you find in the clearing will be jumbled and difficult to follow, but if you search a few yards back into the surrounding timber you will locate where the animals' trails come together and can pick out a specific group to follow.

203. Pick the Right Caliber for Elk Hunting

Because elk are so much larger than deer, many hunters think that you need a large-caliber rifle to kill one. This is incorrect. It is not the size of an animal that determines the caliber one should use, but the thickness of the animal's skin. Elk do not have extremely thick skins; most experts agree that the minimum caliber one should use when hunting these animals is a .270.

204. Call Back Elk from a Busted Herd

If you flush a herd of elk while still-hunting and it splinters into multiple groups, you can use the animals' desire to herd back up to call them to you. If the animals did not smell you when first flushed, they will slow down and take stock of the situation from a few hundred yards away. Get out your cow call and blow it softly, imitating the sounds other cows make when they're regrouping. If a cow answers you, answer back, though wait for a few seconds first. If you do this right, the elk will think you're part of the group and will work back slowly in your direction.

205. It Takes Two to Tag a Called-in Elk

The textbook method of calling a bull into bow range requires two hunters. One serves as the caller, the other as the shooter. The shooter sets up in the shadows of a tree or some other type of cover with a good view of the path the bull should take. The caller sets up twenty to thirty yards upwind of the shooter. Since most bulls will approach the caller by circling downwind, they should appear directly in front of the shooter.

206. Athletic Animals

"Elk can run as fast as 40 miles an hour and have been known to outsprint horses in short footraces. They can jump 8 feet vertically."

—Dave Hurteau, www.fieldandstream.com

207. Critical Time When Your Bull Is Down

After you've made a good shot on an elk, give him plenty of time to bleed out. An hour is good. An hour and a half is better. Unlike a mortally wounded deer that will quickly lie down again after you've jumped him, a wounded elk rarely gives you a second chance. He'll likely be in the next county when he final gives up the ghost.

208. Locate Bulls with a Cow Call

If you're hunting an unfamiliar area or just an unexplored section of your normal hunting grounds, blow softly on a cow call every few minutes as you walk through the forest. Rutting bulls will often bugle in response. If one does, keep calling, move toward him, and don't be afraid to break a branch or two on the way. You want to make him think there's a new cow in the area and that she's receptive to his attentions. Once you're sure you've piqued his interest (ideally he'll be moving toward you at this point), set up in cover with a clear view of where you think he'll appear.

209. Carry Multiple Calls When Hunting Elk

If you plan to keep hunting for a bull you've been calling that has spotted you, winded you, or otherwise discovered your presence, do not continue to use the same call. He will be able to identify it easily and will be unlikely to respond to the same one again. The good news is that each call makes its own unique sound; you can avoid this problem by carrying multiple calls.

210. Hunt Thick Timber near Roads

The best place to look for elk if you're restricted to country that's near an open road is thick, forested terrain where pressured animals will retreat for security. Look for mature forest with both a thick upper canopy and a dense understory of young trees and shrubs. These are great places to still-hunt, especially if you find fresh tracks leading into them. If possible, post some other hunters along the edges of this cover so that they can shoot any bulls you flush while stalking through it.

211. The Best Time to Hear an Elk Bugle

According to T. R. Michels, author of *Elk Addicts Manual,* elk bugle most frequently in the morning from forty-five minutes before to forty-five minutes after sunrise. Bugling peaks within a half hour of sunrise. However, on cloudy days bugling generally increases and peaks later than normal.

212. A Hot Weather Hot Spot for Daytime Elk

When the weather is hot, look for elk taking shelter in forests of mature evergreens that have few low branches. The forest canopy protects the animals from direct sunlight, while the open understory lets in cool breezes.

213. Stay in Town to Collect Elk Hunting Intel

There are lots of great elk hunting opportunities quite close to easily accessed roads in the Western states, especially in units where tags are strictly limited and hunting pressure is correspondingly low. If you're lucky enough to draw a tag in such a unit and are planning a do-it-yourself hunt there, consider staying at a motel or a bed & breakfast rather than pitching a tent at a local campground. Many of these establishments cater to hunters and are operated by people with good local knowledge of the area you're hunting (and of where others may already be hunting). This information can make the difference between going home empty-handed or with a cooler full of meat.

214. Find Elk in the Open after Bad Weather

Under most conditions, it is unusual to see elk feeding in the open during the middle of the day. The exception to this is if a period of strong winds or heavy rain or snow lets up at this time, or if the sun peaks through the clouds and warms up a slope that's been very cold. Elk will have been hunkered down, waiting out the bad weather, and will often feed heavily for a few hours once conditions improve. These are great times to glass food sources, trails, and bedding cover for movement.

215. Catch Elk Leaving the Lowlands

Elk are spread evenly across most elevations throughout their habitat before the season begins, but those down low will retreat quickly up the mountains to avoid hunting pressure shortly after rifle hunters arrive. You can ambush these elk by setting up on passes or saddles that the animals must cross to reach higher-altitude refuges.

216. Check Grazing Schedules before Planning a Hunt

Before planning a hunt on public grazing land, make sure to contact the local BLM or U.S. Forest Service office and ask them if any livestock are scheduled to rotate into the area. Mule deer are less likely to use range that's occupied by lots of sheep or cattle. Domestic herds are the last thing you want to see after you've traveled a long distance to hunt land you've spent time and money researching.

217. The Deadly "Whippersnapper" Elk Call

If you're going to call a herd bull, stick with higher, more shrill tones. These replicate the call of an immature bull. A bull elk will move his harem away from a fight with a legitimate challenger. But if he thinks the caller is a young whippersnapper, he may just run over to kick his butt.

218. Bugle Up Bulls after the Sun Sets

According to Tracy Breen, author of "Oddball Elk Tactics" (realtree.com), professional elk hunter Jerrod Lile believes that call-shy bull elk are often wary only during the day. Instead of calling to them when it's light out, Lile prefers to bugle after dark, then sneak close enough that he's within stalking distance of the bulls he hears once the sun rises. "I usually try to shadow a herd of elk in the middle of the night and do my best to stay close to them," he says. "If I can stay close, at daylight I will probably know where they are and be able to get within bow range."

219. Types of Elk Calls and When to Use Them

According to T. R. Michels, author of *Elk Addicts Manual,* "Determining what call to use when you are hunting elk is not a matter of what time of the year you are hunting, but which sex and age class elk you want to attract." He breaks calls down into four categories. These are:

1. Calls that work on cows: distress call, contact call, cow/calf mew, and fighting squeal.
2. Calls that work on any elk: contact call, cow/calf mew, fighting squeal, and contact grunt.
3. Calls that work on any bull: contact call, cow/calf mew, contact grunt, fighting squeal, subdominant bugle, loud inhale/exhale, and glug.
4. Calls that work on dominant bulls: contact call, cow/calf mew, contact grunt, fighting squeal, roar, dominant bugle, chuckle, loud inhale/exhale, cough, dominance grunt, gurgle, and glug.

Michels notes that the dominant bull calls are not as effective after the rut because the bulls are exhausted, not as aggressive, and not as interested in breeding.

220. Bootless Hunting Can Pay Off

When stalking elk or mule deer in rocky terrain, kick your shoes off when you get within 100 yards. Your socks should keep your feet warm enough for a while. Your steps will be virtually silent on rock and hard ground, and you will able to feel potential noise makers underfoot much better. The extra stealth may be all you need to get close enough for a shot.

221. Don't Use Too High a Magnification Power on Your Rifle Scope

Be wary of using scopes with very high magnification. High-power scopes decrease your field of view, making it hard to pick up moving targets. They magnify the impact of inadvertent movements you may make as you hold your rifle on target. They also work poorly on very warm days by magnifying the distortion caused by heat waves rising through the air. A 4- or 5-power magnification is more than adequate for nearly any elk hunting situation.

222. Stalk in Your Socks

The next time you go bowhunting for elk, stuff three extra pairs of thick socks into your pack. When you spot a bull and need to stalk silently into shooting range, take off your boots and pull on the socks instead. You'll be able to place your feet much more quietly, and you'll feel any branches that might snap beneath your weight in time to adjust your foot placement. But be very careful if using this method in snake or cactus country.

CHAPTER 3

Mule Deer Hunting

223. Let Low Light Show You Hidden Deer

The best time to glass for mule deer is as the sun first appears early in the morning. The low-angle light causes the hair on their coats and light-colored rumps to glow, and will also gleam on the tines of a big buck's antlers. Low-angled evening light is also good for locating mule deer, but glassing in the late afternoon leaves you little time to stalk within range before the sun goes down.

224. Good Way to Spot Mule Deer

When glassing high-country canyons for mule deer, look as much for the deer's steamy breath as the deer itself. Also glass for tracks in the snow. Follow them optically. There might be a deer where the tracks end.

225. Hunt Where the Wind Doesn't Blow

Deer and elk don't like being out in the wind any better than you do. So on windy days, hunt deep canyons and pockets of dense cover—any place that provides some protection. That's when the game will be.

226. That Curious Mule Deer Gait

". . . One got a clear idea of the extraordinary gait which is the mule-deer's most striking characteristic. It trots well, gallops if hard-pressed, and is a good climber, though much inferior to the mountain sheep. But its normal gait consists of a series of stiff-legged bounds, all four feet leaving and striking the ground at the same time."

—Theodore Roosevelt, *Outdoor Pastimes of An American Hunter,* Scribner's, 1905

227. Pick a Banker to Pay for Your Road Trip

Road trips are great ways to explore the wide open spaces that make good public-land muley habitat when you're hunting on a budget. You can make your money go further by putting together a group of buddies to help share common costs such as fuel, lodging, and bulk staples. But watch out for conflicts over money. An easy way to avoid them is to designate one person in your group as a "banker" and have everyone chip in an equal amount of cash to the group's "account." The banker will use this money to pay for everything, saving everyone the trouble of keeping track of receipts and arguing over who's turn it is to buy a tank of gas.

228. Keep Your Glass Clean

It won't matter how much money you spend on optics for spotting mule deer if you don't take proper care of your glass. Dirty lenses will obscure movement and make you lose focus on the terrain. Keep your lens caps on your binoculars and spotting scope when they're not in use. Bring a small bottle of alcohol and a piece of cheese cloth to clean them if they do collect dust or moisture, and avoid touching them with bare skin, which can leave a smear of oily residue that is very difficult to remove.

229. Search the Same Kind of Cover You're Glassing From

"If it feels too hot to be sitting in the sun glassing you will not be glassing deer out in the open. If you move to the shade of a tree to glass, look in the shade of a tree for bedded deer."

—"Ask Dr. Mule Deer," www.kingsoutdoorworld.com

230. Talk the Right Lingo out West

Most western hunters count antler points separately for each side of an animal's rack. A buck with four points on each antler is therefore called a "4x4" buck. Most eastern hunters add up the total number of points when describing their trophies. That same buck with four points on each antler out east will be called an eight-point buck.

231. Glass Your Route before You Stalk

Spotting mule deer is perhaps the easiest part of spot-and-stalk hunting. The stalk is just as important, and much more physically demanding. If you spot a bedded buck, don't immediately start moving into shooting range. First make sure that you're familiar with the route you're planning to take to get there. The best way to do this is to glass it thoroughly before packing up and moving out. Pick out landmarks you'll be able to identify (look for ones that can be recognized from multiple angles), and make sure to remember where they are in relation to where the animal is bedded down. Start your stalk once you've established a clear mental picture of the path you think will put you in a downwind location with a clear shot at the buck.

232. Block Their Escape

Mule deer prefer to flee uphill when spooked. If you startle one while working down from a high elevation it may become confused, hesitating before breaking to the left or right rather than running straight away down slope. This will generally offer the prepared hunter a broadside shot. Be ready.

233. Meandering Tracks Mean Beds Are Close

If a mule deer is traveling from a food source to bedding cover its trail will generally lead in a straight line (taking terrain into account). But as the animal approaches its bedding site it often starts to meander through the cover, nibbling on twigs and looking for a spot to lie down. If you're tracking a muley and see its trail start to wander, turn around and backtrack for a few hundred yards, then climb above where you think the animal has bedded down so that you can approach from a higher elevation. You'll get closer to the deer and will have a better shot at the animal if you spook it.

234. Don't Shoot Deer You Can't Reach

One of the worst mistakes a mule deer hunter can make is shooting a buck on the other side of a ravine or canyon without knowing whether it's possible to retrieve the animal. Vertical cliffs, deep rivers, and maze-like canyons are difficult obstacles to negotiate, and some are impossible to cross. Make sure you know the terrain you're hunting before you take a shot like this.

235. Caching Extra Water for Early Season Hunting

How far you can hunt from your vehicle, especially in early season, often depends on how much water you can carry. Consider packing in a couple gallons of extra water on one of your pre-season scouting trips. Having a water stash will keep you in the field longer when the season comes in.

236. "Power Up" for an Afternoon Muley

Taking a catnap mid-day isn't the worst think you can do on a mule deer hunt. Unless it's the height of the rut, bucks will probably be holed up then. Your eyes could use the break from constant glassing, and a short power siesta will leave you refreshed to go hard until dark.

237. Mule Deer Prefer Sagebrush

If you're hunting in unfamiliar territory, one of the best places to look for muleys is in thick patches of sagebrush. Mule deer seem to prefer this plant throughout their range. Pay special attention to patches you find in places where sagebrush is relatively rare; the plant will act like a magnet for muleys in the area.

238. Trade Home-grown Gifts for Tips to Find Big Bucks

Not all scouting takes place out in the sagebrush. Some of the most valuable information you can find will come from people you meet in communities near where you plan to hunt. Ranchers, oil workers, cow hands, and sheepherders often do not hunt themselves but are out on the range enough to know where big bucks can be found, and won't be shy about sharing. It's a good idea bring a stash of gifts to reward such information. Choose items that are endemic to where you're from—cherries from Michigan, maple syrup from New England, oranges from Florida—your gifts will be more memorable if you do, and could lead to lifelong contacts that open up unexpected opportunities.

239. Why Summer Bucks Are Easier to Find

One reason most people see more mule deer bucks during the summer than they do during the fall and winter is that bucks in velvet require more food to maintain the growth of their antlers, and so must feed more often. After they shed their velvet their nutritional demands are somewhat lessened, and they will bed down more quickly during the daylight hours.

240. Get in a Mule Deer's Zone

According to Dennis Wintch, mule deer editor for *Hunting Illustrated* magazine, most mule deer habitat can be broken up into three distinct zones: a high zone (8,000 to 12,000 feet), a middle zone (5,000 to 8,000 feet), and a low zone (1,000 to 5,000 feet). Mule deer cycle through these zones depending on weather, hunting pressure, and food availability. The trick is to figure out which zone they're currently inhabiting. If you're hunting in a new area, look for fresh tracks and follow them until you're confident you know which level the deer are currently using.

241. How to Field-judge a Mule Deer

If you're looking for a record-book typical mule deer, you should glass until you find at least a five-by-five buck. This means the animal will have four points per side, plus eye guards.

242. Don't Let Other Deer Spoil Your Stalk

Before beginning your stalk, always make sure that you've carefully glassed your route for any other bedded deer in the area. If you see one, adjust the path you plan to take so that you circle downwind of them, or you'll end up spooking your target.

243. Read Their Pee

One way to determine the sex of a deer whose tracks you've found in snow is to follow the animal's trail until you find a spot where it urinated. Bucks will pee forward into the snow, in the same direction its tracks are moving. Does will pee straight down or in a reverse direction.

244. Build Endurance the Cheap Way

You don't have to purchase an expensive gym membership in order to get into shape for a mule deer or an elk hunt. All you really need is access to a high-rise building. Nothing will build up the muscles you'll be using when humping weight through the mountains like carrying a heavy backpack up (and down) ten to twenty stories worth of stairs every day.

245. Getting the Range Right under the Big Sky

The most difficult adjustment easterners make when hunting the West for the first time is adjusting to the scale of thing. Deer tend to be significantly larger than what East Coasters are used to. Elk are five or six times better. Guesstimating ranges is a real crap shoot. Better depend on a rangefinder when hunting the wide-open spaces.

246. Catch Bucks Seeking Shade in the Middle of the Day

While the most productive times to glass for mule deer will be during first hours of morning and the last hours of the day, you can still spot deer moving during the middle of the day if you know where to look. Bucks will often change bedding sites during the middle of the day as shade shifts with the sun's movement, sometimes browsing for a few minutes before they lay down again. You'll be most likely to catch this movement if you're already glassing cover for bedded deer. Look under trees and around brush for anything that seems out of place with it surroundings. When a buck stands up you'll be focused in the right place.

247. Make the Sun Work for You

If you have the choice, glass for mule deer with the sun behind you. Direct sunlight is sharper and you'll see more detail. Deer will have a much harder time spotting you in the backlight.

248. Find Hidden Water Sources in Dry Muley Habitat

Because mule deer often live in arid environments, hunting funnels that lead to water sources can be a very productive tactic. Some sources, such as stock ponds, are easy for a hunter to identify, but because of this they're also more heavily pressured. You may have more luck searching out hidden seeps and springs. Don't be afraid ask for help finding them. Foresters, wildlife biologists, ranchers, and sheepherders are all excellent sources of information on where to look.

249. Catch a Mule Deer Napping

One good tactic for tagging big mule deer is to locate one by glassing from a high vantage point early in the morning, then watch from a distance until he beds down for the day. Mule deer will often remain bedded in the same spot until the afternoon, when they get up to stretch and then feed. You can use the hours when the buck you've spotted is resting to sneak to within shooting range.

250. Look for Big Bucks on Mesas When It Rains

"If it has rained a day or two before you get to your hunting area, big bucks will often move out to the end of long points on lone mesas. The feed is better there and they can get water for a short time in the slick rock."

—Dennis Wintch, from "How to Hunt Mule Deer—Hunting in a New Area,"
Hunting Illustrated magazine, August/September 2003

251. Creep Closer before Rattling

Here's a good tip from Scott Haugen, author of "10 Big-Game Bowhunting Tips" (*Game & Fish,* August 2003). According to Haugen, rattling does work on mule deer, but big muley bucks seem reluctant to travel far if they hear a fight in progress. "The closer you can get—preferably around some brush for cover—the greater your odds of pulling him in."

252. Glass for Bucks in Comfort

It is very important that you situate yourself comfortably when glassing for mule deer. Choose a place to sit that has a solid back support, such as a big rock or a stump, and bring foam pad, or, if you can spare the weight, a small, folding tripod stool to keep your butt off cold, hard ground. You should also invest in a tripod with adjustable legs for your binoculars and/or spotting scope, which will reduce the strain on your arms. Never spot for deer with your rifle scope; you'll end up pointing the muzzle of your gun at targets you do not want to shoot.

253. Let the Wind Settle into One Direction

Wind currents can be fickle before the sun rises, so it's a good idea to wait until later in the morning before planning a stalk on a buck you've spotted. In most open-country habitat, the wind will usually settle as the air heats up, blowing in a consistent direction that makes staying downwind of your target much simpler.

254. Age Tracks in Cold Snow

If the temperature is lower than 28 degrees mule deer won't leave clear tracks in the snow, but you can still age their prints. The trick is to feel the edges of their tracks. If there's no crusted snow around their rims the tracks are less than 15 minutes old. If there's a light crust (you'll feel it as a slight resistance before the track's edges crumble), the track is 15 to 40 minutes old. If the tracks are crusted enough that chunks of snow break off the edges when you apply pressure to them, the track is at least 40 minutes old.

255. Set Up away from the Field Edges

When mule deer are keying on alfalfa, avoid setting up hard on the field edge. You stand a better chance of ambushing a good buck if you take a stand farther back from the field along travel corridors from bedding areas. The deer are more relaxed as they move toward the feeding area, sharpening their radar as they move into the open.

256. See How They Run—and Stop!

"When we came on these Colorado mule deer suddenly, the generally behaved exactly as their brethren used to in the old days on the Little Missouri: that is, they would run off at good speed for a hundred yards or so, then slow up, halt, gaze inquisitively at us for some seconds and again take to flight."

—Theodore Roosevelt, *Outdoor Pastimes of An American Hunter,* Scribner's, 1905

257. Tag Team a Spot-and-Stalk

One of the best ways to stalk within range of a bedded mule deer is to leave a hunting partner behind at the place you first spotted the animal. Your partner can then use hand signals to guide you as you sneak into shooting range. He'll need to far enough away from the bedded deer to not startle it when moving his hands, so bring a pair of binoculars and use them to check on him for instructions at regular intervals.

258. Don't Let Your Bow Keep You from Creeping on Your Stomach

Creeping to within shooting range of an open-country mule deer is one of the most difficult and exciting challenges in all of bowhunting, especially when there's only an open stretch of tall grass between you and the buck you're stalking. To close with your target in such terrain you'll need to inch forward on your stomach, keeping your head down and using only your elbows to pull yourself forward. But it can be difficult to remain silent when you're carrying a bulky, awkward bow in your hands. You can keep your arms moving freely by placing the bow on your back. When you're close enough to shoot, simply slide the bow into your hands, knock an arrow, sit up on your knees, and shoot quickly.

259. Don't Wear Cheap Orange

A common mistake many hunters make is to spend lots of money buying top-notch camou-flage outerwear that's quiet, waterproof, and well matched with the terrain they are hunting, then purchase a cheap nylon hunter-orange vest to layer on top of it. Cheap fabric is often quite noisy. Put as much thought into buying your blaze orange gear as you do the rest of your clothing.

260. Use Your Truck to Decoy Other Hunters

If you're hunting public land that gets lots of pressure, consider parking your vehicle some distance away from where you plan to hunt, even if it's possible to drive much closer. The noise made by your truck or ATV might spook deer, and it can serve as a decoy to keep other hunters from knowing about the spot you've worked so hard to find.

261. Don't Waste Time Hunting in Thick Brush

"Don't hunt in areas where you can't see. If the side hills are so thick a snake will get a pug nose crawling through it, you are wasting your time. You can't shoot what you can't see."
—Dennis Wintch, from "How to Hunt Mule Deer—Hunting in a New Area,"
Hunting Illustrated magazine, August/September 2003

262. Don't Hunt from a Newly Placed Blind

Blinds can be extremely useful tools for bow hunters chasing mule deer, especially on active trails that muleys use to travel from bedding cover to food sources or water holes. But make sure to set one up at least a week before you plant to hunt from it; it takes time for mule deer to grow used to the new addition to the landscape. You can speed up the process by spreading brush around the blind in order to break up its outline.

263. Stalk When the Wind Blows Strongly

If you spot a buck bedded in grassy, open terrain, wait to stalk it until the middle of the day, when the wind usually blows steadiest and strongest. The strong wind will wave grass, leaves, and branches back and forth, and you can use these natural movements to camouflage your progress into shooting position. Wear a ghillie suit for further protection from a mule deer's sharp eyes; the loose strips of fabric attached to the suit will move with the wind, making you look that much more like a part of the landscape.

264. Beating the Cold for Muleys

In super-cold weather, pay special attention to south facing slopes when glassing for muleys. Those slopes get the most direct sun, so the snow cover tends to be a bit lighter. And deer seem to like the extra warmth the direct sun provides.

265. Use the Right Binocular/Spotting Scope Combination

Large, 11x80 or 20x80 binoculars of the type designed for stargazers make excellent mule deer spotting tools because they gather a great deal of light, giving you an excellent picture during the twilight hours, which is when most muleys will be moving. But if you're hiking long distances to reach your hunting areas, you won't want to carry such heavy glass. A good compromise is to use a smaller pair of 10x50 binoculars and also bring a small, 20- or 25-power spotting scope. The combined weight of both these optics will be less than the weight of the larger binoculars, and you can break the weight up by storing your scope in your pack as you hike. Use the binoculars to spot movement at long range, then use the scope to get a closer look at whatever caught your attention.

266. Guess Mood from a Mule Deer's Tracks

You can gauge a mule deer's mood by reading its tracks. Well-defined, evenly spaced prints that don't disturb the snow or dirt usually indicate a calm animal that's not interested in traveling very far. Widely spaced tracks that slide forward at the end of each step indicate a deer that's looking to cover some ground, either moving from feeding to bedding sites or, if it's a buck during the rut, searching for does to breed.

267. Be Prepared to Hike Long Distances

Always wear a daypack when you hunt mule deer. You often have to cover long distances to find them in the open country they live in, and you don't want to get stuck far from your truck without the proper equipment when the weather changes suddenly, as it often does in the mountains. Make sure your pack fits well and is roomy enough to carry a change of clothes, rain gear, a good knife, rope, binoculars, a compass, a survival kit, and extra food and water. Bring your pack even when you think you'll be hunting close to your camp or your vehicle; you never know when a fresh track might take you deep into the backcountry.

268. Look for Sandy Basins to Find Mule Deer

"If there ever was just one thing to see or look for in a new area for deer, 'white sand' is one of the 'gold nuggets' of success. For some reason deer love a little basin with white sand in it. It always has the best bitterbrush and is more open. If I'm in a new area and I see 'white sand,' I'll start hunting right there, right now."

—Dennis Wintch, from "How to Hunt Mule Deer—Hunting in a New Area,"
Hunting Illustrated magazine, August/September 2003

269. Locate Clear-cuts to Find Feeding Mule Deer

One of the best places to hunt mule deer in evergreen forest habitat is a recently logged clear-cut. Deer-friendly shrubs and plants grow rapidly in these clearings as their roots penetrate the disturbed soil and their leaves soak up sunlight normally blocked by large trees. You may have to walk a few miles to reach such clear-cuts, as most logging roads on public lands will be closed to public vehicle traffic, but with unpressured, top-notch feeding habitat as your reward, the hike will be worth the effort. Contact your local BLM or Forest Service office to get information on where these cuts have taken place (you want cuts that are 10 years old or younger), and plan your hunt accordingly.

270. Wintertime Habits

"While the sun was strong, they liked to lie out in the low brush on slopes where they would get the full benefit of the heat. During the heavy snowstorms they usually retreated into some ravine where the trees grew thicker than usual, not stirring until the weight of the storm was over."

—Theodore Roosevelt, *Outdoor Pastimes of An American Hunter,* Scribner's, 1905

271. Use Thermal Currents When Stalking Bedded Bucks

Early morning air that has been cooling all night tends to flow downhill; later in the morning, as this air heats up in the light of the sun, it will reverse direction. These uphill/downhill flows are called thermal currents, and they are important to remember when stalking hot-weather bucks. If you're glassing a clearing for feeding deer at first light, make sure you're positioned so that no downhill currents will carry your scent to the animals. Later, as the deer move uphill to bed, plan your stalk so that you approach them from above.

272. Look for Bucks in Edge Cover on the North Sides of Ridges

A great place to look when you're spotting for bedded mule deer is edge cover (thick brush lining clearings or other openings in which deer can remain concealed while still enjoying a good view of their surroundings). Look first along the north sides of ridges, which generally get more shade. Since deer here will already be bedded down, try to pick out pieces of the animals. Ear flicks, hind-leg scratches, and antler-glints may be the only clues you'll have to find the buck you're hunting.

273. See and Be Seen

When glassing for mule deer, keep in mind that if you're sitting in a place with a 360-degree view of the surrounding terrain, deer on all sides will have a good view of you, as well. Make sure to hide your silhouette by sitting with a rock, some brush, or a stump at your back.

274. Follow the Farthest Track

Mule deer are very alert to the sounds and smells of animals following their back trails and will spook easily if they see you before you see them. To make sure you get the drop on an animal you're tracking, avoid looking too closely at its individual prints. Instead, keep track of the overall trail by picking out the furthest clear track you can see, then still-hunting up to it, keeping your eyes peeled for movement in the distance. Repeat until you find your target.

CHAPTER 4

Bear Hunting

275. How to Tell a Grizzly Bear from a Black Bear before Taking a Shot

When hunting bears in the western states you must be very good at distinguishing between black bears, which are huntable, and grizzlies, which are protected under federal law. Color is not a determining characteristic; many black bears exhibit the same blonde coloration often associated with grizzly bears, and many grizzly bears come in darker colors. Instead, a hunter should look for two things. The first is the presence of a distinct hump on the shoulders; grizzlies have one, black bears do not. A hunter should also try to get a good look at the animal's face in profile. A black bear's nose slopes down from its forehead in a straight line. A grizzly bear's forehead dips inward from the forehead before pushing out into its nose, giving its face an indented, slightly concave appearance.

276. Don't Track a Gut-shot Bear in the Dark

If you find bits of intestinal matter in the blood of a bear you're trailing it means you've shot the animal in the gut. Trailing a gut-shot bear can be dangerous. It's a good idea to avoid following one too quickly—you want to give the animal time to stiffen up and/or die. If you shot the bear in the morning, you should wait at least four hours before picking up its trail. If you shoot a bear in the gut in the evening, you should wait until the morning. Avoid tracking a gut-shot bear in the dark.

277. The Black Bear Wants Your Food

"A good thing to remember is that all blacks are pirates and have a mighty yearning for the white man's grub. A camp left unguarded in black-bear country is a sure invitation for trouble. For some unfathomable reason blacks have never learned to recognize a tent entrance. Or maybe they prefer to make their own entrances and exits. At any rate, whichever the case, they always tear a large hole in one side of your tent going in, and another large hole in the opposite side going out."

—Russell Annabel, "Plenty of Bear," *Field & Stream,* 1937, reprinted in *The Field & Stream Reader,* Doubleday, 1946

278. Spring Bears on Winter Kills

Winter takes a toll on elk and deer herds. If you know the spots where winter kills are concentrated, that is the perfect place to look for a spring bear to stalk.

279. A Bear of Many Colors

Not all black bears are black. They come in many color phases, including blonde, cinnamon, chocolate, and even pure white or blue. Hunt the eastern states if you want a black phase black bear; other color phases are rare east of the Mississippi. Hunt the western states for a brown, cinnamon, or blonde-phase black bear. White phase bears (known as Kermode or spirit bears) and blue phase bears (known as Glacier bears) are found in British Columbia, but are protected from hunting by law in the province. Glacier bears, however, are also found in Alaska and can be hunted there.

280. Where to Punch a Bear

If you're attacked by a bear that seems intent on eating you, the best place to hit it when trying to fight it off is square in its sensitive nose.

281. When Bears Head to Dens

Bear denning is governed by a combination of factors, including the availability of food, average temperature, and whether or not the animal is a pregnant female. The following list showing average denning dates by state and province comes from Richard P. Smith's *The Book of the Black Bear* (© 1985, Richard P. Smith):

Alaska: Early to mid-October
Alberta: Early November
Arizona: Late November
California: Mid-December
Colorado: Late October/early November
Idaho: Late October/early November
Maine: Late November/early December
Michigan: Mid-November
Minnesota: Early November
Montana: Early November
New York: Late November/early December
North Carolina: Late December
Ontario: Late October/early November
Virginia: Late December/early January
Coastal Washington: Early December

282. Help Bears Find Your Bait Pile

If you're planning to hunt over bait you've just set out, it's a good idea to tie a dead couple of dead fish or a rancid slab of bacon to a length of rope and drag it along trails that lead toward the pile. Bears have excellent noses, and if they encounter such a scent trail will be likely to follow it directly to your bait, even if the wind is blowing in the wrong direction.

283. Look for Crop-raiding Bears

If you live in a state that will not allow you to hunt bears over bait, you'll need to figure out where the animals are naturally feeding. One easy way to do this is to canvas farmers in the area you're hunting to see if any of them are having problems with bears raiding their corn fields, gardens, or other crops. You'll get a head start on the scouting process, and get the added bonus of expanding the amount of land on which you have permission to hunt.

284. Wait for the Big One

If you see a smaller bear acting nervous around your bait pile, it could mean that there's a larger, dominant animal nearby. Hold your fire for the bigger bruin.

285. Go Buy a Hound Dog

"All serious black bear hunters should own at least one hound for trailing purposes."

—Richard P. Smith,
The Book of the Black Bear, 1985

286. Chill Your Bear before Butchering

If you plan to butcher your bear on your own, always try to chill the carcass before deboning and separating the meat into steaks, chops, roasts, and other cuts. The cooler the meat, the easier it is to work with.

287. The Best Time for Bear Pelts

The earlier in the spring you can shoot a bear, the better quality its hide will be. Bears shed their winter coats as the weather warms up, often rubbing against trees, rocks, and fence posts to scrape off unwanted hair. If you shoot one later in the spring it may have a patchy, scruffy-looking hide. Catch them close to when they leave their dens you'll get a much better-looking pelt.

288. Make Sure Your Bear Is Dead

When approaching a downed bear, always look to see if its eyes are open or closed. If its eyes are open, the animal is likely dead. If they are closed, the bear may still be alive and should be shot again.

289. When Black Bears Attack

"Indian hunters will tell you that a fighting black is more to be feared than either the grizzly or Kodiak, for the reason that the latter two species seem always to be in a frantic hurry about mauling a man, while a black will rip and tear at a victim as long as there is a spark of life remaining. This explanation of the Kodiak's tactics may account for the number of men who have lived to tell the tale after being mauled by the big brownies."

—Russell Annabel, "Plenty of Bear," *Field & Stream,* 1937, reprinted in *The Field & Stream Reader,* Doubleday, 1946

290. The Curious Eating Habits

"Black bear generally feed on berries, nuts, insects, carrion, and the like; but at times they take to killing very large animals. In fact, they are curiously irregular in their food. They will kill deer if they can get at them; but generally the deer are too quick. Sheep and hogs are their favorite prey, especially the latter, for bears seem to have a special relish for pork. Twice I have known a black bear to kill cattle."

—Theodore Roosevelt, *The Wilderness Hunter,* 1893

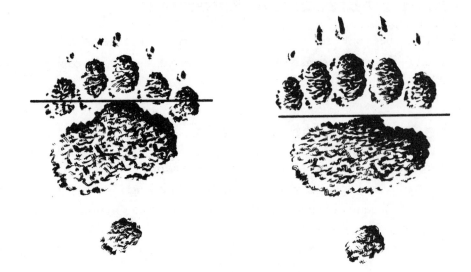

291. Tell Black Bear Tracks from Grizzly Tracks

You can't tell a black bear's tracks from a grizzly's based on size alone. Large black bears will have tracks as big as medium-size grizzlies, and variations in sex and age make this an even more unreliable indicator. And while grizzlies usually have longer claws than black bears (translating into claw marks further from the tips of the toe imprints), not all surfaces pick up claw marks. The best way to tell which animal left a track you've found is this: find the imprint of the bear's front foot and draw a straight line across the base of the toes so that it's just touching the top of the front pad. If it's a grizzly track, most of the toes will be above this line. If it's a black bear the inside toe will be mostly below this line.

292. What You Can Learn from Bear Droppings

You can tell a great deal about a bear from the droppings it leaves behind. Bear droppings dry out quickly, so if you find moist dung you'll know it was deposited recently. You can tell what the bear has been eating, and plan to hunt over the food sources it's been visiting. And you can tell how large the bear was that left the scat by estimating the diameter of its droppings; smaller droppings were usually left by small sows or cubs; anything over two inches in diameter should have you looking over your shoulder for a monster.

293. Biggest Black Bear Ever

The heaviest wild black bear on record was taken in 1885 near Stevens Point, Wisconsin. It weighed 802½ pounds.

294. Distract an Overly Curious Bear by Dropping Your Pack

One way to distract a bear that's showing a predatory interest in you is to drop an item that you're carrying as you're backing away from the animal. A backpack, hat, or even a glove may distract the bear long enough for you to evacuate the area, especially if it has some food in it.

295. Leave Human Scent behind to Scare Unwanted Predators away from Your Bait

Wolves and coyotes are quite common in bear country, and can do a great deal of damage to a bait pile, a real problem when you have to carry fresh bait deep into the woods far from a road. One good way to keep them from scavenging your set up is to leave an old, dirty sock or two near the bait pile. The human scent left on the socks should be enough to frighten off wary canids, but won't bother the bears at all.

296. Don't Bother Hunting in a Heavy Wind

Because a bear's sense of smell is so keen, it can be nearly impossible to hunt them when the wind is blowing heavily and/or changing direction often, especially if you're hunting in a stationary stand over a bait pile. Windy days are good days to find a different activity.

297. Use Your Ears to Find Feeding Bears

If you're still-hunting a bear, following a fresh trail in new snow, or otherwise looking for bruins by sneaking through the forest on foot, make sure to keep your ears uncovered and alert. Bears often make a great deal of noise while eating, breaking branches, flipping over logs, and destroying rotten stumps. They'll also make noise when moving through the forest, and are one of the only other creatures in the woods that snap large branches when walking.

298. Get a Dog on the Trail Right Away

If you own a tracking dog, or know somebody who does, don't wait too long before putting him on the trail of a bear you've shot. The dog will follow the freshest trail it can find, and if there are other bears nearby you don't want to give them time to spread their scent over the area.

299. Carry Tracking Line to Mark a Blood Trail

According to Richard P. Smith, author of *The Book of the Black Bear*, one of the best ways to keep track of a bear's blood trail is to carry a couple of spools of Game Tracker line. This line is more commonly used by bowhunters (it attaches to their arrows and spools out after they shoot) but is also very helpful for hunters carrying guns. If you're trailing a wounded bear, simply allow the tracking line to pay out behind you. You'll get an easy to follow, continuous record of the trail you're following, and you won't have to break your concentration in order to tie bits of surveyors tape to branches or mark the trail some other way.

300. Never Salt a Hide You Plan to Freeze

If you're planning to turn your bear's hide over to a taxidermist but can't get it to the shop within 24 hours, you'll need to store it in a freezer in order to keep it from decomposing. Keep your freezer on its coldest setting, and never salt the hide first; the salt will prevent it from freezing.

301. Why Late Season Is a Great Season

Fall bear hunting generally gets better later in the season. One reason is that bears move more often in cooler weather. Another is that in states or provinces where baiting is legal, hunters will often stop maintaining their bait piles after they fill their tags. Animals that were feeding on such bait will actively search for new food sources, making your own pile that much more attractive. Last, if you kill a bear in the late season, when the air is usually cold, you'll have an easier time of getting your meat out of the woods before it sours.

302. The Bear's Main Alarm System

Both black bears and grizzly do not have great eyesight. Oh, they can see all right, but sight is not their most powerful sense. Their noses, however, are amazing. There's an old Indian expression that sums it up: "The pine needle fell in the forest. The eagle saw it fall. The deer heard it fall. The bear smelled it fall."

303. When Black Bears Can Be Dangerous

"In the spring, soon after the long winter sleep, they are very hungry, and are especially apt to attack large beasts at this time; although during the first days of their appearance, when they are just breaking their fast, they eat rather sparingly, and by preference the tender shoots of grass and other herbs, or frogs and crayfish; its not for a week or two that they seem to be overcome by lean, ravenous hunger. They will even attack and master that formidable fighter, the moose, springing at it from an ambush as it passes—for a bull moose would be an overmatch for one of them if fronted fairly in the open."

—Theodore Roosevelt, *The Wilderness Hunter*, 1893

304. Attract Ravens to Call in Bears

It's always a good idea to leave some extra food scattered about in open areas near your bait pile. Such leavings often attract ravens, which in turn will bring in bears attracted to the loud croaks and caws they make when feeding.

305. The Differences between Boars and Sows

It can be very difficult to determine the sex of a black bear in the field. Male black bears, called boars, are generally much larger than females (sows) and have larger heads and longer bodies. Female bears rarely reach 350 pounds; boars commonly grow to 500 pounds or more. However, the only sure way to tell a younger male from a female is to look for a penis. This is easy in the spring and summer months, but can be difficult in the fall, when a bear's belly hair will be quite long.

306. Size a Bear by Looking at Its Tracks

You can get a good idea of how large a bear is by looking at its tracks. Average-sized black bears (150 to 200 pounds, dressed) will leave front tracks that are 3½ to 4 inches wide, and rear tracks that are from five to six inches long. The tracks left by a trophy-sized animal will be much larger, with front pads five to six inches wide, and rear pads eight inches or longer.

307. Be Patient with Your Bait Pile

If you suddenly stop seeing sign around an active bait pile, do not assume that the bears in the area have been spooked. Bears will often stop feeding on bait temporarily when new food sources become available, but will return once those sources have become exhausted or are no longer in season.

308. Stimulate a Bear's Predatory Instinct

Try calling in a bear by imitating the sound of a prey animal in distress. The squalling of a rabbit or bleat of a distressed fawn can be the best way to bring a bear you've spotted in thick cover out into the open, or to bring one that's too far away to within shooting range.

309. Where to Shoot a Bear with a Gun

The best place to shoot a black bear with a rifle, shotgun, or handgun when the animal is broadside to you is directly in the center of its shoulder. If you're using the right caliber rifle (.270 or higher) this shot should break both of the animal's shoulders and penetrate its lungs. If the bear is facing you the best place to shoot it will be directly in the center of the chest. If it's facing away from you, shoot it in the center of its back, directly between the shoulder blades.

310. Anatomy of a Grizzly's Charge

"I saw a grizzly put on the greatest display of courage and vitality I ever witnessed in the wilds. The bear had been shot through the heart with a heavy soft-nose, and its chest cavity reduced to a mass of exploded tissue. In this condition, apparently running blind, it charged fifty yards down a broken shale slope, missed us, and pitched over a rimrock and piled up dead in the timber below. Medical friends tell me the charge was pure reflex, like a chicken running with its head off. But it wasn't reflex that headed the bear in our direction. That was fighting courage, a last-ditch attempt to even the score."

—Russell Annabel, "The King of Bruins," *Hunting and Fishing in Alaska,* Knopf, 1948

311. Give a Bear Time to Die

Be careful when trailing a bear you've shot if you're only hunting with a bow. Pay attention to where your arrow hits the animal, and delay tracking it until you're confident that the bear has had time to die. Wait at least a half an hour if you hit it in the lungs, an hour if you hit it in the liver, and at least four hours if you shoot it in the gut. If possible (and legal), bring along a friend with a gun.

312. Don't Contract Trichinosis

Bears are known carriers of trichina worm larvae, and bear meat should never be eaten raw or undercooked. Always make sure any bear meat you eat has been heated to at least 140 degrees Fahrenheit for at least two minutes.

313. The Best Weather for Bears

According to Richard P. Smith, author of *The Book of the Black Bear*, the best conditions for seeing bears are when it's raining lightly or misting and there is little to no wind. He believes that bears know fewer hunters will be out in such weather, and that they move more because the air is generally cooler and because they can stalk prey more quietly.

314. Grizzly on a Kill—Look Out!

Other than a sow bear with cubs, probably the most dangerous animal in the Great Outdoors is a grizzly that has made a kill. Sometimes the great bears will cover the carcass (likely to be a moose) then lie right on top. Other times they will be in the brush, upwind, guarding their kill. When a man approaches, they might run away. Then again, they may not! They may charge like fury from hell. The casualty lists are high in this situation.

315. What a Bear Trail Looks Like

Because bears will generally step in the exact same places when taking familiar routes, well-used bear trails often look like old, deep footprints worn into the forest floor rather than the smooth, groove-like paths normally associated with game trails.

316. Trail a Drive to Bag a Trophy

One of the best ways to bag a big bear when putting on a drive through thick cover is to post a couple of shooters behind the drivers. Older bruins do not startle easily and will avoid leaving their security cover if at all possible. Instead of running out ahead of the drivers as a younger bear might do, a big bruin will often simply circle around them. Hunters following the drive stand a good chance of seeing bears that behave this way.

317. Bowhunting Black Bears

Time was when only the top experts even thought about taking a bear with a bow. Not today. Many of the same bowhunters who bag whitetail bucks with their bows are on the hunt for black bears—mostly over bait in Canada. Opportunities to bag a bear with a bow abound in Canada. When Googling for information, make sure you type in the province you're interested in, and, of course, look for the guides and outfitters who have solid records in bowhunting.

318. Black Bear Sizes in Roosevelt's Day

"The black bear does not average more than a third the size of the grisly; but, like all its kind, it varies greatly in weight. The largest I myself ever saw weighed was in Maine, and tipped the scale at 346 pounds, but I have a perfectly authentic record of one in Maine that weighed 397, and my friend, Dr. Hart Merriam, tells me that he has seen several in the Adirondacks that when killed weighed about 350."

—Theodore Roosevelt,
The Wilderness Hunter, 1893

319. How to Measure a Trophy Bear

"Boone & Crockett recognizes four species of bear in North America: the Alaska brown bear, the grizzly bear, the black bear, and the polar bear. All are scored the same way, by measuring a dry skull's greatest width and adding it to its greatest length. The minimum scores required to make the all-time B&C books are:

Alaska brown bear—28 inches

Polar bear—27 inches

Grizzly bear—24 inches

Black bear—21 inches."

—Tom McIntyre, www.fieldandstream.com

320. Sex a Bear by Reading Its Tracks

While it can be very difficult to tell if a bear track was left by a young male or a female animal, you can be reasonably confident that you're following the tracks of a male bear if its front foot pad measures at least four inches across. Most female bears will not grow large enough to leave tracks that wide.

321. Hunting Black Bears over Bait

If you've ever taken as few as three paces into spruce, alder, and birch forests of Maine or Canada—the "Bush" as it is known—you know why the black bear is hunted over bait in the region.

322. Where to Shoot a Bear with a Bow

The absolute best shot on a bear with a bow is when an animal is angling away so an arrow can be placed behind the shoulder blade and into the lungs.

— Richard P. Smith, *The Book of the Black Bear*, 1985

323. Talk Loudly to Avoid Startling Bears

According to Richard P. Smith, author of *The Book of the Black Bear*, a hunter should rarely sneak when hiking in to hunt a bait pile. If a bear is already feeding there, the sudden appearance of a human may startle the animal, which could cause it to avoid the bait in the future, or to feed on it only at night. Instead, the hunter should warn any bears in the area of his approach well in advance of arriving at the bait. Whistle and talk in a normal, calm voice on the way in; this will notify the bear that you're on your way before you're close enough to startle the animal. Bears know that bait is left by humans and while they will move away off to avoid being seen when they hear people approaching, they will not be spooked as long as they are not taken unawares, and should return once they think you are no longer in the area.

324. The Right Size Dog

The best size for a bear dog is between 40 and 70 pounds. Hounds of this size are large enough to frighten bears into running, fast enough to keep up with them over long distances, and quick enough to dodge when a bear is cornered.

325. Smaller Targets

A black bear's lungs are not as large as those of a whitetail deer and are located further forward in the animal's chest cavity.

326. The Grizzly on Your Kill—It Can Happen!

In grizzly country, the elk or moose or deer you've killed and have been dressing out and packing out may become the property of a wandering grizzly. If it does, and you approach it without your rifle, or without being alert, you just might be on your last hunt. Another good idea is to make plenty of noise as you approach your kill.

327. Practice Judging Bears at the Zoo

One of the best ways to practice field judging black bears is to observe them at your local zoo. Try to guess the sizes of the animals in the exhibit, then find a zookeeper and ask him how much the bears weigh.

328. Be Careful When Hauling a Dead Bear

You should wrap the carcass of a bear you've shot with hunter orange material if the animal is small enough to carry out of the woods slung across your back.

329. Avoid Surprising Brown and Grizzly Bears

According to the Alaska Department of Fish and Game's web site, it's important to make your presence known when hiking in bear country "especially where the terrain or vegetation makes it hard to see. Make noise, sing, talk loudly or tie a bell to your pack. If possible, travel with a group. Groups are noisier and easier for bears to detect."

330. Don't Play Dead if a Black Bear Attacks

Grizzly bears are territorial animals, and when one charges you it is likely more interested in defending its territory than it is in eating you. Black bears are less likely to attack humans, but when they do are more likely to be looking at them as a potential meal. If you are charged by a grizzly, stand your ground while maintaining a non-threatening posture, then slowly back away. If the animal knocks you down, curl up into a ball, lock your hands over the back of you neck, and play dead until the grizzly loses interest. If a black bear attacks you, however, you should always attempt to defend yourself. Grab a stout branch and make yourself appear as large, loud, and intimidating as possible. If the animal knocks you down, fight back. Playing dead will only encourage the bear to start feeding.

331. Don't Let Other Hunters Sit on Your Bait Pile

When hunting where baiting is legal, the most important first step is to determine where to place your bait. It's a good rule of thumb to always do so at least a quarter mile from the nearest road or access point. This will reduce the chances that other hunters will discover your baiting site.

332. The Oldest Black Bear Ever

The oldest black bear ever recorded in the wild was shot in New York in 1974. It was 41½ years old.

333. Don't Pee near Your Bait Pile

Avoid urinating near a bait pile. Other human scents rarely scare bears away from bait, but animals use urine to mark territory and warn off others. It makes little sense to send such a message to an animal you're trying to attract.

334. Train Bear Dogs on Raccoons

One of the best ways to train a young hound for bear hunting is to start it out hunting raccoons. Raccoons behave much like bears do when chased by dogs, but they don't run as fast and they tree more quickly. These less-demanding chases are easier on both puppy and hunter, and make for less frustration all around.

335. Pick Out Landmarks with Your Ears

Always listen closely to the sounds a bear makes if it runs away after shoot it. Bears make a great deal of noise when moving quickly through the forest. If you can associate visual land-marks with the sounds you hear you'll have an easier time of following the trail of a wounded animal.

336. Use Multiple Knives When Trimming Bear Fat

Bears spend the summer and fall months building up a thick layer of fat in preparation for their winter dormancy. If you shoot one in the fall, you'll need to trim off this fat before storing the animal's meat. The meat will keep longer and take up less space in your freezer, but the process takes time. Save some by having a few spare knives and a sharpening tool handy.

337. Don't Plan a Spring Hunt Too Early

Watch the weather when planning a spring bear hunt. A warm spring will get bears moving earlier in the season, but an unseasonably cold one will discourage them from leaving their dens. If you're traveling out west or to Canada to hunt spring bears, it's a good idea to build a bit of cushion into your schedule in case winter lingers longer than normal.

Photo courtesy of Jay Cassel

CHAPTER 5

Pig Hunting

338. Distinguish Hog Tracks from Deer Tracks

Although hog tracks and deer tracks can be the same size, it is not difficult to tell them apart once you know what to look for. Hog tracks are blockier than deer tracks and have rounded rather than pointed tips. Deer tracks are teardrop shaped; hog tracks are square in both front and back, and have a more uniform width.

339. Confessions of a Pig-hunting Addict

"I have a curious claim to fame, one that's not jealously contested by anyone I know. Some persons are great sheep hunters—Jack O'Connor, for example—others are great bear, deer, or lion slayers. Me, I'm big on pigs. All kinds of pigs. Small, large, European, African, Asian, American, it makes no difference. For some strange reason, fate has provided me with more varieties of pig hunting than could be thought possible. I've been in Arizona and Texas for javelinas, Georgia for feral (razorback) hogs, North Carolina for European wild boars, Mozambique for red forest pigs and warthogs."

—Jim Rikhoff, "Big on Pigs," *Mixed Bag,* The Amwell Press, 1979

340. Mississippi Haven for Wild Boars

"The Chickasawhay River swamp in Greene County, Mississippi, may have one of the oldest populations of feral pigs in the nation. The area has no record of a time when this river-bottom swamp hasn't homed hogs. Fences and property lines never have bound the free spirits of these feral hogs—just like the wild boars of old. They roam at will, foraging for food, hiding out in the big cane thickets and briar patches along the edges of the river bank and wreaking havoc on croplands by night. Hunters with packs of hounds and live traps and sportsmen with rifles and bows never have eliminated these free-roaming pigs. They have become as much a part of the land as the earth itself."

—John E. Phillips, "John's Journal," Night Hawk Publications

341. Load Your Feeder with Lots of Bait

When setting up a feeder to attract pigs, it's always a good idea to load it with lots of bait. The more bait you use, the less often you'll have to haul in a refill, which spreads more of your scent around the area and could lead to hogs that will spook more quickly.

342. Hunt Small Herds to Find Unpressured Pigs

If you know there are pigs in the area you're hunting but find only minimal amounts of sign, do not get discouraged. Smaller herds of pigs can be more predictable (and thus easier to hunt) because they are generally less pressured than larger groups, whose obvious trails and numerous wallows attract many more hunters.

343. Invest in Good Snake Boots

Always wear snake boots when hunting pigs in rattler, cottonmouth, or copperhead habitat. They will protect you from strikes that hit you below your knee, the most common type of bite.

344. Wild vs. Feral

Very few of the hogs in North America are truly wild—most are descended from domestic pigs, and should be referred to as feral. A true Russian wild boar has a much longer nose and legs than a hog descended from domestic stock, it will have a pronounced ridge of hair running down the center of its back, and its tail will be straight.

345. Control Your Scent When Hunting Hogs

Todd Triplett, author of *The Complete Book of Wild Boar Hunting*, believes that scent control is a vital element of any successful hog hunt. "Always wash with scent-free soap before heading afield, especially from late spring through early fall," he says. "Put on scent-free anti-persipi-rant and use scent-eliminator sprays . . . on your gear and clothing. Wear boots that don't leave scent, preferably an all-rubber design."

346. Shoot to Kill Quickly When Hunting Hogs

A hog's vital organs are located lower in its body cavity than are vital organs in the body cavities of ungulates. To ensure a killing shot, always aim directly behind the shoulder as well as slightly lower than you would aim on a white-tailed deer. Be very sure of your shot before pulling the trigger or releasing your arrow. You do not want to have to follow one far after hitting it; hogs have a thick layer of fat beneath their skin that can quickly plug a wound, making blood trailing difficult, especially if you shoot the animal in a wet, swampy environment.

347. The Challenge and the Prize

"A challenge for the early hunters to take, the wild hog remains one of the most sought-after game animals in America. As one hog hunter explained, 'To know the nature of a wild hog, start with just plain hog. Then add a constitutional leanness and an ability to run all day—fast. Add skill at gutting hounds, willingness to charge a man, the fleetness of a deer, the cunning of a bear and the elusiveness of a fox.'"

—John E. Phillips, "John's Journal," Night Hawk Publications

348. Spot-and-Stalk Hogs in Open Country

In fairly open country, spotting wild pigs from a distance and then stalking them can be an effective method. Start out by trying to situate yourself you where you have a commanding view and the wind is coming toward you. If pigs are seen at a distance, walk slowly and quietly toward them, keeping the wind at your face and using available cover. Since wild pigs have poor eyesight, you may be able to get fairly close without being detected.

—www.jesseshunting.com

349. Follow the Plows to Find Feeding Hogs

A great place to hunt pigs during the summer is near a freshly-plowed garden or crop field. Hogs visit these locations looking for fresh roots that have been turned over by the plow's blade.

350. Bowhunting for Hogs

As you would expect, bowhunters are just as fired up to try hog hunting as rifle hunters. The guides and outfitters are out there, and you can find them on the internet by Googling "wild hog bowhunting guides." One of the sites we like for information is Strictly Bowhunting, www.strictlybowhunting.com.

351. Hunt Hogs over Acorns

One of the best places to set up a stand or ground blind for hog hunting is in or near an oak tree that is producing lots of acorns. Look for red, white, or live oak trees that are producing a good crop of the nuts and set up your stand downwind of where the acorns have fallen. Remember that acorn production is cyclical; a tree that produces lots of acorns one year may not drop any the next.

352. Look for Thickets to Find Bedded Pigs

Wherever you hunt pigs, you can be confident that they'll spend their days holed up in the thickest vegetation to be found. Look for palmetto thickets in swampy bottomland, laurel tangles in the mountains, and grown-over clear cuts in forested country that are near a good source of food, such as an old orchard or grove of acorn-producing oaks. Set up your stand on trails that lead from their bedding cover to where they eat and make sure you're sitting in it long enough for the scent you left on the way in to disperse by the time they head out to feed in the evening.

353. Wild Boar Hunting: A Link with History

"About 40 million years ago, the pig-like mammals became two families, the Old World pigs, which lived in Eurasia and Africa, and the New World pigs, the peccaries, which did and still do live from the southwestern U.S. to southern South America. Tales abound of the danger of both families of pigs. In India alone in one year's time, wild boars killed fifty people. Ancient mythology commemorated boar hunting. Homer wrote the world's first account of a boar hunt centuries before the birth of Christ. Hercules and King Arthur both hunted boards. Throughout the Renaissance, hunting wild pigs remained a popular sport of royalty."

—John E. Phillips, "John's Journal," Night Hawk Publications

354. Here He Comes!

"When a wild boar means mischief, he makes his run with his head down. It is by a sudden thrust upward of his tusks that he does his deadly work. When he charges with his head high, he probably means that he just wants gangway."

—Archibald Rutledge, *An American Hunter,* Lippincott, 1937

355. Don't Enter a Hog's Core Bedding Area

When still-hunting for hogs, always avoid entering the core of a known bedding area. Though the goal during midday is to find a bedded hog, accidentally stumbling into a group could push them out of the area for several days.

— Todd Triplett,
The Complete Book of Wild Boar Hunting, 2004

356. The Best Boar Hunting Story of Them All

Like to read a wild boar hunting story that's off the chart in excitement and excellence? Then check your local library or the internet and get hold of a copy of the novel, *Home From the Hill*, by William Humphrey. This novel of a young man in the southwest contains descriptions of hunting down a legendary wild boar. The novel was made into a movie, by the way, but no movie-making could ever come close to William Humphrey's excellent prose version of the hunt.

357. Find Faint Trails to Ambush Big Boars

If you're hunting for an old tusker, avoid the temptation to set up on the most obvious hog trails in your area. These trails will be heavily used by young boars, sows, and juveniles who travel in groups; older males tend to be solitary and often take their own routes from food sources to bedding cover. Look for a faint trail that's not cluttered with different-sized tracks and hang your stand in the best location for an ambush.

358. Use a Blind When Hunting with Your Kids

The next time you take a child hunting, consider using a blind. Kids have a hard time sitting still for extended periods of time; a blind lets them shift positions without getting caught.

359. Look for Wallows When Scouting for Hogs

Wallows are muddy or dusty patches of ground where pigs roll to cool themselves off, remove parasites attached to their skin, and cover themselves in dirt to keep off biting insects. These are great places to look for when scouting, because you can use them to identify the sizes and numbers of animals in a herd. Tracks are easy to find in such places, and you can get an accurate read on a hog's size by measuring the imprints left by its body in the mud.

360. Hunt over Bait during the Evening Hours

Hunting over bait during the warm summer months is a great way to find pigs that might otherwise be feeding unpredictably on the variety of widely dispersed food sources found at this time of the year. But don't bother waiting over your bait pile or feeder during the morning or the middle of the day. Evening hunting will be far more productive, as hogs that are leaving their beds stop by for a snack on their way to nocturnal foraging.

361. See More Hogs by Hunting from a Boat

Since hogs prefer habitat that is low-lying and wet, two of the best places to hunt them are in deep swamps and along river bottoms. These can be extremely convenient places for hunters to find them, because you can use a boat to sneak into prime hunting cover without snapping and crackling your way through thick brush.

362. Wild Boars: What You're Hunting

Wild boars in America are a mixture of feral (born wild) pigs from domesticated stock running loose in the woods for decades, even centuries, and of original European wild boars brought into this country and planted at different locations. One of the main plantings was by a man named George Moore who in 1912 put fourteen European wild boars on his 1600 acres of timbered land surrounding Harper's Bald, a mountain peak in the Snowbird Mountain Range of North Carolina. Moore thought of his land as a preserve, but, of course, the hogs roamed into the countryside and have been there for decades, plus spreading elsewhere in the Great Smokies. The pure European wild boars have also been imported in places ranging from New Hampshire to California to Georgia.

363. Hunt Hogs near Old Homesteads

One of the best places to look for wild hogs is around an abandoned homestead. Pigs like these sites because they often contain abandoned orchards, overgrown gardens with wild-growing vegetables, and are located close to open meadows or overgrown pasture that offer a range of other food sources.

364. Wild Boars up North

In case you're thinking wild boar hunting is strictly a southern thing, check out this Wild Boar Reserve about 60 miles northwest of Toronto: www.bigtusks.com, (619)-323-3506. You'll find other wild boar hunting opportunities in Canada by Googling "wild boar hunting in Canada."

365. Don't Stalk One Spot Too Often

When still-hunting for hogs, it's a good idea to avoid walking through a specific area too often. Hogs quickly wise up to human sign and will become very wary if they think people are using their home territory. Hunt the area from a tree stand as often as you like, but only stalk through it once every three or four days.

366. Read a Pig Rub to Find Big Boars

Hogs often rub their bodies on nearby trees when they're done using a wallow, smearing sap on their hides to provide further protection from biting flies. Keep your eyes peeled for these rubs, because they can also give you clues to the size of any boars using the area. Look for the scars left by a big boar's tusks; if you find them you'll know you're hunting in the right place.

367. The Two Best Ways to Hunt Pigs in Summer When You Don't Have Bait Are . . .

During the summer months, most pigs feed nocturnally to escape heat and insects during the middle of the day. If you're not planning to hunt over bait, you'll have a hard time finding these animals. The two best tactics to use in such situations are, first, to hunt behind dogs, which is the easiest method. Second best is still-hunting, which can be productive because pigs are ranging widely to feed on many different food sources.

368. Scout for Scat to Learn What Hogs Are Eating

Always analyze hog scat closely. You can determine a great deal about what a pig is eating from both the consistency and composition of its feces. Wet, loose stools indicate rich, moist food sources such as fresh tubers. Look for undigested bits of food for further clues to the animals' diet, and adjust your hunting to fit what you learn.

369. Sizing Up Wild Hog Country

"Remember when hunting wild hogs that they have an extraordinary sense of smell, a good sense of hearing and considerable intelligence—but poor vision. Although wild hogs can move at a trot and are good simmers, they can gallop only for a short distance. Wild hogs frequent regular paths connecting their resting places, feeding areas, water holes and wallows and particularly the salt licks. They must have water available for bathing in mud, which is of great importance to their well-being and gets rid of parasites."

—John E. Phillips, "John's Journal," Night Hawk Publications

370. Size Matters!

Several wild boar hunting lodges charge by the size boar you wish to hunt—the bigger the more expensive. Typical of this type operation is Cumberland Mountain Hunting Lodge near Cookeville, Tennessee: www.cmhl.com, (931)-456-9025. Their hunts are for three days for boars starting at 170 to 249 pounds and going up to 350 to 500 pounds.

371. Still-hunt for Pigs When They're Bedded Down

If you're hunting pigs in thick cover, avoid still-hunting during the early morning and late evening. Hogs are easier to approach when they're bedded down than when they're actively moving and feeding, and they are naturally more active during low-light conditions.

372. Don't Hunt Pigs near Their Bedding Cover

Be very careful when hunting anywhere close to a [pig's] bedding area. Most hogs will already be in the security of their lairs by early morning; any intrusion could cause them to abandon that core area temporarily. And if you repeatedly push hogs from these areas, they may leave permanently.

— Todd Triplett,
The Complete Book of Wild Boar Hunting, 2004

373. Kill Quickly When Hunting Summer Pigs

Shot placement is very important to summer pig hunters. If you hit an animal and it runs long distances before dying, it can be very difficult to find it before its meat goes sour. Make sure to always place the shot through the heart and/or lungs, and follow up quickly to retrieve your kill.

374. Don't Use a Scoped Gun When Hunting Hogs with Hounds

Shooting a bayed boar is difficult when dogs are darting around and harassing the animal. Don't carry a gun mounted with a scope in such a situation. It's easy to make sure you have a clear shot when you're shooting with open sights, but a scope restricts your field of view, making it hard to know if a dog is about to jump in front of your muzzle before you pull the trigger.

375. Focusing on Hog Habits

"When hogs feed on acorns, they eat the nuts as soon as the nuts hit the ground. Often, you won't see any sign of where they've fed. Although deer leave many droppings in their feeding area, hogs primarily leave their dung around their bedding regions. That's why you have to know where and how hogs move to hunt them."

—Lee Taylor of Leakesville, Mississippi, in interview with writer John E. Phillips, "John's Journal," Night Hawk Publications

376. Find Hog Wallows in Fine, Silty Soil

If you're looking for a hog wallow, start by searching in areas where the soil is rich with clay or other fine silt. This soil coats a hog's skin better than coarse, sandy soil, leading to better protection from insects and parasites.

377. Bait Pigs without Getting Winded

If you're setting up a bait pile to attract wild or feral hogs, always wear gloves to mask your scent. Pigs have excellent noses and may be wary of human sign, especially if they've been hunted before. Spread your bait along trails you know pigs use, creating a trail that leads to the larger pile where you plan to set up, and make sure your stand is downwind of the pile.

378. Look for Boars When You Hear a Pig Squeal

If you hear a pig squeal for several minutes in the evening, it's likely the sound of a sow being bred. Chances are good she has a large boar with her. Pigs do not have large home ranges; you'll have a good chance of seeing this boar if you make a note of where you heard the sow squealing and hunt that area later.

379. Watch out for Snakes When Hunting Pigs in the Summer

According to Todd Triplett, author of *The Complete Book of Wild Boar Hunting*, one of the most worrisome aspects of summer pig hunting is the fact that venomous snakes are very active at this time of the year. You can reduce the risk of an encounter in snake country by walking on dry, open ground, and avoiding low hanging branches snakes use to sun themselves. Also make sure to check carefully entering a blind, stand, or vehicle; snakes often crawl into such structures to hide.

380. Don't Shoot a Trophy If You're Looking for Meat

One of the best things about hog hunting is the meat you get after shooting one. There are few things tastier than tender, fresh, preservative-free wild pork. If you're hunting for the table, however, look for a young pig. Avoid old boars in particular; the taste of a hog's meat diminishes quickly as an animal approaches 200 pounds.

381. Bring a Big Enough Gun to Kill Big Boars

Hogs are tough-skinned animals, especially mature boars, which develop thick pads of gristle beneath the scarred hides on their shoulders as protection against the tusks of other males. It's a good idea to carry a fairly heavy caliber when hunting one. Good choices are the .30-06 and .300 Winchester in open country, and brush guns such as the .450 Marlin when hunting in swampy lowlands and river bottoms.

CHAPTER 6

Moose Hunting

382. Make Your Own Moose Thrasher

Here's how to make a simple, easy-to-transport call used for imitating the sound of a moose thrashing its antlers in thick brush. Take a 40-ounce plastic bottle and insert a one-and-a-half foot length of wooden dowel about five inches into the mouth of the bottle. Wrap duct tape around the neck and the dowel until the dowel is secured to the bottle, then cut off the bottom of the bottle with a pair of scissors. To use, simply hold the call by the wooden handle and rake it through a bush or across the ranches of a sapling.

383. Don't Glass from the Same Spot You Call

It's always a good idea to change your location after you've finished an extended calling sequence so that you are glassing the area from a spot upwind of where you were calling. If there's a bull in the area, you can be sure he will have heard you and will remember the exact spot your calling came from. When he eventually comes in to investigate it's likely he'll first circle downwind of where he heard your calls. Switching spots lets you stay undetected if this happens.

384. Observations on Charging Moose

"Under ordinary conditions, however, there is very little danger, indeed, of a moose charging. A charge does not take place once in a hundred times when a moose is killed by fair still-hunting . . . Yet there are now and then found moose prone to attack on slight provocation; for these great deer differ as widely as men in courage and ferocity. Occasionally a hunter is charged in the fall when he has lured the game to him by calling, or when he has wounded it after a stalk."

—Theodore Roosevelt, *The Wilderness Hunter*, 1893

385. Pick the Right Bullet

You do not need a heavy caliber rifle to kill a moose; you need a bullet that will penetrate deep enough to reach the animal's vitals. Choose a long, tough, heavy-for caliber bullet with a high sectional density; such a bullet won't expand too quickly and will hold together well after impact. Pick the right bullet and you can use any centerfire cartridge from 6.5 × 55 on up.

386. Be Patient When Calling in Moose

Moose are curious creatures, but they can take their time satisfying that curiosity. Even during the peak of the rut it can take days for a moose that's heard your calling to decide to investigate. Be patient. There will be rare occasions when a nearby bull that's crazed with lust comes crashing into your setup right away, but most calling won't pay off until many hours later.

387. You Don't Need a Big Knife to Field Dress a Moose

Big knives can be useful tools in many situations, but they are not necessary equipment for field dressing North American big game, including moose. All you really need is a 4-inch blade. Anything longer becomes awkward to handle within an animal's body cavity, and you run the risk of cutting through the animal's viscera.

388. Walk like a Moose

Moose have sensitive ears and a keen sense of smell. It is very unlikely you'll be able to approach one on foot without it hearing you, even if you're working into the wind. Fortunately, you do not have to be completely silent. Instead, try to sound like a moose. First, make sure you're wearing no clothing that makes unnatural rustling sounds when brushed against branches or grass. Second, make sure any metal items you're carrying in your pockets, on your gun sling, or clipped to your jacket or pants are tightly secured so that they don't clink or clank while you're walking. Last, do not try to sneak. Predators sneak, tensing up their bodies in order to perform deliberate movements designed to minimize motion and reduce the sounds of their steps. Moose know what sneaking sounds like, and most humans are not capable of sneak quietly enough to fool one. You'll have more luck if you step as quietly as possible while still maintaining a loose, natural stride. Any sounds you make will likely be mistaken for the sounds of another moose, elk, or deer moving at a relaxed pace through the brush.

389. How to Recognize a Pissed-off Moose

When a moose is irritated by your presence, it will use its body language to warn you that it's upset, pulling its ears back and flaring the long hair along its neck and hump, much the way a dog will when looking for a fight. It may even growl at you and lick its lips. When you see this, back away quickly and try to get a large obstruction between you and the animal.

390. Russell Annabel on Alaska Moose Hunting

"Sheep hunting is great sport, bear hunting is packed with adventure and thrills, and there is a definite kick in risking your neck climbing the windy crags of the goat country—but for downright fun, I'll take a moose hunt any old time. Like grouse shooting, it's a sport that goes with bright leaves tingling down through the branches of old trees, with quiet noonday watches on sun-drenched hillsides, with cautious sallies through the shadowy green-gold enchantment of deep forest aisles, and with campward horseback rides in the purple, star-shot dusk of mountain evenings. It is a sport for the man who appreciates the wilderness at its best, who has an eye for color and beauty—and yet it also has its taut, pulse-quickening moments."

—Russell Annabel, "In the Moon of the Painted Leaves," *Field & Stream*, 1936, reprinted in *The Field & Stream Reader*, Doubleday, 1946

391. Wintertime Habits

"A 'yard' is not, as some people see to suppose, a trampled-down space, with definite boundaries; the term merely denotes the spot which a moose has chosen for its winter home, choosing it because it contains plenty of browse in the shape of young trees and saplings, and perhaps also because it is sheltered to some extent from the fiercest winds and heaviest snowdrifts. The animal travels to and fro across this space in straight lines and irregular circles after food, treading in its own footsteps, where practicable."

—Theodore Roosevelt, *The Wilderness Hunter*, 1893

392. Break Some Brush to Call in a Bull

Bull moose will often thrash bushes, saplings, and small trees with their antlers to display their dominance and spread their scent around an area during the rut. One of the easiest ways to call in a big bull is to imitate this behavior. Find a dead evergreen and break off a few of the dry branches at its base to make sharp cracking sounds, use an axe to chop at dry, dead saplings, or thrash bushes with heavy stick. Dominant moose in the area will often come running to investigate.

393. Calling Moose Is Not for the Faint of Heart

Always use extreme caution when attempting to call a moose. If you're imitating the sounds of a bull, you run the risk of bringing a rut-crazed, 1,000-pound beast with huge antlers charging into your setup. As if that weren't frightening enough, you'll also be imitating the sounds of a primary food source for brown, black, and grizzly bears. Be prepared to take quick action if you attempt this hunting method.

394. When to (and When Not to) Use a Big Scope

Oversize, 50mm objective lenses will always collect more light than standard-size rifle scopes, giving you a distinct advantage in low-light conditions—brighter, sharper images of the animals you're aiming at. This does not mean, however, that you should always carry such a scope on your rifle. Oversize lenses are great choices if you're hunting from a stand or spotting and stalking in country where you expect to take long shots at unsuspecting moose. But if you plan to do much still-hunting, they can be a liability. There are two reasons for this. The first is that oversize scopes require higher mounts than standard scopes, which means it's more difficult to acquire a proper sight picture when you need to make a quick shot. The second is that oversized scopes are heavy! You'll be much happier if you mount standard-sized optics on the gun you use for still-hunting.

395. What to Do if You're Attacked by a Moose

The best thing to do if you're charged by a moose is to run away as fast as you can. Most moose won't chase you very far once they see that you're no longer a threat. It's also a good idea to put a tree between you and the animal; moose can't circle trees as fast as you can. If the moose knocks you down, it may continue running or start stomping and kicking with all four feet. Curl up in a ball, protect your head with your hands, and hold still. Don't move or try to get up until the moose moves a safe distance away or it may renew its attack.

396. Moose Hunting in a Big Wind

Upland bird hunters hate days of the howling winds. Duck hunters love them. Moose hunters should love them. Working your way into position for a shot at moose is much easier in a big wind, if you plan your hunt to approach from downwind. First, the moose isn't going to catch your scent. Secondly, they can't hear much with the wind howling.

397. Grunt like You Mean It

Bull moose grunt when challenging each other and when trying to win cows in a herd. These grounds are short, deep, and occur every two to three seconds. The best way to imitate one is to use your grunt call like you would a musical instrument. Don't just blow sound through the call, put feeling into it. Be pissed-off. Tell the woods about your ugly mood; pick a fight with a tree. If you can communicate these feelings using simple "ugh!" "ugh!" grunts, you'll be right on target.

398. Unstoppable in Snow

"Snowdrifts will render an ordinary deer absolutely helpless, and bring even an elk to a standstill, offer no impediment whatever to a moose."

—Theodore Roosevelt, *The Wilderness Hunter*, 1893

399. Flash a Moose with Your T-shirt

If you see a bull moose in the distance that is either too far away or in cover too thick to shoot through, try "flashing" the animal. A bull will often shake his head at a rival, "flashing" him with the white of his antlers in a display of aggression. Since a moose's eyesight is relatively poor, you can imitate this display by simply waving a light-colored piece of fabric, such as a t-shirt or even a plastic bag. The sight of these "antlers" can be all it takes to bring your bull into range.

400. Stop a Startled Bull with a Cow Call

If you spook a bull, try making a long, loud cow call as he runs away. There's a good chance he'll stop to figure out where the sound is coming from, giving you an opportunity to make a quick shot.

401. Keep Your Scope Fog-free

It's a good idea to avoid keeping your rifle in a warm tent or cabin overnight. If the next morning is cold and damp the inside of your scope could fog up, and you won't be able to wipe it clear. A better place to store your gun is locked in the trunk of your car or the cab of your truck. In the morning the scope will be at the same temperature as the air outside, and condensation will not occur.

402. Watch for a Camp Bull

Always keep a sharp eye out near camp if you're hunting moose in the backcountry. Bulls will often be attracted to the sounds made by you or your guides chopping wood, pounding in tent stakes, or breaking branches when clearing the ground at your campsite.

403. Watch Out for Your Dog in Moose Country

According to the Alaska Department of Fish and Game, moose consider dogs to be their enemies and will sometimes go out of their way to kick at them, even if the dog is on a leash or in a fenced yard. Give moose an extremely wide berth if you have a dog with you, as your pet might cause the animal to react violently.

404. When Moose Charge

It is most unusual for a moose to charge a hunter, in the manner of say a grizzly charging. But well-documented cases of moose charges do exist—and far from just on hunters. Ranchers are sometimes charged by moose deciding to reside in their feed lots; actual Alaska Railroad locomotives have been charged by moose; hikers have been terrorized by a bull in rut. They're not a real menace, but moose do charge folks sometimes.

405. One Enormous Animal

Moose are the largest members of the deer family on the planet, and the Alaska-Yukon moose is the largest kind of moose (there are seven different subspecies, with four—Alaska-Yukon, Shiras, eastern, and northwestern—living in North America). The heaviest moose ever killed by a hunter was an Alaska-Yukon bull that weighed 1,697 pounds.

406. Call like a Cow Using Only Your Voice

Cow calls are high-pitched groans that can be best described as a high, moaning "eerrrrrrrr" sound. These calls can be relatively short in duration, or can last for up to two minutes. You can imitate the sound using your voice alone. To do so, pinch your nose (a nasal sound does a better job of imitating a cow), cup your hands over your mouth, and start your "err" sound at a lower pitch, gradually raising pitch in the middle of the call, holding the "r," and wavering your tone a bit before lowering the pitch as you taper off into silence.

407. Take a Second-chance Trophy

According to Wayne Kubat, an Alaska Master Guide and owner of Alaska Remote Guide Service, it's always a good idea to return to an area you know holds good bulls, season after season, even if you missed or otherwise startled an animal the season before. "If you botch a chance on a good bull during one hunting season, consider spending a little extra effort looking for him in the same area during the next season," he says. "Moose, like many other animals, are very consistent in their seasonal movements from year to year.

408. Brighten up Your Sights

If you hunt with open sights you know that it can be difficult in low-light conditions to quickly align your front sight in the rear sight's notch. You'll have a better chance of keeping your shot from going high when taking quick shots if you paint the top of your front sight with fluorescent fly-tying lacquer (or even your wife's fingernail polish). Make sure to remove the bluing from the sight first (use an emery cloth), then paint the bare metal (pink is a good color).

409. How to Field-judge a Moose

According to Boone & Crockett's *Field Guide to Measuring and Judging Big Game*, the best view for judging a moose's antlers is from the front, when a bull is holding its head so that the rack is nearly vertical (imagine a bull moose feeding and you'll have a good idea of what to look for). Top-scoring antlers generally lie flatter instead of cupped up. Since it's hard to count points in the field, judge racks based on overall antler mass. Note that width is not as important as well-developed palmation, and look for broad brow palms with three or more points.

410. They're Bigger Than You Think

"People who have never seen a full-grown bull moose in the flesh seldom realize how big they are. Some bulls have stood eight feet high at the shoulders, with the great head and antlers towering several feet higher. The average bull runs to about 1,200 pounds, but many go as heavy as 1,800 pounds. A few guides have claimed 2,000-pound bulls, but the weights were estimated and could not be verified with scales in the remote wilderness."

—Eric Cameron, "Moose Are Mighty Dangerous," *Field & Stream,* September, 1953

411. Why Moose Are Called Moose

The name "moose" comes from the Algonquin language and means "eater of twigs."

412. Piss Off a Big Bull

One way to convince a moose that there's a rival in his territory is to imitate the sound of another bull pissing. Get a large container such as an empty plastic milk jug, fill it with water, then pour it back into the water from around the height of your chest. Subtle sounds like this can be very effective if you use them sparingly and are patient enough to wait for a curious bull to investigate.

413. Moose by Canoe

Moose love water, and so do many moose hunters. This is because there are few ways to access unpressured moose habitat more quietly and with less effort than by paddling into it. And there are few ways of packing out moose meat more efficiently than by carrying its quarters in a canoe. Scan banks and shorelines for moose standing hidden in the brush, and pay close attention when paddling up or floating down rivers that connect ponds and small lakes—moose travel along these streams because they often flow through flat terrain that's easier for them to traverse.

414. Hang Your Stand on the Eastern Side

If you can only hang one stand overlooking a clearing you think moose are using, it's a good idea to hang it on the clearing's eastern edge. The prevailing winds in most moose habitat blow from the west, putting you be downwind of your target in normal weather conditions.

415. Make Cheap Trail Markers out of Clothespins

You can make your own reusable trail markers by wrapping the wings of simple wooden clothespins with half-inch strips of reflective tape. Simply clip them to branches along the route you use to get to your stand in the dark and use a flashlight to pick them out on your way in in the morning. You can also waterproof the clothespins by dipping them in polyurethane, a good idea if you plan to leave them in the woods for any length of time.

CHAPTER 7

Caribou Hunting

416. Alaska's Caribou Herd

According to Alaska's Department of Fish & Game, the state has almost twice as many caribou as it has people. Alaska's human population numbers around 600,000, while there are over one million caribou in the state

417. Where Caribou Range (and Used to Range)

Although caribou are found almost exclusively in Alaska and Canada, they once ranged widely in northern North America and in Northern Europe. But overhunting and habitat destruction led to their eradication from Germany during the Roman era, Great Britain during the Middle Ages, and Poland in the sixteenth century. Caribou were gone from most of the United States by the beginning of the twentieth century.

418. Caribou Migrate the Furthest

Some caribou migrate more than 3,000 miles each year—farther than any other land animal. They travel in herds every fall and spring from their wintering to their calving grounds, and arrive just in time to think about heading back.

419. Multi-purpose Hooves

A caribou's hooves are wide, concave, and act like snowshoes, distributing the animal's weight on snow, ice, and melted muskeg. These hooves also work like paddles when caribou need to swim across fast-flowing rivers, or even large lakes. But they don't slow the animals down. Caribou have been recorded running faster than 50 miles per hour.

420. Caribou Never Stop Moving

Caribou are not the wiliest game animals a man can hunt, but that doesn't make them easy prey. First you have to find them. Then you have to decide whether or not to wait to shoot a trophy. You can't pattern a caribou because it never stays in one place. The herd you're stalking today might be miles and miles away the next. If you see a bull you like, pull the trigger, because you never know what tomorrow will bring.

421. Make Sure You're in Shape

"Stories of caribou shot from the tent lull some hunters into believing a caribou hunt takes no physical effort. But selective hunting for big bulls almost always does. You may hike as little as several miles a day or go on a really prodigious walk. Bad weather can add to your fatigue, as can a full pack. If you are not in shape when you go, you will very quickly wish you were."
—Wayne van Zwoll, "Caribou: Noble and Mobile," www.fieldandstream.com

422. Bring the Right Optics

Unless you're a bush pilot, hardest part of hunting caribou will be finding the herd. Bring high-power binoculars (at least 10 × 42) and carry a spotting scope. Make sure to use top-quality glass or you'll lose your ability to hunt during the morning and evening hours.

423. Don't Spook the Herd

"When you're sneaking up on a bull, keep track of other caribou. They seem to float in from nowhere just when you want to move. Though caribou won't jet away like a whitetail buck when you surprise them at a distance, they will jog off and take other caribou with them. Then you have two options: Stay put and hope they stop so that you can stalk them again, or run after them. In my experience, spooked caribou seldom give you an easy second hunt."
—Wayne van Zwoll, "Caribou: Noble and Mobile," www.fieldandstream.com

424. The Cows Have Antlers

"Caribou are the only deer in which both sexes have antlers. Males shed their antlers following the fall breeding season (young males retain their antlers longer that mature males). Pregnant females shed their antlers soon after the calves are born in the spring. Non-pregnant females shed their antlers during the winter."
—Alaska Department of Fish & Game

425. Average Caribou Weights

Mature caribou bulls weigh, on average, about 400 pounds, but they can grow to as large as 600 pounds. A cow caribou's average weight is about 250 pounds.

426. Trophy Caribou Criteria

According to fieldandstream.com, Boone & Crockett recognizes five different caribou categories. All are judge by the same criteria; only the sizes vary. Minimum all-time scores are 400 for barren ground caribou, 390 for mountain caribou, 375 for Quebec-Labrador caribou, 295 for woodland caribou, and 360 for Central Canada barren ground caribou.

427. Antlers by Subspecies

"Antler configuration can vary greatly between the subspecies. While woodland bulls of eastern Canada typically have smaller racks, the Quebec-Labrador bulls can grow significantly larger and wider. Central barren-ground bulls are perhaps the most diverse in configuration and can grow to be very high and wide. Mountain caribou are typically the most massive, with trophy-class specimens boasting the largest circumference measurements of all six subspecies."

—Kevin Wilson, "Caribou Hunting," biggamehunt.net

428. How to Field-judge a Caribou's Antlers

When trying to guess the length of a caribou's antlers, use the animal's shoulder as a measuring stick. Most shoulders will be between 48 and 54 inches high. Look for antlers with curved main beams, which will generally be both longer and wider than straight ones (though they may look shorter from the side). A trophy animal's shovels will be broad, have multiple points, and extend far out over the muzzle. Kicker points, the spikes that grow off the back of a caribou's antlers, will add to the score, as will palmation and extra points at the tops.

429. Tasty and Healthy

Because caribou do not store much of their fat in muscle tissue, their meat is leaner than beef. Caribou meat is considered more healthy than beef, and is quite tasty.

—Alaska Department of Fish and Game

430. How Old Do They Get?

Male caribou can live to reach seven or eight years in the wild. Females live slightly longer, to 10 or more years. These numbers are not averages, as many caribou die within the first year after they are born.

431. The Largest Herd of Caribou

"There are currently three very large herds of caribou, the Western Arctic herd in northwest Alaska, the George River herd in northern Quebec, and the Taimyr Peninsula herd in Siberia. Each herd is currently estimated at close to 500,000 or more individuals. Due to different census techniques and schedules, as well as annual fluctuations in populations, it is not possible to say which of these three herds is currently the largest."

—Alaska Department of Fish and Game

432. How to Read a Caribou's Body Language

"When caribou are not alarmed, they walk quite slowly, extending the head forward and downward. When alarmed, caribou perform a special behavior to warn other caribou of danger. They'll do this if a predator gets too close, but isn't about to catch them (or after they figure out that you're a person sitting on a rock). An alarmed caribou will trot with the head held high and parallel to the ground, and the short, normally floppy tail held up in the air."

—Alaska Department of Fish and Game

433. A Good Gun for Caribou

While a good shot won't need more than a .270 to take down a thin-skinned animal like a caribou, the animals are much larger-bodied than most whitetail deer. It can help to shoot a bigger gun when you're reaching out to knock one down at the long ranges you'll often find when hunting in the tundra. One great caribou cartridge is the .338 Win Mag. Loaded with a 200-grain bullet, the cartridge will hit three inches high at 100 yards. Elmer Keith loved this chambering for both caribou and elk, and you will, too.

434. Make Those Long Shots

Make sure to pack a good rangefinder and a pair of shooting sticks when heading north on a caribou trip. Long shots of up to 400 yards are common on the tundra. Practice these shots at the range in advance of your trip, and use the rangefinder to confirm all distances before you shoot after you've arrived.

435. Find Caribou Where It's Cold

"Caribou will usually frequent the coldest, highest spots around, except in the dead of winter when they are seeking protection in the valleys and lowlands. This is good to remember when you're scouting for them. Look for them to be on the windy, exposed mountain heights or standing in the snow patch that has never melted from last winter's storms."

—Tom Brakefield, *The Expert's Book of Big Game Hunting in North America*

436. Winterize Your Caribou Gun

Always make sure to keep your gun clean, moisture-free, and either grease-free or treated with synthetic lube designed to function in extreme freezing temperatures. The last thing you want when firing your rifle at a caribou after a long, freezing, late season stalk is for the hammer, firing pin, or trigger to malfunction because your gun's oil congealed in the cold.

437. Don't Put Wet Bullets into a Freezing-cold Rifle

Always carefully clean any cartridges you've dropped on the ground if you're hunting in the far north during the late season. They make pick up moisture that causes them to freeze to the inside your gun's chamber, reducing your expensive rifle to a single-shot firearm.

438. See and Be Seen

When glassing for mule deer, keep in mind that if you're sitting in a place with a 360-degree view of the surrounding terrain, deer on all sides will have a good view of you, as well. Make sure to hide your silhouette by sitting with a rock, some brush, or a stump at your back.

CHAPTER 8

Pronghorn Antelope Hunting

439. Vision and Speed: The Pronghorn's Defense

"His eye is larger than that of cow or horse, nearly as large as that of an elephant; they give him somewhat the appearance of a huge beetle. He can see half or three-quarters of a mile away, with a range of vision keener than that of an 8-power glass. . . . I've seen a herd fairly fly across the plains up to the foothills and trees, then scorn the cover they have reached and circle back and back again, as if playing a game of tag with your bullets. The pronghorn is a real sportsman. He runs, but he never hides."

—Major Robert E. Treman, "Wyoming Antelope," *Field & Stream,* 1937, reprinted in *The Field & Stream Reader,* Doubleday, 1946

440. Wear Knee Pads and Gloves for Pronghorns

Knee pads and leather work gloves should be part of the antelope hunter's arsenal. Available at home improvement stores, they are the ticket when you have to scramble on your hands and knees over rocks and cacti to get into range of a 'lope.

441. Pronghorn on the Run

Pronghorn antelope have been authentically clocked at speeds exceeding 55 miles per hour.

442. The Pronghorn Alarm System

The white rump of the Pronghorn has white hair that can be raised at will (the Bighorn Sheep has the same type). The hair is raised in alarm—a perfect signal to all its kindred that danger is stalking the herd.

443. The Old Pronghorn Flagging Trick

Indians did it, and now modern-day hunters sometimes fool pronghorns by flagging them from ambush. The trick takes patience, sweating out the teasing movements as the pronghorns come nearer, then ease away, then come nearer again, then ease away again.

444. How Big Is That Buck?

It's tough to gauge the size of an antelope buck from a half-mile away, but if you can detect an especially pronounced black spot on the side of his head, you can bet he's worth a stalk.

445. The Pronghorn Challenge

"Antelope shooting is the kind in which a man most needs skill in the use of the rifle at long ranges; they are harder to get near than any other game—partly from their wariness and still more from the nature of the ground they inhabit . . . Even good hunters reckon on using six or seven cartridges for every prong-horn they kill; for antelope are continually offering standing shots at very long distances, which, nevertheless, it is a great temptation to try, on the chance of luck favoring the marksman."

—Theodore Roosevelt, *Ranch Life and the Hunting-Trail,* The Century Co., 1888

446. Feel Lucky?

"As in all other kinds of big-game shooting, success in hunting antelope often depends upon sheer, downright luck. A man may make a week's trip over good ground and get nothing; and then again he may go to the same place and in two days kill a wagon-load of venison.

—Theodore Roosevelt, *Ranch Life and the Hunting-Trail*, The Century Co., 1888

447. The Well-placed Shot

"Antelope are very tough, and will carry off a great deal of lead unless struck in exactly the right place; and even when mortally hit they sometimes receive the blow without flinching, and gallop off as if unharmed. They should be followed up a little distance after being fired at . . ."

—Theodore Roosevelt, *Ranch Life and the Hunting-Trail*, The Century Co., 1888

448. Set Your Decoys with Stealth

When hunting pronghorns with a bow, a decoy can make the difference between a fruitless stalk and a successful hunt. The trick is to creep close enough to set one up, and then to set it up without being spotted. Wait until the buck you're hunting is busy chasing a doe, or obscured from view by a clump of sage or other brush. If he sees your decoy rise up out of the grass he may grow suspicious of the unnatural motion and fail to come closer to investigate.

449. The Double Decoy Setup

If you are able to carry two decoys with you when stalking a pronghorn with your bow, bring one imitating a small buck and another that looks like a doe. You want the herd buck to think that a smaller rival has stolen one of his girls.

450. Roost Pronghorns like Turkeys

According to Mark Kayser, whitetail columnist for *North American Hunter* magazine (and an avid antelope bowhunter), it is possible to roost antelope the way you roost a turkey. "If you locate a herd of pronghorns and watch them until dark, odds are high they'll be in the same general location at sunrise," he says. "You can get in close before shooting light and fool him more easily in the dim light of dawn."

—"Pronghorn Lessons From The Prickly Pears," *Bowhunting World Annual*, 2004–2005

451. No Country for Pronghorn Stalking

"For successful stalking, you need to hunt country with rolling or broken topography. Wash-outs, gullies, ridges and gumbo buttes provide plenty of topography for a sneaky bowhunter to get within 40 yards of a lone buck that has yet to join a herd. Targeting lone bucks is the key. Pronghorns have unmatched big-game eyesight, and a herd is like a Hubbell telescope on legs, offering reduced stalking success."

—Mark Kayser, "Pronghorn Lessons From The Prickly Pears,"
Bowhunting World Annual, 2004–2005

452. Learn to Draw while Kneeling

"It pays to practice drawing your bow from a kneeling position. You need to bring the arrow to full draw with the bow in a horizontal position. You may want to invest in a new rest to keep the arrow from falling off when holding at the canted position."

—Mark Kayser, "Pronghorn Lessons From The Prickly Pears,"
Bowhunting World Annual, 2004–2005

453. Don't Let Him Spot You

"Before you come up to range [a buck] or release [your arrow], make sure the buck is looking directly away. If he is looking any other direction, he'll pick up on the movement quicker than a Labrador spots an accidental food scrap falling from your table."

— Mark Kayser, "Pronghorn Lessons From The Prickly Pears,"
Bowhunting World Annual, 2004-2005

454. Sit over Water

You can avoid strenuous stalks during midday heat if you switch to hunting a water hole. Pronghorns are creatures of the dry, high plains, but they need to drink periodically, and will often show up during the hottest hours to slake their thirst. If you know which water sources they've been using you stand a good chance of ambushing one.

455. Hang Your Stand on a Windmill

A great way to hunt pronghorns is from an elevated stand over a water hole, but there aren't many trees on the high plains on which to hang your stand. If you can't find a convenient cottonwood, try climbing up a windmill. Ranchers use these to keep stock tanks and ponds full of water, which means they're often conveniently located for hunters looking for a thirsty speed goat.

456. Give Your Blind Time

If you plan to hunt from a blind overlooking a water source, make sure the blind has been in place for a few days before you plan to sit in it. Pronghorns will be wary of this new addition to the landscape after it first appears; you want to hunt from it after they grow comfortable enough with its presence to wander within bow range.

457. Wait until They Drink

"The key to a successful pronghorn setup [when hunting over a waterhole] is locating the corner of the waterhole where pronghorns frequent the most, then wait until they begin gulping before you release. Most shots are less than 30 yards. On a good water-hole setup, you may have more than 50 animals visit you during the course of an afternoon."

—Mark Kayser, "Pronghorn Lessons From The Prickly Pears,"
Bowhunting World Annual, 2004-2005

458. You Don't Need Long Shots

"The key to getting up on [pronghorns] lies in the seemingly flat land they inhabit, which is actually broken, cut, and intersected by coulees, ravines, gullies, washes, draws, ridges, hills, and divides. A smart antelope hunter can take advantage of this tortured topography to get close—almost always less than 200 yards, and very often less than 100."

—David E. Petzal, "Choosing the Right Rifle for Pronghorn Antelope,"
www.fieldandstream.com

459. Rangefinders Help

"Most misses on antelope occur because hunters don't believe they're as close as they are and shoot way over them. The cure for this is a laser rangefinder. . . . As a Montana guide said to me, 'Hunters don't believe me when I say it's a 200-yard shot, but if the rangefinder says it's 200, they buy that.'"

—David E. Petzal, "Choosing the Right Rifle for Pronghorn Antelope,"
www.fieldandstream.com

460. The Best Goat Gun of All

"Very possibly, the .25-06 is the best goat gun of all. It's a wonderful, light-kicking round that has plenty of velocity (but not so much that it will destroy the animal) and enough bullet weight, and it can double very nicely for mule deer if you're hunting them on the same ticket."

—David E. Petzal, "Choosing the Right Rifle for Pronghorn Antelope,"
www.fieldandstream.com

461. Use a Heavy Gun

Most pronghorn stalks will not take you deep into the backcountry, and so you do not need to carry a light rifle to save weight. Bring a heavier gun instead. It will shoot steadier, especially when prone or over shooting sticks, the way most shots at goats are taken.

462. An Antelope That's Not

"Although sometimes called antelope, pronghorn are not closely related to the animals of African plains. In fact they are so different from other hoofed animals that they are the only members of the family Antelocapridae. Their head ornaments set them apart from deer and elk whose branched, solid antlers are shed each year, and from goats and cattle whose hollow horns are made from hair and are not shed. Pronghorn have branched, hollow, hairlike horns that are shed annually. They are the only animal with this combination."

—Facts About Pronghorns, U.S. Fish & Wildlife Service, www.fws.gov

463. Glass from Your Truck

Most pronghorn antelope have yet to associate vehicles with the hunters who drive them. This makes your truck an idea platform from which to glass for a trophy. Once you've spotted a buck you want to stalk, glass out the route you plan to stalk, then drive your truck far enough away that the animal won't see you getting out.

464. The Pronghorn Antelope's Range

"True Americans, pronghorn are found only on the plains and grasslands of North America. Like bison, seemingly endless numbers once covered the west, stretching from Saskatchewan to just north of Mexico City. And like bison, they nearly became extinct. Populations declined from an estimated 30–60 million in the early 1800s to less than 15,000 by 1915. A moratorium on hunting lasting until the 1940s and a federal tax on firearms and sporting goods funding conservation efforts are credited with stopping the decline. Today there are almost 1 million pronghorn. Five subspecies are recognized: American/common (found in most of range, Canada, and northern Arizona); Mexican/Chihuahuan (found in New Mexico, Texas, formerly southeastern Arizona); Oregon (found in southeastern Oregon); peninsular (100–250 animals, found in Baja, Mexico); and Sonoran (endangered, 500 animals found at Cabeza Prieta National Wildlife Refuge and Sonora, Mexico)."

—Facts About Pronghorns, U.S. Fish & Wildlife Service, www.fws.gov

465. Some Facts of Pronghorn Biology

A male pronghorn weighs, on average, about 120 pounds. Females are slightly smaller, averaging 105 pounds. The animals are not large, standing approximately 3 feet at the shoulder. Both males and females have horns, though the male's are significantly longer, averaging 13 to 15 inches compared to the female's 3- to 5-inch horns. Pronghorns can live up to nine years in the wild.

466. How to Field-judge a Pronghorn

A trophy antelope's horns will be longer than thirteen inches, which is the distance from the base of an average pronghorn's ear to the tip of its nose. Horns that appear to be twice as long or longer than the animal's ears are likely to break the Boone & Crockett record books, especially if they are curved, crooked, and look wider at their bases than the width of the animal's eye. Look for horns that split into prongs above the tips of an pronghorn's ears. You want an animal whose front prong extends at least 4 inches forward from the main horn.

CHAPTER 9

Wild Sheep and Mountain Goat Hunting

467. "Pocket Hunting" for Big Sheep Heads

Their numbers have dwindled over the years, but the hunting that calls to the bold, sheep hunting, is still answered by strong hunters and resourceful guides and outfitters. Tucked in a classic from the stories of legendary Alaska hunter and writer Russell Annabel (see our Tip on Annabel in "Beyond the Basics") is this gem of advice to sheep hunters: "When scouting for sheep in new country, a useful formula to remember is that the better rams almost never are found on the 'front' slopes of a valley; they range back to the heads of tributary streams—in the high hanging basins. They like to feed below glacier ice, where constant summer-long seepage keeps the vegetation green and succulent." Annabel went on to say that the heads of clearwater creeks will four times out of five have no sheep on them.

—Russell Annabel, "Pocket Hunting for Big Sheep Heads,"
Hunting and Fishing in Alaska, Knopf, 1948

468. Alaska's Sheep Rules

"In most of Alaska's hunting districts, a legal ram must meet at least one of three requirements: (1) both horns are "broomed," or broken; (2) one of the horns shows at least eight annuli, or annual growth rings; or (3) one of the horns is full curl, describing a 360-degree circle when viewed from the side. These requirements describe only about 3 to 8 percent of the sheep population across the seven Alaskan mountain ranges where they live."

—Steven Rinella, "The Ghost of Sheep River," www.fieldandstream.com

469. North America's Native Wild Sheep

There are two species of wild native sheep in North America, the bighorn sheep and the Dall sheep. There are three subspecies of bighorn: the Rocky Mountain bighorn *(Ovis canadensis canadensis)*, the Sierra Nevada bighorn *(Ovis canadensis sierrae)*, and the desert bighorn *(Ovis canadensis nelsoni)*. There are two subspecies of Dall sheep: the Dall sheep proper and the Stone sheep.

470. Glass in the Morning

Although sheep move most during the morning and evening, it's generally a bad idea trying to find the animals late in the day. Sheep live in high, rough country. Unless you're prepared to spend the night, you don't want to get caught on the side of the mountain in the dark.

471. Watch for Their Rumps

"Bedded sheep will almost always get up and move around a little . . . between noon to around 1 PM. They may feed for a few minutes, or move from one group of beds to another nearby. Or they may only get up, stretch, turn around and lie back down in the same bed. If you are watching the right spot at the right time, you'll see their white rumps and know exactly where they are."

—Bob Hagel, *The Expert's Book of Big Game Hunting in North America*

472. Glass near Good Grass

Sheep are grazers, and will always be found near the green spots in the high country. Hunt for their sign near high basins and cliff-side seeps rich with grass.

473. Sheep Bed in Rock Slides

Sheep trails are generally well used and can be spotted from long distances as distinct lines crossing rock slides. Look near the center of these slides for rams bedded in the shelter of large boulders.

474. Glass from the Other Side

"If the country [you're hunting] contains a considerable amount of green timber, overhanging ledges and vertical cliff faces, your vision is very limited from above. The best vantage point in that kind of terrain is the ridge on the opposite side of the canyon. From there you can look into the little pockets under the cliffs and under the trees."

—Bob Hagel, *The Expert's Book of Big Game Hunting in North America*

475. The Colors of the Mountain

Bighorn sheep come in a variety of colors, from light tan to dark brown to a deep blue-gray. These colors vary from region to region (and sometimes within a single region). Because the animals tend to bed in spots that match the colors of their coats, it's a good idea to have a sense of the common shades found in the area you plan to hunt. Look for ground that matches these colors, then look for sheep hidden there.

476. How to Field-judge a Mountain Goat

Identifying a trophy mountain goat is not easy. The differences between a good billy's and a record-book animal's horns will often be less than an inch. The first step to finding a record is to make sure the animal you've spotted is, in fact, a male. Billies have high, humped shoulders, and shaggier coats than nannies. Once you've found an old male goat, straighten out his horns in your minds eye and compare that length to the length of the animal's head. If the stretched horns reach from the animal's nose to the bottom of its eye, they are less than nine inches long. If they reach from the nose to the base of the ear, they are at least nine inches long and will qualify as a true trophy.

477. Creep across Crests

When stalking sheep and goats, be extremely careful to never silhouette yourself against the skyline. If you must cross the crest of a ridge or a saddle, do so on your hands, knees, and belly, and move as slowly as you can.

478. Hide in Their Blind Spot

If you spot a group of sheep lying down, always try to glass out a route to stalk that lets you approach the animals from a higher elevation. Sheep almost always bed perpendicular to the slope they're on so that they can survey the land below, which leaves a blind spot behind and above them.

479. How to Field-judge a Trophy Sheep

When glassing for a record-book sheep, always look for a full, curling horn that's bottom extends below the line of the lower jaw. You want heavy, thick horns with broomed tips, which will score higher than unbroomed horns of the same length.

480. Use Those Binoculars

"Find a good vantage point and glass the area thoroughly—glass, glass, glass, glass. Many new sheep hunters walk too much and don't glass enough. Don't be discouraged if you don't see rams right away. They can be tough to find—so keep looking."

—www.huntingbc.ca

481. They Don't Sit Still

"If you make a stalk and the rams are gone don't panic but carefully look around. They may have just moved a short ways to get out of the sun or flies and are still close by."

—www.huntingbc.ca

482. Scan for a Silhouette

Sheep easily spot a skylined hunter's silhouette, especially when the hunter is moving. But the reverse is also true. When glassing for sheep, always keep a close eye on the tops of ridges, cliff edges, and the skyline over a saddle. Scanning for silhouettes is the easiest way to spot these animals.

483. Look for Big Rams near Small Ones

"If you find a young ram or two laying out on a rock ridge or shelf, don't be too eager to write them off as little guys and move on. Many times these little fellows are just sentries for the mature rams are laying in the shade fighting flies."

—www.huntingbc.ca

484. Don't Educate the Herd

If you're hunting with friends or as part of a guided group and are lucky enough to kill a sheep, don't immediately rush in to claim your kill after the shot. Stay hidden, watch to see where the animal falls, and wait to retrieve it until the rest of the herd has left the area. Avoid startling them and other hunters in camp will have a much easier time of stalking sheep in the area.

485. Some Cheap Mountain Camo

There's a reason Dall sheep and mountain goats have white coats; there's often snow year round in the mountains where they live. The next time you're planning a high country hunt for these animals, bring along a pair of white painter's overalls. Pull them over your hunting clothes when planning a stalk across a snowfield and you won't need to buy expensive, snow-colored camouflage.

486. The Ground Grows Trophies

"Look for an old loner goat living on mineralized slopes, the minerals contributing to horn growth."

—Tom McIntyre, "New Big Game Field Photos" from *Boone & Crockett's All-Time Trophy Record Books*, www.fieldandstream.com

487. Don't Drop a Goat off a Cliff

Be very careful before shooting a mountain goat to identify the place you expect the animal to expire. Goats live in extremely rough country. If you shoot one off the side of a cliff it may fall a long, long ways, ruining much of its meat and possibly damaging its horns. Worse, it may land on a ledge or some other feature of the terrain that you can't reach without a helicopter. The last thing you want is to shoot an animal you can't retrieve.

488. Account for the Hump

Don't let an old billy goat's hump throw off your aim. This massive growth of fat and hair covers a ridge of finlike vertebral spines and gives the animal a unique profile when compared with other big game. When preparing to pull the trigger, don't put your crosshairs roughly halfway up a mountain goat's body the way you would on an elk or a deer; the animal's vitals will be located in the lowest third of its body. Hold at the top of that lowest third to ensure a killing shot.

CHAPTER 10

Turkey Hunting

489. Learn to Shoot Turkeys from Both Shoulders

One of the most difficult situations in turkey hunting is having a bird sneak up behind you when you're sitting at the base of a tree. It can be extremely difficult to twist your body around far enough to make an accurate shot, and it's nearly impossible if the bird is behind your right shoulder if you're a right-handed shooter (and vice versa if you shoot with your left hand forward). It's a good idea to practice shooting your turkey gun from your opposite shoulder before the season starts. If you're comfortable taking shots this way your chances of getting a bead on a turkey without spooking it will improve dramatically.

490. Control the Volume of Your Box Call

If you're working a gobbler with a box call and he hangs up in the distance, you may be calling too strongly. Box calls are notoriously loud; the tom may think the hen you're imitating is closer to him than you want, and will often stop and wait, thinking that she will come to him. One way to get him moving is to reduce the volume of your call. Hold the call upside down, with the handle on the bottom, and slide your thumb up the sides to increase pressure on the call and gradually dampen the vibration. The gobbler will think the hen is moving away from him and may give chase.

491. Five More Reasons Gobblers Are Easy to Miss

Need more reasons to miss a gobbler within 30 yards? Try these: (1) The bird is moving, and you panic slightly, raising your head from the gunstock just a bit; (2) You gun is new, unfamiliar, or one you haven't shot in weeks or months; (3) You're wearing gloves, deadening your touch, and you pull the trigger like it's a rusty nail; (4) Your guide or companion is doing the calling, and he whispers the command "Shoot!" to you. You instantly obey, even though you're not ready; and (5) You try for a head shot. Any of these reasons is enough to make a grown man cry.

492. Removing Old Chalk Makes a Box Call Sound New

If your box call starts to sound dull and lifeless, it could mean that the chalk used to increase friction between the paddle and the sides of the call has become gummed up with foreign material. You can recondition your call by applying a fresh coating, but make sure to remove the old chalk residue first using a green scrubby. Do not use sandpaper or you will damage your call.

493. Use Decoys Late in the Season

The best time to use turkey decoys is after most hens are already sitting on their nests. A decoy is much less effective early in the breeding season when most toms will already be attended by hens.

494. Bust a Roosted Flock in the Spring

If you're hunting a gobbler that you know is roosting with a bunch of hens, try busting up the flock off the roost the evening before you plan to hunt. The turkeys won't go far, and they won't be grouped as usual, which could make the gobbler much more receptive to your calling in the morning than he would be if he were following his normal routine.

495. The Best Place to Set Up on a Roosted Gobbler

If you've done your scouting homework, you'll often know where a gobbler has roosted for the night. If you've done your extra credit, you'll know where he goes after he flies down. The best place to set up to call him in the morning will be between these two places, about 100 to 200 yards away from his tree (distance depending on how well leafed out the trees are). Get there well before first light, and sneak in as quietly as you can. Roosted birds are alert to unusual sounds and can pick up movements even in very dark conditions.

496. Don't Let a Hot Gobbler Get Too Close

The next time a gobbling tom comes trotting into your setup, don't wait too long before taking the shot. Most turkey load patterns open up at around 20 to 30 yards; this is the distance at which you have the best chance of putting a pellet into his brain or spine. If you let him get to close your pellets may be packed so tightly together that a slight miscalculation will cause all of them to miss.

20 yrds.

10 yrds.

497. Locating Roosting Gobblers

When your calling or scouting has located a roosting area (and you've been careful not to spook the birds!), you'll hear them fly up into the trees—big wings flopping, a great deal of noise. Be aware, however, that they don't pick the limb they wish to roost on from the ground, then fly up to it. It's after they are in the trees that they move around to a favored spot to spend the night.

498. When Gobblers Get Lonely

Many turkey hunters miss out on bagging their bird by not being alert to a hunting opportunity that takes place in the middle of the day. Sometimes around eleven o'clock in the morning, hens have left the gobbler to go to their nests. That's when the toms get lonely—and start to gobble, betraying their location. You can get into position, set up, and call in your bird.

499. Rake Leaves to Call in Hung-up Toms

The next time a gobbler hangs up in the distance, responding to your calls but refusing to approach, stop calling and start imitating the sound of a feeding hen by raking a hand through the leaf litter at your feet. If all goes according to plan, the gobbler will grow frustrated, wondering why the hen he can hear scratching for food won't respond to his calls, and will often come closer to investigate.

500. Get Ready to Shoot When a Tom Shuts Up

If a gobbling turkey falls silent, don't assume right away that he's lost interest. Resist the temptation to crank him back up with the call. Instead, get your gun ready. When turkeys shut up, it often means they're on the way to you.

— Philip Bourjaily,
The Field & Stream Turkey Hunting Handbook, 1999

501. Fake a Flock of Fall Turkeys

Most hunters use turkey decoys to stimulate a gobbler's mating or competitive instincts during the spring season, but decoys also work well for fall turkeys. The trick is to use lots of them to simulate a small flock. If you can figure out where the turkeys you're hunting roost, and where they feed, set up your fake flock between them and use a couple of different calls to imitate the sound of a few feeding hens.

502. Box Calls Work Best Out West

Hunters chasing Rio Grande and Merriam's turkeys in the wide-open spaces of their western habitat will frequently encounter situations in which loud calling is necessary, such as when a strong wind is blowing, or when turkeys are located far away across an open stretch of prairie. A box call is the ideal call to use in such situations. Make sure you bring more than one so that you can switch to the second if they get tired of the first.

503. Circle Gobbling Birds Hung up behind Obstacles

Gobbling turkeys hang up for lots of reasons, but one of the most common is that there's an obstacle between him and you. Streams, fences, and ravines will often keep a turkey from following up on the promise of a ready hen. In many cases you'll have the best luck killing your bird by crossing these barriers yourself. Using a crow call to keep him gobbling, circle around him until you're 180-degrees away from where you were set up before. He'll be more likely to return along a path he's already used than he will to work through less familiar territory, and you'll know there won't be any other obstacles on this trail that might obstruct his progress.

504. Spooking Roosting Gobblers

In the pre-dawn darkness, it's very easy to get too close to the area where you "roosted" a gobbler the night before. Slip into a calling site at a safe distance from the stand of trees where the birds roosted.

505. Faking Out a Gobbler: A Desperation Tactic

When a gobbler plays hard to get, and nothing else has worked try walking straight away from him, calling occasionally as you go. If he thinks his potential paramour is leaving him, he just might come running.

506. Pause after Loud Noises to Hear Distant Gobblers

Turkeys gobble to all sorts of loud noises—sirens, gunshots, foghorns, thunder—you should always pause and listen after any loud noise in the woods to see if it's startled a bird into gobbling.

— Philip Bourjaily,
The Field & Stream Turkey Hunting Handbook, 1999

507. Cover Ground to Find Mid-day Gobblers

Turkeys gobble more in the early morning than they do during the middle of the day. This makes them easier to find, but it does not mean they are easier to hunt. Most toms will gobble in the morning even if they're with hens, which means you stand a good chance of spending all morning talking with a bird that has no reason to come to your calls. If you find yourself working a bird that refuses to come to you, don't give up hope. Instead, go looking for a more accommodating tom. It is true that turkeys gobble less frequently when the sun is high, but the flip side of this behavior is that if you find one that does gobble, he is much less likely to be with a hen and will be far more willing to come in to your calls. Hike through your property and call every 100 yards or so until you get a response.

508. Don't Get Mistaken for a Turkey

Never wear any clothing or carry any accessories that contain the colors red, white, or blue. You should also keep your hands and head camouflaged when calling, and wear dark-colored socks and pants long enough to keep bare skin fully covered. These colors are found on the heads of wild turkeys, and you do not want to be mistaken for a gobbler by another hunter.

509. Make a Gobbler Jealous

You can use a decoy to simulate a breeding hen by pushing a hen decoy's stake deeply enough into the soil so that the decoy's belly touches the ground. Hens take this position when they're ready to mate. Put a jake decoy behind her (a jake is an immature male turkey), as if he's about to breed her, and the tom you're hunting may become so upset that he approaches your setup with much less caution.

510. Bust a Roosted Flock in the Fall

The most common tactic used by fall turkey hunters is to find and then scatter a flock of the birds and then sit down to call them back in. Turkeys will naturally want to regroup, and if you

call well enough to imitate a lost bird, they will use you as a homing beacon. One good way to find a flock to bust is to identify where the birds roost. Scout the woods for large hardwood trees with lots of fresh droppings at their bases, and head out the evening before you plan to hunt to listen for the sounds the birds make as they fly up for the night. Creep into the woods before sunrise the next day, and then rush the flock as soon as it flies down.

511. Coping with "Shut-mouth" Gobblers

If pressure has forced spring gobblers into silence, try patterning a long beard like you would a deer. He'll have favorites route he takes to favored strutting areas and feeding spots. So glass open areas until you find where the birds are using, then set up an ambush.

512. Practice for Turkey Season with Light Trap Loads

Do your shoulder and wallet a favor and practice [shooting your turkey gun] with light trap loads. Just be sure to try a few magnums before the season to make absolutely certain they shoot to the same point of impact.

— Philip Bourjaily,
The Field & Stream Turkey Hunting Handbook, 1999

513. Don't Waste Time on Henned-up Birds When You Can Hunt Somewhere Else

If you've got lots of land to hunt, don't waste time trying to bring in turkeys that aren't that interested in your calling. When a bird gobbles once in response to your calls but won't move any closer after 15 to 20 minutes, it's likely he's still with hens. Make a mental note of your location, then move on to search for another, lonelier bird who will respond with more enthusiasm. Later, however, if you still haven't filled your tag, return to the spot you were calling in when you first heard him gobble and try calling again. His hens may now be on their nests, and he'll be wondering what happened to the one that wouldn't come see him earlier in the morning.

514. Find Unpressured Turkeys by Hunting from a Boat . . .

Many reservoirs are surrounded by a strip of property that's managed by the U.S. Army Corps of Engineers. This land is generally open to public use, but is often itself surrounded by private property and therefore hard to access on foot. The best way to hunt this unpressured public land is to use a boat. Simply motor along the shoreline early in the morning and stop to call at every likely location. If a gobbler responds, beach your boat, circle around behind the bird, and call him into your setup.

515. . . . And from a Mountain Bike

Another great way to access unpressured public turkey land is to use a mountain bike. Most turkey hunters won't walk more than two miles from where they park their trucks. Look for a forest service or timber-company road that's gated to keep out motorized vehicles, then ride your bike deep into the property, stopping to blow a locator call or yelp loudly every few hundred yards. Keep your ears open even while riding—with no noisy engine masking the sounds of the woods you'll be able to hear turkeys even while moving.

516. Why Gobblers Are Easy to Miss

How do hunters miss a big target like a wild turkey standing within 30 yards? My personal pet theory (and I've done it myself!) is that the shooter is so enthralled by the scene before him that he raises his head from the gunstock just slightly. Do that, and you'll miss every time.

517. Call to the Hens to Bring in Flocked-up Western Turkeys

When hunting western birds such as Rio Grande or Merriam's turkeys, you'll often be glassing open country for gobblers that have gathered lots of hens in a flock. A good tactic to use in such a situation is to call to the hens rather than the gobblers. If you can convince a hen to investigate a noisy rival (you), the gobbler that's with her may tag along into shooting range.

518. Securing Your Box Call

When a box call you've stowed in a pocket of your turkey hunting vest shakes accidently, giving out a scrape sound just as your sneaking to a turkey roost before dawn, your hunt may be over almost before it starts. Secure those box calls.

519. When Roosting Gobblers Fly Down

When you hear hens fly down from the roost, while a gobbler lingers on his limb, still calling occasionally, your nerves will be as tight as they can get. But don't start thinking your bird is as good as in the oven. Next, a scenario can take place that virtually dooms your hunt. The hens may start walking away in a direction away from your setup. The gobbler flies down and joins them, oblivious to your calls.

520. Hide Your Position by Imitating a Moving Hen

When calling turkeys with a diaphragm call, it's always a good idea to throw the sound to one side or the other by cupping your hand to your mouth and turning your head to the left or right. Turkeys have acute visual and auditory senses, and you don't want them keying in on your exact position. If you make it sound like the hen you're imitating is moving back and forth to either side of you the gobbler you're calling will be less likely to see you before it gets within shooting range.

521. Watch out for the Spurs!

Never pick up a gobbler you've shot before he stops thrashing. Male turkeys have sharp spurs of bone on their lower legs, just up from their feet, which they use when fighting to establish dominance over their rivals. The last thing you want as you celebrate your kill is a nasty gash in your palm. Always step on your bird's neck until he stops twitching and you'll be safe from this last line of defense.

522. Not All Turkeys Gobble When Excited

Hot gobblers don't always gobble. A fired-up tom will frequently strut, spit, and drum his way toward your setup without making any other sounds. Make sure you listen closely for the low-frequency, rumbling hum that tells you there's a strutting bird in the area.

523. Store Your Mouth Calls Properly to Preserve Their Sound

You can make your favorite mouth call last longer by storing it in your refrigerator during the off-season. The latex reeds will be less likely to warp, which could ruin the sound you've come to rely on. You should also insert a flat toothpick or two between the reeds so that they don't stick together.

524. Avoid Bumping into a Moving Gobbler

Be careful when using yelps to locate gobblers in the forest. A hot tom may respond by moving quickly toward your location, and if you're doing the same thing, you run the risk of bumping into him before you're set up. It's a good idea to first use a crow or owl locator call, which allows you to get a fix on his location without giving him any motivation to search out the source of the sound. If these calls don't work, then switch to yelps of increasing volume, and move cautiously when setting up on any birds that respond.

525. Stop Calling to Attract a Tough Tom

One way to bring in a difficult gobbler is to avoid calling at him at all. Let him know there's a hen in the area by flapping a turkey wing and scratching in the leaves at your feet, then shut up. Yelping in response to his gobbles may only encourage him to stay put because he thinks the hen you're imitating is interested in him, which would normally mean she's heading his way (hens usually move toward gobblers, not the other way around). If you don't call at all he'll wonder what he's doing wrong, and may come closer so that he can attract your attention using visual rather than auditory means.

526. Don't Call in the Fall like You'd Call in the Spring

In the fall, gobblers, jakes, and hens all gather in separate flocks. Calling like a hen to fall gobblers brings no response; to upset the pecking order, you need to be a new gobbler. Same thing with jakes and hens.

CHAPTER 11

Duck Hunting

527. Wind and Your Decoy Setups

The truth is that you can spread your duck decoys just about any way you wish, as long as you leave an open area for the birds to land into the wind. No matter which way they come from, or how much they circle, their final move down will be into the wind. No wind at all? It becomes a guessing game.

528. The Toughest Shot in Duck Hunting

Shooting a cripple on the water is duck hunting's toughest shot. You'll see your shot pattern absolutely smother the bird, yet it will swim on.

529. How Fast Are They? Let's Ask Hemingway

" . . . You can remember duck shooting in the blind, hearing their wings go *whichy-chu-chu-chu* in the dark before daylight. That is the first thing I remember of ducks; the whistly, silk tearing sound the fast wingbeats make; just as what you remember first of geese is how slow they seem to go when they are traveling, and yet they are moving so fast that the first one you ever killed was two behind the one you shot at, and all that night you kept waking up and remembering how he folded up and fell."

—Ernest Hemingway, "Remembering Shooting—Flying," *Esquire* magazine, February 1935

530. "Special Effect" Decoys

Decoy makers today have waterfowl hunters covered from every possible angle, including sleepers (actually resembling sleeping birds), feeders (with necks outstretched), and bobbers (rear ends of ducks feeding under the surface).

531. Mack's Prairie Wings: Don't Miss It!

Down in Stuttgart, Arkansas, the Command Center of classic, tall-timber mallard gunning, the waterfowl emporium Mack's Prairie Wings has everything the serious waterfowl hunter could hope for. Named after Richard Bishop's classic Prairie Wings book about the area, Mack's options include fantastic links that just take you into the current state of waterfowling everywhere.

—www.mackspw.com.

532. Guide's Advice I Don't Want to Hear

In the duck blind, you'll often hear your guide urge you to, "Stay down. Keep your head down. Don't watch the birds! I'll do the watching." Well, if you're not watching the birds, you're losing part of the joys of the hunt. Your blind should be good enough for you to peer through the stalks or brush just as the guide is doing. When the ducks are passing right overhead, neither one of you should be looking skyward. You'll spook the birds for sure.

533. Take 'Em? Or Let Them Circle?

"Mallards, blacks, gadwalls, widgeon, and pintails all like to circle a decoy set once or twice before they decide to come in. Two or three birds may leave the flock and pass in nice range. Take 'em! Never mind the flock."

—Ray P. Holland, *Scattergunning*, Knopf, 1951

534. A Waterfowl Hunter's Classic Book

A Book on Duck Shooting by Van Campen Heilner is the magnum opus of waterfowl hunting books. Illustrated in color and black-and-white by the legendary Lynn Bogue Hunt and complete with a huge selection of photographs, the book is a total portrait of duck hunting from the far North to South America and even Europe. Originally published by Penn Publishing, Philadelphia, in 1939, the book can be found on used book sites like Amazon (www.amazon.com) and Alibris (www.alibris.com) and others. A new edition has been published by Premier Press, Camden, South Carolina, with an introduction by Jim Casada.

535. Local Birds: Use Small Decoy Spreads for Small Bunches

Make a distinction between the resident ducks you hunt in early season and the large flocks that migrate in later on. You'll spot resident birds in pairs and small flocks, so decoy them accordingly and don't burn out any one place by hunting it too often. Save the big spreads for when the birds from up north show up.

536. Why Cans Are Number One

"Now, the canvasback is the king of ducks in the old hunter's book, and an epicure's delight in the bargain. He is the hardest of them all to hit as he hurtles hell-bent across the sky. The big bulls remind you of a jet fighter with their bullet heads and sharp, small, swept-back wings. Those wings claw air at such a furious clip that they send the big, fat bodies racing along faster than any other duck. They are straightaway speedsters made for a big track, and they never flare or dodge."

—Jimmy Robinson, "Bull Cans of the Delta," *Sports Afield,* 1938, referenced in *Autumn Passages,* Ducks Unlimited and Willow Creek Press, 1995

537. The Making of a Duck Caller . . . Sort Of

You might say I'm a Clint Eastwood-Dirty Harry, sort of duck caller. Clint said, "A man has got to know his limitations." My own call rests in my pocket mostly, because I'm not very good with the thing and because, like Blanche in *A Streetcar Named Desire,* "I've always depended upon the kindness of strangers," meaning guides and hunting-camp hosts who really know their stuff when it comes to tooting on a duck call. In Arkansas and Tennessee, the calling lanyards these guys wear aren't just for showing off duck bands.

538. Pothole Sneak Attack

If you've scouted out a promising pothole or small pond and you're planning to jump-shoot the ducks that are resting there, try to sneak up on them with the wind at your back. When the ducks jump into the wind (which they most certainly will do), you might get a shot before they re-orient themselves and fly the other way.

539. Mix 'Em up If You Want To

So you're thinking about adding some bluebills or canvasbacks (diving ducks) to your decoy setup of mallards, pintails, and gadwalls (puddle ducks) to give your spread more visibility. Go right ahead. It won't hurt your chances a bit.

540. Gloves for Setting out Decoys

Gloves that stretch almost to your elbows and keep your hands dry are a must for setting out decoys. Shuck 'em off and wear your regular gloves when you get into the blind. See the "Midwest PVC Decoy Glove" at Mack's Prairie Wings, www.mackspw.com. Check other favorite waterfowl gear vendors for other options.

541. Too Hidden for a Good Shot

When you're hunkered down in a blind so that you can't see the ducks you're working, when it comes time for someone to exclaim, "Take 'em!" you come up with your gun and have to find the birds before you get down to pointing and swinging the barrel. It won't be an easy shot.

542. Wait out Those Gadwalls

Gadwalls can be tricky when they're working your decoy. In his classic book *Scattergunning*, legendary *Field & Stream* editor and water-fowler Ray P. Holland advises, "Gadwalls are particularly prone to circle and circle. Keep your head down and don't move, and they will come within range when ready."

543. Jump-shooting Joys

Jump-shooting ducks from a canoe or john-boat is a great way to hunt some creeks and small rivers. The best way is with a partner, one hunter with the gun at the ready, the other on the paddling. Stay quiet, anticipate the sharp bends where you may surprise a few mallards, blacks, or other puddle ducks. Listen carefully as you go. You just might hear the birds before you get to them.

544. Pond Shooting at Sunset: The Way It Used to Be

Waiting for ducks at sunset beside ponds where the ducks would be coming to roost was once a mainstay of hunting tactics. Local wood ducks, mallards, and black ducks, puddle ducks of all sorts that had migrated into a particular area—they all come hurtling into the ponds after sunset. Sometimes the shooting was so late, the birds had to be outlined against the western sky. Today, shooters who try this are easy marks for wardens waiting nearby to hear the sounds of gunshots after legal shooting hours. If you want to just watch the show (and you should!) leave your guns in the truck.

545. Northeast Arkansas: They've Got the Ducks

I've had wonderful duck hunting with Charles Snapp around Walnut Ridge and the Cache River area of northeast Arkansas, near the Cache River. The region has tremendous rice-producing activity, and today is said to "short-stop" a lot of the ducks that would be heading on down to the famous Stuttgart area. Look for duck guides and camps in Northeast Arkansas.

546. Movement—Not the Blind—Wrecks Your Chances

Most of the time, when ducks working toward your decoys decide to flare away, it was movement that spooked them, not your blind, no matter how flimsy.

547. Dreams of a Duck Caller

I admit to being a card-carrying Calling Wannabe, bitten by the bug in my youth when I opened a package from Herter's. Inside were my first duck call and a 78-rpm record on using it—complete with the recorded sounds of an actual hunt. That big, beautiful wooden call became a prized possession. I played that record constantly, soaking up the notes of the Highball, the Comeback Call, the Feeding Chuckle, even the harsh Brrrrr, Brrrrr used on diving ducks. Suddenly, duck hunting became more fun than ever—even on blank days when not a duck turned to my call or fell to my gun.

548. It's All about Visibility, Visibility, Visibility

Unless you're gunning a tiny creek-bottom or river location, surrounded by high trees, most of your duck-hunting locations will be in open areas where you hope passing birds can see your decoys and come on in. Anything you can do to increase the visibility of your spread will make a difference. Black decoys show up better from a distance. Magnum-size adds visibility. Canada geese decoys add visibility, whether you're hunting geese or not. Movement devices (the ones that are legal where you hunt) are critical if there's no wind blowing: spinners, battery-driven shakers, pull-cord movers—whatever you've got.

549. Using Double-barreled Guns in the Blind

Despite their status as classic smoothbores, side-by-side and over-and-under double-barrels have two issues with some waterfowl hunters. First is the two-shot limit. Some consider that a liability. They want three shots. Next is the fact that doubles must be broken open for feeding, and that can sometimes by cumbersome in the blind.

550. Take My Hand!

Duck and goose hunters are around water, docks, boats, slick boards to walk on, slick steps to climb—all sorts of uneven, unsteady spots to negotiate. Seniors who hope to keep enjoying hunting as long as they can should not hesitate in asking someone to "Take my hand!" It's a lot better than ruining your day.

551. The Great Blue Heron Decoy Trick

Many of the old-time waterfowl market hunters swore by the trick us having a Great Blue Heron decoy in their spread. The Heron is a wary bird that won't allow anything to approach it very closely, therefore the old-timers felt a Heron in the decoys was a real confidence booster. Today you can buy a heron decoy from several major waterfowl gear providers and try out the trick yourself.

552. Speaking up for Mallards

"I glowed with elation at the prospect of matching wits again with the mallard. One does well to select it as his favorite duck. . . .There are faster ducks and those less reluctant to decoy. The mallard lacks some of the patrician qualities of the canvasback, the bluebill's dash and the brilliant flight performance of the teals. But its intelligence seldom sleeps. When it spills from the skies, wing-bars flashing iridescently, a feather or two floating in the wake of the charge that struck it down, no gunner, no matter how often he has centered such a target, fails to respond in a feeling of satisfaction and achievement."

—Kendrick Kimball, "Pintail Point," *Field & Stream,* 1935, reprinted in *The Field & Stream Reader,* Doubleday, 1946

553. Duck Hunting's Outer Edge

Maine sea duck hunting, in coves of freezing rough water and along rocky coasts of pounding surf, can be so risky that I once ran an article when I was editing *Sports Afield* called "Ducks of the Deadly Ledges." Despite the dangerous implications, this can be fantastic hunting for eiders, scoters and assorted puddle ducks. The eider, by the way, makes a wonderful trophy mount. Just type the words "Maine sea duck hunting" into Google and you'll get lots of sites.

554. When It's Bluebills We're After

"Into this rocket-minded world the speedy bluebill fits most admirably. If there is jet propulsion among birds it all started with him. As he rides the northern gales he comes with the speed of a bullet, and he is gone before the slow-minded hunter can get his gun to his shoulder. For those who love duck hunting the time of the bluebill is the high mark of the year. Few birds are speedier, few offer a more sporting target. And, above all, few are more obliging in responding to decoys. For the bluebill, 'scaups' to the hunters on the Eastern Shore, is a gregarious little bundle of energy. He loves company and he will arrow into your stool with the greatest of confidence, even eagerness. Another high recommendation for him is his edibility."

—Jimmy Robinson, "Rockets of the North," *Sports Afield,* 1937, referenced in *Autumn Passages,* Ducks Unlimited and Willow Creek Press, 1995

555. Magnum or Super-Magnum?

Over-sized decoys certainly increase the visibility of your spread. The choice of Magnum or Super-Magnum boils down to visibility versus carry. You can carry more Magnum decoys in your bag than Super Magnum.

556. The "Hole" Is the Thing

No matter what shape of decoy spread you decide is right for your hunting location and conditions, it must contain a hole or two for the birds to land.

If the water in front of the blind is solid with decoys, the birds will land on the outside of the spread, at long range or even out of range.

557. Winchester's Model 12: A Waterfowling Treasure

The Winchester Model 12 pump is one of the greatest guns that ever went duck hunting. If you possess one of the originals, consider yourself a lucky gunner.

558. Waterfowl Hunting's Most Important Tip

You won't bag any ducks or geese unless you're hunting where (choose one, or all) they're flying, feeding, or resting. Today! If you don't see birds in the fields, in the water, or in the air, you'll have to set up at a spot where you've seen them before (like yesterday, perhaps) and hope for the best.

559. Considering the Risks

The reality of waterfowl hunting is that it can be rather daunting—even downright dangerous in certain conditions and situations. The big waters, the swift rivers, the wind and rain and ice and fog, all that gear to be managed—it's not always easy hunting. If you're a senior or disabled, you have to consider hunting only when you have a buddy along.

560. The Outer Gun: The Key Position

The Outside shooter on the upwind side of permanent duck blinds or lay-out blind setups is in the key position and can absolutely ruin the shooting for everybody with him. It's happened to me more times than I can remember. The ducks, or geese, are coming into the spread against the wind, from his side. If he starts shooting too early, around the corner, the guns in the center and other side will get no shots, or shots at widely flaring birds only. Sometimes, to top off this little drama, the outside offender will turn to the other guys and say, "Why didn't you guys shoot?" Advice: Put an experienced shooter in that outside position, a shooter with the judgment and nerve to wait until the birds are into the spread enough so everybody can shoot.

561. Where'd the Mallards Go?

When you're on a marsh in the early morning where you reasonably expect a flight of mallards, don't be surprised if they don't show up until later in the morning. Your local birds, or even visitors from the north, may be feeding in the fields.

562. Black Ducks—Red Letter Day

My calling aspirations reached a sort of pinnacle years later. I was hunkered on an icy creek on the marshes of the Chesapeake Bay, near the famous Susquehanna Flats. A pair of black ducks flew down the creek, very high and in a big hurry, headed somewhere with express tickets. They clearly were not interested in my modest decoy spread, but when I hit them with my old Herter's call and the Highball, they turned like I had 'em wired. Interested then, they circled warily while I scrunched down. Now I started rattling off my Feeding Chuckle, and a few moments later they were cupped and committed. I could finally say that I knew how to call ducks.

563. Waterfowl Hunting with Sean Mann

From his headquarters on the Eastern Shore of Maryland, Champion caller and call-maker Sean Mann runs waterfowl hunting adventures on the Shore and hunting ducks and geese in Alberta that is some of the finest this author has ever seen. Some of the photographs in this book taken by photographer Tim Irwin were made when hunting with the author and Sean in Alberta, at his camp outside Edmonton. Sean runs a quality operation, with leases that put the gunner where the birds are regardless of the time and conditions. Bag limits in Canada are generous, and the shooting simply spectacular. For complete details, go to Sean's Web site, www.duck-goosecalls.com, or phone Sean Mann's Hunting Adventures for brochures at (800) 345-4539. Sean starts hunting in Canada in September, so book early.

564. As the Season Goes On . . .

If you're a serious duck hunter and you don't already know this, you soon will: As the season progresses the ducks will fly higher and higher, and you will keep having to add decoys to your spread to attract their attention.

565. Remington's 870 Wingmaster Pump

As a "working man's" choice for a great waterfowling gun, the Remington 870 Wingmaster pump has brought down a lot of ducks and geese for a lot of folks without breaking the family budgets. It was the favorite gun of *Sports Afield*'s legendary Jimmy Robinson.

566. An Unusual Duck-hunting Safety Reminder

Bangor, Maine outdoor writer and waterfowling veteran Tom Hennessey received what may be the ultimate reminder on duck-hunting safety. Although the subject is dead serious, as we've pointed out above, this one is funny. On the way out the door with his lab Coke, Tom heard his wife Nancy say, "Who are you going hunting with?" He answered, "I'm going alone." Tom says Nancy's pause and reply were as chilling as the pre-dawn darkness: "If something happens to you, how will Cokie get home?"

567. Jump-shooting on Western Rivers

"So you jump the islands by floating down from above, scanning carefully with binoculars to see if any mallards or Canadas are resting in the lee water down at the tail . . . Then you paddle like hell to put the island between you and the birds, beach at the upper end, then sneak down through the mini-forest."

—John Barsness, *Western Skies,* Lyons & Burford, 1994

568. Where the Birds Want to Be

Pushing into a cove in the marsh or along a big river or lake, in the first pre-dawn light, you flush a big bunch of ducks or geese. Away they go, gabbling and honking. Never mind trying to follow them or heading for another spot. Set up right there. It's the place the birds want to be.

569. "Take 'Em!"

Few moments afield are as thrilling as those when a big flock of ducks sweeps into your decoys. You'll shoot a lot better when you are aware whether your birds are diving ducks—like bluebills and canvasbacks—or puddle ducks—like mallards and pintails. Diving ducks will bore straight past when the shooting starts, while puddle ducks will bounce skyward as though launched from a trampoline.

570. Tall-timber Trick

When gunning the hole in the tall timber with a few decoys out, give the water around your tree a good kick when birds are passing or circling to imitate splashing and feeding activity.

571. You Really Ought to Join DU

There are so many good reasons for a serious waterfowl hunter to join Ducks Unlimited (DU) that we can't list them all. Their Web site for hunters, www.ducks.org/hunting, will tell you all about membership benefits, including a wonderful magazine, hunting tips, videos, and the great work DU does to preserve waterfowl habitat. You can phone them at (800) 45-DUCKS.

572. When Ducks Are on the Way In

When your calls have gotten the attention of a passing flock, and the birds have turned and are in the way in, there are two opposing views on what to do with your call next. One (the majority, by the way) says to cease all calling and let them come on. The other warns that if you've been doing the feeding chuckle, keep it up as the birds come on. To stop now might spook them.

573. Don't Forget to Plug That Gun

The most frequent ticketed waterfowl hunting violation is failure to plug pumps and autos to three shots. Many hunters have this happen simply because they haven't checked their gun properly.

574. Tell Your Guide about Your Calling

When you've been putting in a lot of time and practice on your duck calling, don't let the guide's obvious skill keep you from doing your thing. You've paid for the trip, and you ought to have a chance to see what you can do while you're in an area where the ducks are flying.

575. Avoiding a Deadly Leap

"To see a retriever hit the water in one of those long, hell-bent leaps is, without question, an impressive sight. Fact of the matter, though, is that it can be downright dangerous. Often waterlogged and floating just beneath the surface, long splinters and stubs of stumps and fallen trees can impale your dog. Common sense dictates that deadwood snags or other such obstructions should be removed from the area in front of the blind."

—Tom Hennessey, *Feathers 'n Fins,* The Amwell Press, 1989

576. A Different Type of Decoy Setup

Guide Rick Nemecek told writer Wade Bourne that he doesn't believe in standard decoy patterns like a J-Hook or U: "I believe these patterns become familiar to ducks that see them day after day. Instead, I set my stool in small family clusters with three to six decoys per cluster. Now the overall pattern may be a J or a U, but it's loose. These clusters don't run together to form long strings." (For more tips from Rick Nemecek and other top guides see Wade Bourne's book, *Decoys and Proven Methods for Using Them*, Ducks Unlimited, 2000.)

577. A Cut Above

Freelance duck and goose hunters can run into a lot of stuff that needs cutting fast. Avery Outdoors Avery Quick Cutter is a powerful ratchet-style cutter that will take out the toughest brush or even stray wire. With it you should carry the Avery Speed Saw, with seven razor-sharp teeth per inch. It could help you build you blind anywhere. Break-Up camo pouches or you can get a combo patch that hold both.

—www.averyoutdoors.com

578. Early Morning Pothole Tactic

When ducks are on a pothole in the early morning and have not left for their day's feeding, you have a choice: Try to sneak up on the pothole before they leave, OR try to get a shot pass shooting as they fly over on their way to the fields. The later approach depends on your scouting abilities. Have you discovered the route they take from the pothole to the fields?

579. The First Decoy Spreads—Ever!

In his wonderful book *Decoys and Proven Methods for Using Them*, Wade Bourne reports on the discovery by anthropologists in 1924 of a basket of eleven canvasback-shaped, woven, tule-reed decoys made by Indians in the Humboldt Sink area of west-central Nevada, carefully wrapped and buried 2,000 years ago.

580. Decoy Choices of a Top Guide

In his book *Decoys and Proven Methods for Using Them*, writer Wade Bourne reports on the strategies of Rick Nemecek of Port Clinton, Ohio, longtime guide on the Sandusky Bay marshes on the south shore of Lake Erie. Nemecek says, "I've talked to biologists who fly aerial waterfowl surveys, and they've told me the first thing they notice when they see ducks on the water is their black profiles. So my early season spread will include one-third to one-half black duck decoys. Then the next thing biologists tell me they see is white, so I always set two or three pintail drakes in my spread. My typical early season spread of eighteen decoys includes seven or eight black ducks, three pintail drakes—and the rest mallards. In later season, my spread of thirty-six decoys includes twenty-four black ducks, three pintails, and nine mallards."

581. Choke Tube Add-on

A waterfowl gun decision that comes up all the time is whether to stay with your factory choke tubes or purchase one of the highly-touted add-ons. In an article on the Cabela's Web site, www.cabelas.com, writer Adam Bender says he's been getting patterns more effective than factory tubes with Carlson's Black Cloud Choke Tubes, using Federal's Black Cloud steel shot loads. The Cabela's site offers other choke tube choices as well.

582. Picking up the Decoys the Easy Way

Here are a couple of nifty ways to pick up your duck decoys without having to lean out of the boat. For one, cut a notch in the blade of a paddle. Hook onto the decoy anchor line and lift. As an option, create a special pole from a 5- to 7-ft. dowel rod with a metal hook screwed into the end.

583. The Wind Rules the Direction

Like airplanes, ducks and geese will land into the wind—whatever wind there is, a wisp of breeze or a gale. Plan you blind location and decoy setup accordingly, because this isn't a maybe. They will come in into the wind!

584. Some Realities of Sea-duck Hunting

"Sea-duck shooting—eiders and coots—brought into vogue by the one-a-day limit on black ducks, is educating hunters to dangers that neither they nor their dogs have encountered on sheltered bays and marshes. Make no mistake about it, sea-duck shooting is rough business, and a dog fetching eider ducks from an offshore ledge takes a beating."

—Tom Hennessey, *Feathers 'n Fins,* The Amwell Press, 1989

585. A Must-see Waterfowling Museum

Located on the banks of the historic Susquehanna Flats, at Havre de Grace, Maryland, not far from I-95, the Havre de Grace Decoy Museum houses one of the finest collections of working and decorative Chesapeake Bay decoys ever assembled. The museum was established in 1986 as a private, non-profit institution existing to preserve the historical and cultural legacy of waterfowling and decoy making on the Chesapeake Bay. There are also displays of blinds, boats and shooting rigs. Every serious waterfowl hunter will want to visit this one: www.decoymuseum.com

586. Jump-shooting without a Boat

You don't necessarily have to use a boat to jump-shoot creeks and small streams. If you can stalk the banks quietly, you might get within range of puddle ducks using the stream as a sanctuary during the day when they're not feeding in the fields.

587. Tricks of the Freelance Hunter

With the development of the so-called "Mud Motors," such as the Go-Devil, and portable boat blinds like Avery, freelance duck hunting has been made a lot easier. With your johnboat (a 16-footer ought to be about right) on a trailer, you can go to whichever locations the ducks are using. Use the afternoon hours to scout, scout, and scout—looking for locations where the ducks might be loafing during the day, or an inviting spot along a flyway where you expect them to be crossing the next morning on their way to feed or loaf. (See the fantastic Macks Prairie Wings store and Web site, www.mackspw.com, for mud motors, boats, portable blinds—the works. Also, Cabela's at www.cabelas.com.)

588. Late Season Timber Tactics

"We've learned one thing that's really important for hunting in late season. When the ducks are extremely wary, they'll work into little bitty openings in the thickest, brushiest woods in the area. These are places where we won't use more than 15 decoys plus our shakers. . . . I'll make one short highball on their first pass, then I'll shut up and let 'em work on their own. Once I tell them I'm there, I don't call anymore. I think the biggest mistake hunters make in flooded timber, especially from Christmas on, is calling too much."

—Arkansas Guide George Cochran, interviewed by writer Wade Bourne in Bourne's book, *Decoys and Proven Methods for Using Them,* Ducks Unlimited, 2000

589. It's Not Just Wood Ducks Anymore

Used to be a time when local ducks were almost entirely wood ducks. Mallards and others were visitors from the North. No more. Plenty of mallards and other puddle ducks spend their summers in areas where they can be well scouted prior to opening day. Wood ducks the same.

590. The Romance of Sea Duck Hunting

"You'd have thought the tollers were trespassing on property owned by eider ducks. Flock after flock swung in to investigate. Spent shells twirled in the tide, and Bubba retrieved until his feet were sore from the barnacle-encrusted rocks. In between, we talked about seals and shags, eagles, deer, snow squalls and black ducks and whistlers, and shotguns and steel shot—which, I have to admit, will shoot effectively when you learn to use it."

—Tom Hennessey, *Feathers 'n Fins,* The Amwell Press, 1989

591. Add a Few Decoys to Your Jump-shooting Boat

When you're heading for a day's jump-shooting on a likely stream, don't forget to take along a few decoys. On a day when you're seeing a good number of birds on the move, at a cove or quiet spot, especially on a braided river, you might have the chance to put out your decoys, wait a while, and pull in a flock or two.

592. Don't Push Your Luck with Decoys

Positioning your decoys closer to the blind so your shots will be easier may sound like a tempting idea, but it's not a good one. You won't be getting any shots! Put the closest decoys at least 30 yards from the blind, the others even farther out. If you gun can't handle that distance, it's not a very good duck gun.

593. The Right Time, the Right Place

One of the greatest experiences on earth is to be in your duck blind before daylight, with your decoys out, on a frosty morning without cloud cover. As you sip your coffee or tea, you'll watch

the stars fade away as the shadowy shapes of the nearby terrain begin to take form and color. Hopefully, birds will be flying, heading out to their feeding grounds, or spooked by other hunters somewhere. It's the Grand Parade starting, and you are there.

594. Using the Wind with Your Decoy Spread

Ducks often want to land outside a spread of decoys—even when the setup has left an inviting hole. That's why you want to set your decoys upwind—not directly in front of the blind—so that you'll still have a good shot at the birds coming in against the wind and trying to land on the outside of the decoy spread.

595. Origin of the Word "Decoy"

"The word decoy is a shortened version of the Dutch word EndeKooy, which was a cage-type trap for snaring wildfowl."

—Wade Bourne, *Decoys and Proven Methods for Using Them,* Ducks Unlimited, 2000

596. Fighting Back on Those Bluebird Days

When there's not a cloud in the sky or a breath of wind blowing—a notorious "bluebird" day—even when ducks are moving (which won't be very often!), it's tough to get their attention. Battery-driven shaker decoys and jerk-strings attached to some of your decoys can save the day on bluebird days. If you don't have a chance to study how pro guides set up their jerk decoys, check out Wade Bourne's book, *Decoys and Proven Methods for Using Them.*

597. The Freelance Duck Hunter

It's not easy to be a freelance duck hunter today, hunting on your own, finding good places to put out your decoys, bagging some birds. It takes skill, energy, gear, and planning—and the cold fact is that many hunters just can't pull together all those necessary ingredients. They join clubs that have leases, and they book guides.

598. Yes, Indeed, Ducks Are Hard to Hit

In his classic book *Scattergunning*, Ray P. Holland points out that ducks are harder to hit than any other gamebird because: They are taken at longer ranges, they fly faster, the shots come at more angles, and their protective feathers make them tougher to kill.

599. Sea Duck Hunting: Get the Picture?

"In the lee of the ledge, a dozen of Al's handmade eider-duck tollers bobbed like a string of lobster buoys. To our right, smooth-running swells turned white as they stumbled over a stoop of submerged ledge. Spruces picketed the shores to our left. Gulls skirled, and a sea-tossed salad of kelp and rockweed was so salty you could smell it."

—Tom Hennessey, *Feathers 'n Fins,* The Amwell Press, 1989

600. Tiny Camera, Big Memories

Attach a tiny digital camera to the same lanyard from which you hang duck calls and dog whistles. It will then be at your finger tips to capture the action.

601. Foggy Morning Timber Hunting

In the School of Hard Knocks I've attended, fog means lousy duck hunting. Double and triple that in timber hunting, where bright sunny weather always seems best. (Probably because the ducks can see the decoys in the open pools in the trees but can't see you standing in the shadows.)

602. Don't Be a "Skybuster"

A "skybuster" is the most hated person on any marsh or field where there's duck or goose hunting. The Skybuster blazes away at birds that are clearly out of range, thereby frightening the birds away from the area and ruining chances others might have had on the incoming birds.

603. The Best Decoys Ever

Before they were banned in 1935, live decoys were used by waterfowl hunters, particularly commercial hunters. The decoy birds, which had to be fed and kept all year, were small domestic ducks, resembling mallards, prone to frequent calling.

604. They Love Those Sandbars

Sandbars on the edges of shallow water in clam bays and coves of big rivers will be a good drawing card for ducks and geese to loaf and pick up grit, especially when you've got open water while most region's ponds and lakes are iced-up. When scouting for such locations, one of the most rewarding sights you'll ever see will be birds dropping down over the trees in a bend in the river ahead. That's where you'll want to be setting up.

605. What Discourages Most Duck Hunters

Finding a good place to hunt is the Number One issue for all duck hunters today. Even with special management areas open to hunters, finding a good place to hunt ducks simply isn't easy. In most areas, goose hunting is much easier.

606. You've Got to Lead Them

The legendary duck hunter George Bird Grinnell is often referenced for his famous quote, "Shoot ahead of them . . . Shoot farther ahead of them . . . Shoot still farther ahead of them." And it's a fact: Most ducks are missed by not leading enough.

607. Silhouette Decoy Hole Punchers

The job of putting out dozens of silhouette decoys on hard or frozen ground becomes a lot easier when you use a hole punch like the Real-Geese Stake Hole Punch, available from waterfowl emporiums like Mack's Prairie Wings, www.mackspw.com, and the Smart Stick, available from www.smartstick.com.

608. Beating the Crowds in Public Hunting

Ducks quickly wise up to blinds on public hunting areas. You score more ducks if you seek out remote corners that see much less pressure. Use just a half dozen or so decoys and call only enough to get passing birds' interest.

609. The Chesapeake Style: Big and Tough

Just as the Chesapeake Bay retriever is generally bigger and stronger than a Labrador retriever, the early-style Chesapeake decoys were heavier and blockier than those being carved elsewhere in the early years of decoy making.

610. The Magic of Calling Your Birds

"To the avid waterfowler, no moment of truth can match the instant when a flock first responds to his call and decoys, the time when this wild, free bird of unsurpassed grace begins a descent from the sky down to gun range. It is a stirring spectacle . . ."

—Grits Gresham, *The Complete Wildfowler*, 1973

611. "Flasher" Decoys—Great but Not Guaranteed Successful

Where legal, the "flasher" movement decoys, like the original "RoboDuk," catch the eyes of ducks flying high and wide off your spread. While deadly in early season, they are considered by most experts to not be as effective in later season on down the flyways, when ducks have been seeing them in just too many decoy spreads. In fact, some hunters go so far as to say they believe the flashers can actually spook ducks.

612. Shooting Ducks in the Decoys

You have to want to shoot a duck awfully bad to let the incomers land in the decoys, and then you blast them on the water.

613. What Shot Hitting the Water Tells You

When you see your shot string hit the water behind a low-flying duck, your most-likely reaction will be that you shot behind it. Not necessarily so. The shot string is hitting the water well beyond the bird and could have been right on target, except too high.

614. Avery's Got the Stuff

Avery Outdoors Inc. in Memphis is where you kind find waterfowling mainline gear like layout blinds, plus gizmos and accessories you've never thought of that will make your waterfowling easier. Check them out at www.averyoutdoors.com.

615. Fetch That Bird!

If you have to hunt ducks on big water without a dog, bring along a spinning rod and a big surface plug. You can cast the big plug a long way, long enough to retrieve down ducks you can't wade to.

616. Your Face Is a Dead Give-away

When using layout blinds in most duck and goose setups, you've got to do something about your shining face. To incoming ducks, it will stand out like a neon sign. Wear a face mask or dab on some camo makeup.

CHAPTER 12

Goose Hunting

617. The Most Effective Way to Set out Goose Decoys

Veteran Maryland call-maker Sean Mann guides early season duck and goose hunting in Alberta and is one of the most successful and experienced in the business. He told DU's Wade Bourne, in a tip for the DU Web site: "To finish more geese when hunting over a field spread, set decoys 10 feet apart (three long steps), and face them in random directions. This set provides a natural, relaxed look, and it also offers incoming birds plenty of landing room inside the spread. By setting my decoys so far apart, I use half the number I used to. I can set up and tear down faster, and most of all, the geese work better. Our hunts are much more productive than when I set decoys closer together. Less really can be more."

618. How to Change Your Luck with Snow Geese

In the October '08 *Field & Stream,* author Dave Hurteau, in an interview with veteran guide Tracy Northup, Up North Outdoors, www.huntupnorth.com, presents a deadly method for changing your luck with those tough, high-flying flocks of snow geese. In a tip called, "Play

the Wind," Northup says. "Snow geese typically fly high and circle straight down, making it difficult to shoot them anywhere but right over a good spread. But a 30–40-mph wind keeps them flying nice and low." Northup recommends scouting out a location of snows where there are ditches or hedgerows a hundred yards or so from the fields where you can sneak into position to pick off the low-flying snows as they pass—without spooking the main flock.

619. Birds in Flight: Looks Are Deceiving

Because they are big, Canada Geese appear to be slow in flight, compared to ducks. And because of their long tails, pheasants appear to be slower than they really are. Swing your gun properly, lead the bird, and keep swinging as you pull the trigger. Or you'll be shaking your head, wondering how you missed.

620. Snow Geese: Playing the Numbers Game

Those large flocks of snow geese weaving across the horizon, clamoring constantly, are hard to pull into normal decoy spreads of just two- or three-dozen birds. The flying geese can see great distances, and they are looking for big groups of feeding birds. Savvy hunters have learned to cope with this by putting out decoys by the hundreds, if necessary, and to do this they'll use all the silhouettes they can haul to the site, plus whatever "rag-type" decoys they can fashion themselves from things like baby diapers and white garbage bags attached to a stake.

621. Layout Blinds Take Getting Used To

When using a layout blind, before the birds start flying take some time to try practicing the move it takes to rise into a shooting position. It takes some getting used to. If you don't practice it, you may not be in a good position with your face well down on the gun during the first critical seconds when it's time to, take 'em!

622. Local Geese, Local Knowledge

We live in an age where many (most!) Canada Geese have never been to Canada and are never going. They have become local birds, and the generous limits and seasons reflect that. Hunting them in early season is pleasant and rewarding, but you have to do your homework in finding a place to hunt where the birds are feeding, resting, or flying past.

623. When the Canadas Sleep Late

In below-zero weather, sleep in an extra hour or two. When it's that cold Canadas will stay roosted and fly out to feed only after the sun has come up and warmed things up a bit. It might be 10 AM before they leave the roost. The only thing you'll get by showing up at dawn is cold.

624. Keep Those Silhouettes Visible

When using silhouette decoys for geese, take care to position them so many of them appear broadside at every angle. When edge-on to the viewpoint of the flying birds, they become invisible.

625. Layout Blinds: You're Part of the Action

You're lying in a field, totally hidden right among the decoys. No brushy blind, no boat, no pit blind, no elaborate box blind, no blind on stilts. Instead, you're tucked comfortably into a well-camouflaged layout blind, made further invisible by attaching brush to the blind's convenient straps and holders. You're wearing camo yourself, including a hat and mask. Even your gun is camouflaged. Unlike hunting from a brush blind where you have to keep your face down—and thereby miss part of the spectacle of flying birds on the way in—you're seeing the whole show, from the time birds appear in the distance, until they coming right into your face. There's nothing like it!

Photo courtesy of Jay Cassell

626. Hiding Your Boat in Plain Sight

The john-boat or canoe you can put into the water and go wherever the ducks and geese are flying has gotten a lot easier to hide with the introduction of today's synthetic camo material. The material, imitating different shades and textures of marsh grass, comes in manageable mats you can attach to your boat, then roll up and put away after your hunt. Cabela's, www.cabelas.com, has a bunch of different patterns, including the excellent Avery, and there's a popular one called Fast-Grass that's available at the Knutson's waterfowling store and site, www.knutsondecoys.com.

627. Don't Let Those Incoming Geese Fool You

"The approach of wild geese to a blind is one of the neatest optical illusions in nature. The geese just keep on coming. You think they are one hundred yards away, and they are two hundred. You think they are fifty yards away, and they are one hundred."

—Gordon MacQuarrie, "Geese! Get Down!," *Field & Stream,* 1941, reprinted in
The Field & Stream Reader, Doubleday, 1946

CHAPTER 13

Ruffed Grouse and Woodcock Hunting

628. Good Hearing Can Pay Off Big

When the leaves in the woods are dry and crinkly, say on a perfect Indian Summer day, you can actually hear the few steps ruffed grouse take to launch into flight. The sound is a sort of dry, "tick, tick." Once you've heard it a couple of times, followed by a flushing bird, you'll know what to listen for.

629. Lend a Hand to Your Bird Hunting

When your upland bird hunting—quail, grouse, pheasant—takes place in thick cover, an old glove worn on your left hand (for right-handed hunters) enables you to ward off vines, limbs and briars as you work through the cover while your gloveless right hand holds your smooth-bore ready for the flush.

630. Grouse Hunting Teamwork

It's fun to hunt grouse with a buddy, but you must know each other's location at all times, and even then you may not be able to take a shot. (That's the very reason most grouse hunters shoot better when they're hunting alone.) In keeping track of one another, use a simple call-out, like, "Ho!" or "Over Here!" instead of constantly shouting sentences like, "I'm over here, Bob, on your right." The more grouse hear of such talk, the more likely they are to flush wild.

631. Spring Training for Rookie Dogs

"Spring woodcock provide the perfect opportunity to steady a young dog up . . . a high percentage of these birds are willing to sit so tight. A secondary reason is that the dog is fairly easy to see due to the lack of vegetation in early spring . . . Seeing the bird depart is of particular good for youngsters. It fills them with more fire and desire for the future . . . tells them inwardly every time that this, bird hunting, is why they're here on earth."

—Nick Sisley, *Grouse Magic*, self-published, 1981

632. A Startling Grouse-kill Discovery

"I kept track for my next 20 grouse kills. I don't like to keep statistics while I'm grouse hunting. . . . However, I did keep track for 20 birds and quit. I found that I killed 16 of those ruffs on what I figured were reflushes, four of them on the original flush. Those statics were startling, even for a guy who has chased the thunder birds for almost two decades."

—Nick Sisley, *Grouse Magic*, self-published, 1981

633. How Far Do Grouse Roam Every Day?

Despite the amount of boot leather hunters wear out in pursuit of their favorite bird every season, grouse are really "stay-at-home" gamebirds, seldom roaming more than a half mile from its home range.

634. Second Shots on Early Season Grouse Coveys

When you flush a couple of early season grouse, and fire only one shot, don't break your gun to reload right away. You may be into an entire group of birds hatched that year, and one of the birds that's been sitting tight will jump late—just when you break open your gun. On the other hand, if you've fired both shells, try to reload as quickly as possible.

635. The New England Grouse Gun Classic

William Harnden Foster, author of the classic *New England Grouse Shooting*, shot a 28-gauge Parker DHE with a straight stock.

636. Keep Track of Where You Shot From

Woodcocks are small birds and their feathers make for excellent camouflage on the forest floor. This can make finding one you've shot hard to retrieve, especially if you're hunting without a dog. After you knock one down, hang your hat on a branch or drop a spent shell on the ground where you were standing when you pulled the trigger. If you get confused about where you thought the bird landed you'll be able to return to the exact place you shot from to restart your search.

637. What Are Your Chances?

"I've kept a detailed journal of my days afield . . . Here are the hard facts: For every twelve grouse flushed, four escape unseen; of the eight the hunter glimpses, four are out of range, disappear too quickly, or otherwise evade getting shot at; of the four shots that the hunter takes, three are misses."

—William G. Tapply, *Upland Autumn: Birds, Dogs, and Shotgun Shells*,
Skyhorse Publishing, 2009

638. Burton L. Spiller's Grouse Feathers

When one first opens the pages of Burton L. Spiller's *Grouse Feathers*, the immediate effect is startling. Opposite the title page, which, in addition to Spiller's name, informs us that the book's illustrations are by Lynn Bogue Hunt, there is a full-page drawing of a ruffed grouse huddled against a pine trunk while a great horned owl passes below. The effect is startling. Instantly, one knows you're about to read a book produced by a writer and artist who love grouse and know what they're talking about. The edition I have was published by The Macmillan Company in 1947, but the original was a Derrydale Press edition in 1935. *More Grouse Feathers*, also illustrated by Lynn Bogue Hunt, followed from Derrydale in 1938, but a new edition was published by Crown Press in 1973, with an introduction by *Field & Stream*'s H. G. Tapply. Burton L. Spiller wrote other books, but he will always be best remember for these two chronicles of hunting the golden New England hills for grouse and woodcock.

639. Cock Bird or a Hen? How to Tell

The black band on the tail of all ruffed grouse tells you whether you've bagged a male or female. The cock bird always has a continuous band, while the hen's is broken. As in all things in nature, there are exceptions sometimes, mostly among young birds.

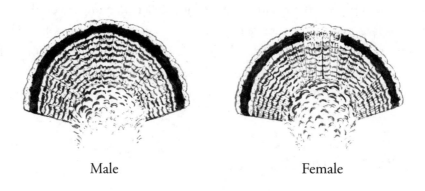

Male   Female

640. Those "Fantasy" Grouse

Sporting scene painters—even the very best of them—invariably picture ruffed grouse flying through the open—clearings in the trees, even along the edges of fields. The artists do that, no doubt, so the audience can see the bird. The reality is that you'll almost never have a chance to look down your gun barrel and see a grouse in huge openings like those in your favorite paintings. You might have a glimpse of a bird in a small gap in the trees and brush, just for an instant—if you're lucky.

641. Noise Flushes More Grouse

Yes, grouse can be a tight-holding bird, but when you're approaching their location with a lot of chatter and constant commands to your dog, you're almost guaranteeing you'll get a wild flush, out ahead of the point.

642. Flushing Dogs as Grouse Dogs

It makes a lot of sense to use flushing/retrieving dogs like Labs, Springers, and Goldens as grouse and woodcock dogs. (Pheasants too, by the way.) In addition to flushing the birds, they retrieve and make great family dogs. When trained properly to hunt close to the gun, these dogs can do a good job for you in grouse and woodcock covers. When not properly trained, running wide distances and out of control, they are worse than useless. You'd be better off walking up your birds alone.

643. Signpost to Good Woodcock Hunting

Look for white splashes on the ground of the covers where you're hoping to find good woodcock hunting.

644. Back on That Legendary "Road"

Field & Stream writer Corey Ford's grouse story "The Road to Tinkhamtown" has become a sort of cult classic, revered in anthologies and close to the hearts of an army of grouse hunters who love the literature of the sport. The story originally appeared in the October 1969, issue, with a superb illustration by the artist Howard Terpning. Ford died of a stroke on July 29, 1969, prior to the publication of the story. As this is written, the original unedited version of the story {written in 1963], returned by writer/editor Laurie Morrow from Ford's handwritten manuscript, is now being featured on the *Field & Stream* Web site, www.fieldandstream.com. Laurie Morrow is the editor of the Corey Ford anthology of stories, *The Trickiest Thing in Feathers*, Wilderness Adventures Press, 1996.

645. The New Englander—Found Just about Everywhere

Although the traditional home of the ruffed grouse is New England, you will find them and their subspecies all over the northeast, down the Appalachian chain to Georgia and Alabama, in all the Rocky Mountain states, and on west to Oregon and Washington. They are found all over Canada, the Yukon, and Alaska.

646. Aspens and Grouse: The Late October Key

Grouse hunting and shotgun expert Nick Sisley tells us that where grouse thrive in aspen country—like the Upper Midwest—look for fantastic gunning in 13–17-year-old aspens in late October, and the grouse are feeding on hazel catkins that thrive in this particular aspen-age stage.

647. Going It Alone

"I like to hunt alone, when there's no one to blame but myself. I have found that picking my way through birdy cover without a dog taps into something atavistic and important that absent when dogs are doing the hunting for me. Hunting without a dog is . . . hunting. I find myself thinking like a grouse, scanning the cover, imagining where a bird might be lurking, how close he might let me approach, which direction he'll choose to fly."

—William G. Tapply, *Upland Autumn: Birds, Dogs, and Shotgun Shells*, Skyhorse Publishing, 2009

648. Walk 'Em Up!

Grouse hunting with no dog is better than grouse hunting with a poor dog. The untrained or poorly training dog will run too far from the gun, flush every bird in the area, then chase them down and flush them again.

649. The Perfect Grouse and Woodcock Gun

When it comes to grouse guns, arguments may rage over the bore—12 or 20 gauge—but you'll find general agreement over these details: lightweight, short barrel, fast swinging, and with a stock that fits so perfectly that it instantly becomes part of you when your face touches the stock.

650. Keep Your Favorite Covers as "Top Secret"

It may go without saying, but this tip is a strong reminder: You must not take someone to your favorite grouse covers unless they are an absolute trusted friend for life. No exceptions! Be warned! If you break this rule, you're going to someday arrive at your favorite cover to find more SUVs than a dealer's lot.

651. Stay after Them!

"Reflushing grouse is a key to success in more ways than one. It's a cornerstone to good, sound, basic grouse hunting."

—Nick Sisley, *Grouse Magic*, self-published, 1981

652. He's Not Alone!

Flush one woodcock, and you're likely to find others not far away. When the flight is on, there should be a good number of birds in the vicinity.

653. The Quiet "Getaway"

In rainy or snowy weather when they're holding tight in the spruces, hemlocks or other conifers, ruffed grouse can launch into flight with hardly a sound, far less noise than the familiar whirr of wings you're expecting. As a bonus, the bird may be eight feet over your head.

654. Avoid Over-training Your Dog

"Because Sam [a setter] was so 'birdy' and easy to handle, I made the mistake of over-training him. I realized it when he began pointing birds other than game species. Whenever we got into a cover where partridge or woodcock were scarce, he would start slamming into stylish but unproductive points. The pup was, of course, trying to please me. I had worked him so often on planted pigeons that he figured whenever I hung a bell on him he'd best point something—and soon."

—Tom Hennessey, *Feathers 'n Fins*, The Amwell Press, 1989

655. Finding Woodcock Covers

"All alders do not attract woodcock, but I have seldom found woodcock in large numbers far from alders . . . On the migratory flight, if it is not alder cover that is used, it will be cover close to water or damp ground . . . I have found woodcock in large numbers on a mountain top, but, as in lowland coverts, it was flat land with alders."

—George Bird Evans, *The Upland Shooting Life*, Knopf, 1971

656. How Grouse Survive the Winter Woods

During the golden days of autumn hunting, ruffed grouse will be found near their favorite foods—among wild berries, in old apple orchards, among acorns and beechnuts. As the snows come and the winter deepens, you'll find them "budding," actually surviving by eating the buds of next year's greenery.

657. The Great Grouse Dog Secret

"The secret to acquiring a great grouse dog doesn't rest in buying one, for the truly great ones are seldom if ever for sale at any price. Nor does the secret lie in selecting a puppy from one of those mythical 'long bred lines' of pure grouse dogs. The secret to great grouse dogs centers around one heck of a lot of both hard work and outright luck."

—Nick Sisley, *Grouse Magic*, self-published, 1981

658. Number One on the Table: It's the Ruffed Grouse

As far as I'm concerned, all upland gamebirds are great on the table, but there is one that stands out as better than the rest. It's the ruffed grouse. No, I don't want to argue about it. It's the ruffed grouse! (Of course the wild turkey is better than anything, but I'm not comparing turkeys to our upland birds.)

659. Marking down Flushed Birds

"Generally, grouse tend to fly farther when they're shot at, not fly as far if they flush wild . . . There was a time when I shot at every bird possible—the old theory that shooting makes them sit tighter on the reflush. Hogwash. The father a bird flies, the less your chances are of flying him again. Birds sit tighter because they're not in familiar territory, not because they've been shot at."

—Nick Sisley, *Grouse Magic*, self-published, 1981

660. The Flight-bird Woodcock Myth

There's an old woodcock saying that will never die, even though it's a complete myth. It's the idea that flight birds are bigger than local birds. They're not. In a particular instance, one bird might be older and bigger than a local bird. But later, when the local birds leave, they too become flight birds.

661. Woodcock Flights and the Full Moon

"Thank God for the moon. Since day one, sportsmen have attributed their success or lack of it to the phases of that celestial sphere. Woodcock hunters are no exception. In fact, if you could produce a deed to the melon-like moon that illumines October nights, I guarantee you, a woodcock hunter would be the first in line to buy it. Why? Because theory has it that the nocturnal travelers always migrate on the full of the moon. I don't buy it. For my money, you can place that theory in the same category as the one claiming that flight birds are bigger."

—Tom Hennessey, *Feathers 'n Fins*, The Amwell Press, 1989

662. Hitting More Grouse: The Big Secret

Here it comes, the grouse-hunting technique that will put more birds in your coat than any other: When you hear the flush, don't stand there looking for the bird, then raise your gun. Your gun should be coming to your shoulder as you look toward the direction of the flush. At the first glimpse of the bird, the barrel should be coming onto what you're seeing, and you fire instantly. There's no tracking, no aiming. It's a "throw" shot, as I prefer to call it, instead of the oft-heard "snap" shot. Of course, this method is assuming a hunting buddy is behind you, out of harm's way.

663. Out of Circulation—and Staying That Way

When the temps really drop and high winds are raging through woods, ruffed grouse—just like the white-tailed deer—can remain holed up in conifers, not using much energy, waiting it out.

664. Equipped on "Stayin' Alive"

The ruffed grouse is one tough dude, well equipped to withstand tough winters and predators. His legs are feathered with hair, and even his feet have fine feathers which act like snowshoes. His plumage so matches the woodlands that he is almost impossible to spot on the ground. In deep winter during storms, the grouse is not adverse into diving into snow banks and spending the night out of harm's way. Sometimes, this move is fatal when the crust freezes on top and they cannot break back through come morning.

665. What Grouse Really Weigh

A serious grouse hunter in Tennessee weighed every bird he ever shot for many, many years. They all weighed between 1 pound, 12 ounces, and 1 pound, 14 ounces.

666. Woodcock Flights: The Real Deal

"Take my share of moonbeams. To get these grand gamebirds moving, give me a good old-fashioned line storm of wind-driven rain. You know, the kind that lacquers leaves into your windows and shimmies the shade of the lamp post across the street. Next morning, let me hunt covers in a river valley where fresh young alders are crowding out tired old fields. Come afternoon, give me birch knolls and poplar hillsides that are mounded with ant hills and moist with spring creeks. Give me that, Sport, and it's a sure bet that on Saturday there's be a woodcock cooking in the beans."

—Tom Hennessey, *Feathers 'n Fins*,
The Amwell Press, 1989

667. The Dead "Giveaway" on Woodcock

"Going into strange woodcock terrain 'cold' can be disappointing. Two coverts may look alike, yet only one many attract 'cock. Whitewash is the best clue, next to seeing actual birds. The white splashing disintegrate rapidly and when you see them you can almost count on woodcock being nearby."

—George Bird Evans, *The Upland Shooting Life*, Knopf, 1971

668. The Penultimate Upland Gunning Experience

The autumn day has been crisp and tangy. The hills and valleys were aflame with color, but now, at dusk, the shadows have dulled the splendor. Your dog's work has not been error-free, but neither has your shooting. Nevertheless, as you walk back to your truck, you feel the puffy heft of a pair of grouse and three woodcock against the small of your back. The day has been filled with exciting action and the deep satisfaction of being a part of the autumn uplands. You're hoping it will be the same on your next time out. But you never know. There are no guarantees, and you don't want any. Just another chance.

669. Grouse Sit Tighter on Reflushes

A grouse biologist shared a theory with outdoor writer and grouse expert Nick Sisley that he believed grouse definitely sit tighter on reflushes. The reason: because they're not in the spots they usually frequent. In their more-familiar, favorite spots, like the one where you first flushed them, they know the best escape routes and use them every time they're disturbed. On the reflush, they're probably in less-familiar cover.

670. Stop Spooking the Grouse

My friend Jay Drake is a superb grouse hunter who is convinced that noise is the greatest problem in getting good shots at grouse. Jay has many times noted tracks in the snow where grouse simply walked away, never flushing, as he approached. Jay likes to hunt alone to reduce the noise of bells, whistles, commands to dogs, shouts between hunters, and even boots on dry leaves and cracking sticks. In Jay's view, you have to use more stealth to bag grouse than you ever thought necessary.

671. Join the Ruffed Grouse Society

For the serious grouse and woodcock hunter, the Ruffed Grouse Society offers a serious list of benefits that include: four issues each year of their very fine magazine; the opportunity to take part in a strong nationwide effort to improve grouse habitat; the camaraderie of associating with serious hunters like yourself; travel opportunities; info sharing; and others too numerous to mention here. Basic opening membership costs $25 a year. Check them out online at www. ruffedgrousesociety.org or call them at 1-800-JOIN-RGS (873-5576).

672. It's an Uphill Climb

Most authorities and experienced grouse hunters agree: a grouse flushed on a hillside will fly uphill almost every time.

673. Best Way to Cook Woodcock: In the Beans

Veteran outdoor writer Tom Hennessey of the *Bangor Daily News*, with several books to his credit, is a grouse and woodcock hunter without peer. Woodcock can be difficult to turn into a great meal he admits, but he has a favorite way of doing just that. Cook a big pot of baked beans just the way you like them, then add in several woodcock breasts to soak and simmer. You'll have a woodcock feast fit for a king.

674. The Woodcock Gourmand

"How I feel about woodcock breasts, quickly sautéed in wine and brown butter, then salted and peppered, can be quickly surmised by the admission that one evening I ate nine birds by myself, washed down with a fine 1959 Saint Emilion. I would have eaten a few more but my wife had her greedy hands in the platter."

—Gene Hill, "Bad Cooks," *A Hunter's Fireside Book,* Winchester Press, 1972, now offered by Skyhorse Publishing

CHAPTER 14

Pheasant Hunting Tips

675. When Ringnecks Sit Tight

Despite their reputation for being track stars, running ahead of the dogs and hunters, pheasants are capable of making themselves invisible and sitting tight when they feel pressured enough. They can hide in the smallest clump of grass, letting you walk right past them.

676. Don't Let That Tail Fool You

Compared to gamebirds like quail and ruffed grouse, the takeoff of a pheasant, while exciting, is rather slow. However, in its initial, vaulting leap, the rooster pheasant's long tail and gaudy colors make the bird seem even larger than it really is, and the shooter fails to take a lead, but merely pokes the barrel at the body of the bird.

677. How "Cackles" Betray Cockbirds

When a pheasant "cackles" as it flushes, it's a cockbird. Every time. Hens do not cackle. This doesn't mean that cockbirds cackle every time they flush. They don't. Sometimes they fly away in silence. But when you hear a cackling bird, even if it's in the sun and you can't see its colors, you know it's a cockbird.

678. Once Is Not Enough

Don't hesitate to hunt a productive piece of pheasant cover once in the morning and again late in the day. Often, more birds will move into the prime habitat throughout the day.

679. Go Late for Western Ringnecks

While the typical western ringneck hunt involves following short tails though long, golden grass in shirt-sleeve weather, some of the best pheasant hunting on prime habitats in the Dakotas, Nebraska, and Montana occurs after Thanksgiving. There is less pressure then, and the winter weather tends to push birds into flocks. Gaining access to great hunting spots is often easier then, with big game seasons ended. So consider a late season pheasant hunt in the West.

680. When Pheasants Fly High and Fast

After the initial flush, when a pheasant gets some distance between itself and the ground, the bird will be flying high and fast. If you're lucky enough to have a bird flying your way that's been flushed by another hunter, you should be ready to take your shot with a smooth, fast swing and lots of lead. On a stand in driven bird shooting, tower shoots, or as a "blocker" at the end of a cornrow, this is the shot you'll be getting all the time. When in full flight, pheasants are fast, and you've got to get your gun barrel out in front.

681. The Key Maneuver

When you work pheasant cover, always work toward a distinct end point, be it an irrigation ditch, road, creek, or open field. The birds will eventually figure they can't outrun you. As you and your dog approach that end point, the birds will flush.

682. You're Walking Past the Birds

Pheasants tend to sit tighter in wet weather, so work cover more thoroughly than you would on a bluebird day.

683. Boots: Made for Walking

If you don't break in that new pair of hunting boots before the season, you're making a big and painful mistake. One that could even ruin your hunt for big game and birds in rough terrain where you can expect to do a lot of walking.

684. Coming up Empty!

Always reload quickly after shooting a flushing rooster; he may have compatriots with him. While you're patting yourself on the back for a great shot, other birds may flush as you stand there with an empty shotgun.

685. The Fox That Flies

Pheasants have been around for centuries and know all about avoiding man once the hunting season opens and the shooting starts. These are foxy birds, with lots of "smarts" and survival instincts.

686. Pheasant "Benefit" Shoots: Watch for Them

On the *Field & Stream* magazine Web site, www.fieldandstream.com, in an article called "Deep in the Heart of Roosterland," T. Edward Nickens describes shoots in the Texas Panhandle where communities sponsor "Community Hunts," held for donations of $150 to $250. The money goes to community needs, and the hunters get shooting over thousands of acres of prime private pheasant land—some shoots for weekends, some fees for access the entire pheasant season. Nickens's hunt takes place in the area around Hart, Texas, but the idea is cropping over in many other prime pheasant areas.

687. Late Season Is Special

"But later pheasant hunting may be as pure a form of hunting as there is. The hunter then becomes a classic searcher and stalker, shooting less and hunting much, much more."

—John Madsen, "Pheasants Beyond Autumn," *Outdoor Life,* October, 1977

688. They Need to Take a Drink

Like four-legged critters, pheasants need a water source to thrive. In dry months in the fall, work cover near watering holes late in the afternoon to find birds.

689. Late Season Escape Hatches

"I don't have much late-season cunning, but one practice that's worked out well is simply getting as far as possible from roads. An obvious reason is that the birds have faded away from roadsides and roadside field edges. Then, too, the very center of a square-mile section of Midwestern corn-land may be the untidiest part. It's where a farmer tends to sweep stuff under the rug, back where passersby can't see small farm dumps, weed patches, messy fence-corners and junk machinery."

—John Madsen, "Pheasants Beyond Autumn," *Outdoor Life,* October 1977

690. After the Season Opens . . .

Hunting pheasants on opening day and then a week later will seem like the difference between night and day. The pheasant's "disappearing act" after opening day is one of the most remarkable in all upland bird hunting.

691. The Slower, the Better

If you are hunting pheasants without a dog, go super-slow. Walking slowly and stopping frequently will make the birds nervous and can key a flush when they're holding tight and waiting for you to walk past.

692. Find the Roosts for a Shooting Treasure

Out on the prairie, pheasants have limited roosting options. Find those roosts and you've got a wing-shooting gold mine early and late in the day.

693. Pheasants in the Tracking Snow

Got snow? Then go track up a pheasant. You don't need a dog, and you'll quickly learn the birds' favorite hiding spots and get a good feel of how many birds are in the area.

CHAPTER 15

Quail Hunting

694. Shooting the Covey Rise

A good covey rise—say twelve to fifteen birds—is one of the most exciting events in all wing-shooting. Alas, it's also the time when many shooters miss on their first shot, then hastily throw their second shot into thin air. From Day One, quail hunters are urged, "Pick out one bird and shoot it." But they have a hard time doing it. The sight of all those birds, particularly wild birds, hurtling toward the trees—or even through the trees—keeps their face from getting down on the stock, which will result in a miss every time. Some hunters do well on coveys by telling themselves that they're going to shoot the first bird that flies—just as though they were shooting singles. In my case, my scores on covey rises improved when I started really hunkering down on the gun, swinging toward one bird, and telling myself, "I'm going to kill that bird." That's the kind of focus shooting covey rises requires, at least in my view."

695. Another Good Reason to Love Bobwhite Hunting

"Apart from his courage and trickiness in the field, the bobwhite has the power of inspiring magnificent nostalgia in the evening, when the fire snaps and the bourbon melds gently with the branch-water."

—Robert C. Ruark, "The Brave Quail," *Field & Stream,* December 1951

696. Point! Be Ready for Wild Birds

If you're fortunate enough to do some quail hunting for wild birds, you'll soon learn that they don't always act like the birds you've seen in paintings. Instead of being right under the pointing dog's nose, they may be some distance out in front, even as much as 10 yards or more. Be ready for that "out-front" flush.

697. Leave That Safety on until the Shot!

In my formative gun-handling years, I learned to leave the safety on until the gun is moving toward my shoulder to make a shot. Many quail hunters take their safeties off when walking in to a point to flush the birds. The practice is dangerous. The birds may have moved, the dog will have to relocate, and you might have a lot more walking before the birds take flight (if indeed they ever do take flight). Walking around through briars and tangles with a loaded gun with the safety off is a prescription for disaster. Train yourself to leave the safety on until a bird is in the air and the gun is moving toward your shoulder.

698. Hunt "inside" the Field Edges

When your pointing dogs run back and to along a field, staying in the open ground, they may be pretty to look at but will only find coveys of birds that are actually in the field, feeding. By carefully working through the woods bordering the field, the dogs will have a chance to trail and find where coveys have been walking to and from the field, and where they spending most of their daytime hours.

699. Let Your Dog Work the Cripples

When it's time to "hunt dead!" the best thing you can do for your dog is to avoid walking through the area where you have dead birds or a cripple. Stay out to the side and let the dog find the birds.

700. Wet-weather Preserve Birds

Rain and wet weather are usually bad news for preserve quail hunting. Quality preserve hunting, with strong-flying birds, always depends on the place you're hunting. Some are great. Some are un-great! But, generally speaking, the flight qualities of preserve birds in the rain will be disappointing.

701. Marking down the Singles

After a covey rise, many hunters make the mistake of diverting their attention to downed birds too quickly, instead of carefully watching the escape routes of the covey's survivors. Even after these escaping birds are seen to cup their wings and sail in a certain direction, they bear careful watching, for they can sail a long way and change direction quickly.

702. Cold Front Moving in—Great Hunting!

There's nothing quite like being in the field in an afternoon when low clouds are scudding about, it's starting to spit just a bit of snow or icy rain, and the temperature has been dropping sharply. Quail will be feeding like there's no tomorrow, leaving strong trails of scent your dogs can easily find. You can bag your limit on a day like this.

703. Make Mine a Side-by-Side

All right, call me "old-fashioned" if you wish. But to me, a side-by-side 20-gauge double is the gun of choice for bobwhite quail. Barrels 26 inches, bored modified and improved cylinder. You can tramp a long time with a light double, enjoying its sweet feel of balance and sleekness, and when the gun comes to your shoulder, the broad sighting plane seems to flow onto the target. I like double triggers, and a straight stock, but again, I'm old-fashioned. For many hunters today, the over-under seems to be the favorite, especially when it's the same gun used for sporting clays. Makes all the sense in the world. But it's not for me in the quail woods.

704. Cancel the "Dawn Patrol"

The "dawn patrol," so popular and necessary in waterfowl and deer hunting, isn't necessary when you're out for bobwhites. Particularly on cold or frosty mornings, quail like to remained huddled together on their roosts until the sun is well up and warming the landscape. Then the birds will be out and about, and your dogs will have a much better chance of picking up scent.

705. Preserve Shooting Dangers: They're for Real!

Every year it happens: A quail shooter on a preserve shoots a companion or a dog. The reason: Preserve birds often run or walk around in plain sight (completely unlike wild birds!), and when they fly they may be so low they're barely fluttering over the bushes. Add to all this the fact that these birds may fly in a direction behind the hunter. If he turns to shoot, he will be blasting his companions, the guides, and the dog wagon, if there is one. The preserve shooter must be calm, cool, disciplined to only take off the safety and raise the gun on strong-flying birds out front. Low birds and birds escaping to the rear are *not an option*.

706. Leave Some for "Seed"

Shooting a covey of wild bobwhites down to two or three birds doesn't make any sense. From a covey of say twelve birds, set your personal take as five or six. No more. Now leave that covey alone for the rest of the season. There's always next year.

707. When You're Headed for a Tough Day

One of the toughest days you can have in quail hunting will be when the temperature is very low and a stiff breeze is blowing over the frozen ground. These conditions make finding birds a tough proposition for even the best dogs.

708. Keep Your Head down on the Stock

Hunters sometimes wonder why they missed a seemingly easy shot—a covey of quail bursting into flight, a flock of mallards right over the decoys, even a wild turkey strutting into plain view. Often the reason is simply because your were so excited and enthralled by what you are seeing, that you lift your head slightly from the gunstock. When you do, it's all over! You're going to miss the shot.

709. Take It Easy, Get More Shots

With a good bird dog willing to "hunt close" under today's tough conditions, quail hunting is not the place to be in a hurry. Instead, just mosey along and take your time, working every nook and cranny along the edges of the fields thoroughly. You'll find lots more coveys than the hunter in a hurry.

710. Why We Miss Them

Although wild quail are fast, they aren't that fast—so fast that it's "now or never" as in ruffed grouse hunting. Far and away, most bobwhite quail are missed by shooting too fast.

711. When Birds Are Running, Keep up with Your Dog

When your dog is pointing for a few seconds, then moving ahead, then moving again and relocating as you come up, you've obviously got some running birds ahead. Try to keep up with the dog as he moves along. Chances are high that this covey is going to flush wild, well ahead.

712. They're Closer Than You Think

"Most quail are killed within sixty feet of the gun. Before you say I am wrong, measure the next ten you kill. The bobwhite fades away so fast on the flush that many men won't shoot at a bird thirty to thirty-five yards away, believing that he is beyond good killing range."

—Ray P. Holland, *Scattergunning*, Knopf, 1951

713. The Best Snakebite Kit

If you're worried about rattlesnakes where you do your quail hunting, remember that the best snakebite kit ever invented is a set of car keys.

714. Havilah Babcock, the Quail Hunting Man

Just as the name Burton L. Spiller is synonymous with grouse and woodcock, the name Havilah Babcock is the one you will see on several classics of bobwhite quail hunting. A South Carolina school teacher with deep love and respect for the Carolina low-country, Babcock wrote about quail and quail hunters with wry humor and deep insight. Beginning with the book, *Tales of Quails 'n Such*, Babcock's main interest was bobwhite quail, but he did not shy away from other low country subjects with which he was deeply familiar—everything from catalpa worm fishing to possum hunting. His stories were mainstays in *Field & Stream*, and they are collected in several books available today. Check www.amazon.com.

CHAPTER 16

Western Grouse and Quail Hunting

715. The Best of the West

Wingshooting in the American West—from desert country to mountain valleys—includes an agenda of birds to warm the hearts of avid bird hunters and their dogs. You have the scaled quail, often called "blue quail" by the locals; the Gambel's quail, the true desert bird; his cousin the California Valley quail, found more in cultivated areas; the mountain quail, the largest quail of all, with a plume that is sharper shaped and stands straight up instead of bending forward like the other western quail; and the Mearns's quail, a colorful, full-bodied quail that hangs out in smaller coveys than the other western quail and lives in the grassland canyons amid brush and scattered trees. All of these quail are a joy to study in photographs and illustrations in books or on the Internet.

716. The Sage Grouse: Now a Trophy Bird

Due to the loss of quality sagebrush habitat, the big, colorful sage grouse has become a trophy bird, available on open-season lists in nine states. They are found in the high sagebrush areas of the Western United States and Saskatchewan and Alberta in Canada. Going back to the time of Lewis and Clark, groups of sage grouse were a common sight throughout the West. Today, they have become a rare sight, except in certain areas. And what a sight they are. With some of the cocks weighing from six to eight pounds, they look as large as turkeys when crossing open ground.

717. The Rattlesnake Question

In a lot of bobwhite quail hunting in places like Texas and Mexico, snakebite-proof boots are preferred. In general, most western quail hunting does not require this precaution. Check with the local hunters.

718. Huns vs. Bobwhites: Which Is Faster?

When bobwhite hunters take their first crack at Huns, they'll usually will say the gray partridge is faster. Most of the experienced hunters who have put in their hours with both birds feel the wild bobwhites are faster. The Huns look faster because they're larger and jump at longer ranges.

719. Sharptails and Gun Dogs

If you'd love to see your dogs work on a great gamebird in open country, then try to take them sharptail hunting. A covey of eight to ten sharptails is a stirring sight to encounter with your dog, then following up the singles will give you a different kind of action, with slow, careful work in cover and tangles.

720. The Ups and Downs of Chukar Hunting

Once you've located chukars, you literally chase them uphill and down, over steep, tough terrain that can stop your heart if you're not in good shape. When the birds are flushed along the bottom of the hills, they fly uphill. Going after them, you'll reach the top only to have them fly back downhill. And so it goes.

721. Here Today, Gone Tomorrow

It helps to remember that Sage Grouse are desert birds, and like desert forbs they can disappear almost completely during drought, only to replicate madly with a little rain . . . some years you find none, while in others they bloom like an irrigated desert, with hundreds of grouse startling local ranchers, who think such numbers of birds must migrate south, or "up the crick," or somewhere in other years.

722. Something Else You Might Need

Carry a tube of Super Glue in your bird vest. A few drops of adhesive can make emergency clothing or gear repairs. In a pinch, it can even close a wound.

723. Made for Walking

Hunting western quail will require the best, well-fitted, completely-broken-in boots can you afford. Rocky, uneven ground, sprinkled with cactus that bites, will challenge your every step. Gun dogs will need constant attention, and many western hunters equip their dogs with special boots.

724. How to Miss Western Quail

They may look like they're flying straight and level, but western quail are almost always rising as your gun comes up for the shot. Blot the bird out and fire, and you'll miss every time. You've got to hold over them slightly.

725. Just like the Name Says

"Sage grouse habitat can be summed up in a word—sagebrush. To say that the shrub is important to the grouse is a great understatement. The grouse eat it, they hide in it, they nest in it, and they perform their annual, age-old courtship displays near it. Without sagebrush, they cannot exist."
—Craig Springer, "The Sage Grouse," Cabela's Field Guide Story, www.cabelas.com

726. Sharptails vs. Ruffed Grouse on the Table

It's no contest: The ruffed grouse not only beats the sharptail but beats almost everything else as well. Still, sharptails are a prize worth bringing home, and there are several ways to enjoy them. One of the most often quoted from hunter-campers is to broil the birds over hot coals in the field.

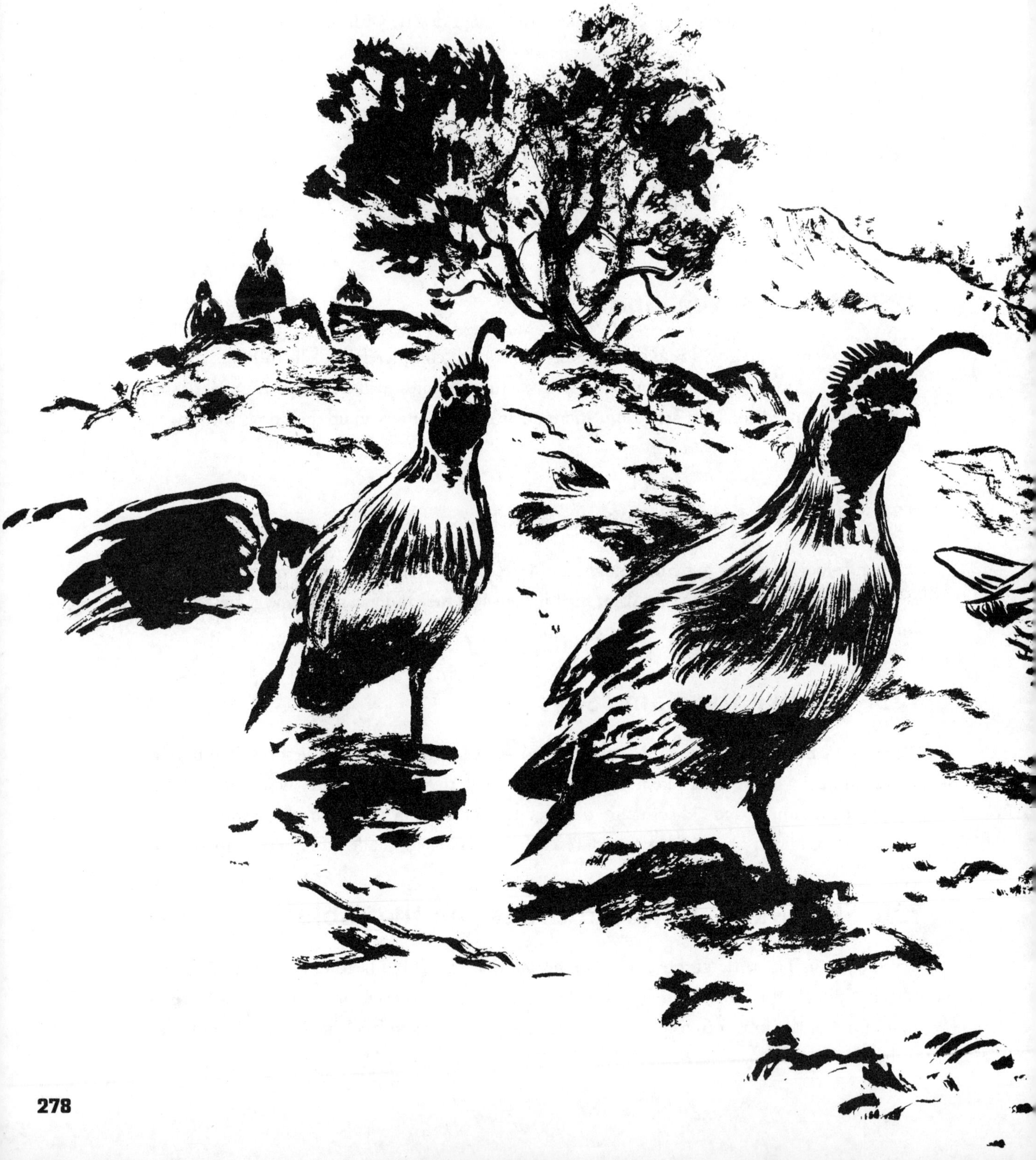

727. When Bobwhite Man Meets Western Quail

The first sight of western quail by a seasoned bobwhite hunter like this writer is apt to be a bit disconcerting, as well as memorable. Try to picture twenty to fifty closely-bunched blue-tinted bodies literally flowing over the ground in a stream-like motion. The covey seems to disappear as it leaves open ground and melds into the cover. Then, as you hurry forward, you spot them emerging from the cover in the distance, still on the run . . . and now you are on the run yourself, trying to get them to flush. These are scaled quail, or possibly gambel's, the track stars of western quail hunting.

728. The Disappearing Chukars

Sometimes chukars can be heard and spotted calling on the tops of hills. Off you go to pursue the covey up the steep slope. When you reach the top, you find they've departed—probably for the cover at the bottom of the other side of the hill.

729. The Great Treasury of Western Bird Hunting

Imagine an entire book devoted exclusively to western bird hunting. Well, it not only exists, but it's written by veteran writer and hunter John Barsness, whose prose is a hallmark in *Field & Stream*, *Sports Afield*, *Gray's Sporting Journal*, and many other publications. The book is *Western Skies,* published by Lyons & Burford in 1994. Look for it at sites like www.amazon.com. Reviewing the book in *Shooting Sportsman* magazine, Robert F. Jones said, "Anyone planning to gun the Great Plains, whether for sharptails or widgeon, ringnecks or teal, should read this evocative book at least twice—once for the fun of it and again for technique. It's all here—told in the wry, loving voice of a native-born Plainsman who knows both his birds and his country."

730. You'll Need Water Out There

Every western quail hunter needs to consider the availability of water in his plan for his hunt. Or to put it another way: Consider the non-availability of water. You, and especially your dogs, are going to need it.

731. Another Way to Carry Water

Photographic supply stores offer collapsible quart and half-gallon jugs made for darkroom chemicals. They make great canteens because you can squeeze the air out of them after you take a drink, which eliminates noisy sloshing.

732. Gambel's or Valley?

Found in similar terrain, the valley and gambel's quail can be hard to tell apart. The valley quail has scaled markings on the breast. Another difference, pointed out by Ray P. Holland in *Scattergunning*, is that the head of the male gambel's is bright chestnut.

733. Habit That Betrays Sharptails

Wherever they are found, sharptails have a strong habit that often betrays them: In the early morning and late afternoon they fly to the fields where they like to feed. They can be spotted at that time, even ambushed if you know their route. I've had great sharptail shooting in Manitoba by waiting behind hay bales for the previously-spotted flock to appear.

734. Sage Grouse on the Table

How do sage grouse taste; Well, it all depends on the way you prepare and cook them, but to many the sage taste is too strong. In the Lewis and Clark expedition in 1805, William Clark wrote, ". . . the flesh of the cock of the plains is dark, and only tolerable in point of flavor."

735. Sharptails in Flight

When a bunch of sharptails bursts into flight, the birds don't explode skyward in the manner of bobwhite quail or ruffed grouse. They're more like pheasants, a little slow on the takeoff but gathering speed quickly once away from the ground. When pass-shooting opportunities come your way, look for the birds to fly in an alternate flapping/sailing manner.

736. Tapping into the Alaskan Ruffed Grouse Bonanza

I lived in Alaska for two years—Fairbanks to be exact—attending my last two years of high school while my father was assigned to Ladd Air Force Base as an officer commanding anti-aircraft radar installations during the Korean War. North of Fairbanks, the gravel Steese Highway wound through hills and tundra toward the Yukon. The stretch from Fairbanks to a place called "Eagle Summit" harbored the best grouse and ptarmigan hunting covers I shall ever see. When one thinks of these northern forests, ptarmigan come immediately to mind, and, of course, spruce grouse. Now "spruce hens" are terrific as a gamebird when you flush them, but they're nowhere even close to being as wary and fast on the wing as ruffed grouse. But we had ruffed grouse too! Yes, real ruffed grouse, up there in Alaska. And while they were not as wary as the grouse you'll flush in, say, Pennsylvania, they were plenty wary enough to provide us some great hunting and legendary table fare.

737. Using Calls to Find Chukars

Coveys of chukars sometimes reveal their locations by calling. Chukar calls and instruction are readily available from Cabela's and others.

738. Chasing down a Hun Covey

You could, in theory, bust an entire covey of Hungarian partridge if you mark their landings after every flush. But you'll have better hunting long-term if you satisfy yourself with three or four flushes. Then go find another covey to work.

739. Uphill? Downhill?

Unlike ruffed grouse, which almost always will fly uphill when flushed on a hillside, western quail will take off downhill, creating a very difficult shot, since most hunters are not accustomed to holding below the bird.

740. The "Ground Sluice" Tactic

Many western quail hunters, frustrated by the running birds and anxious to get the covey airborne and scattered, fire a shot that rake the ground in front of the birds and causes them to flush. Of course, if you're hunting with a dog, this tactic is not an option.

741. Hun Country: Hunting the Prairies

The great prairies of Alberta and Saskatchewan and western states like Montana are home to the European gray partridge (Hungarians, or Huns, as they are known), first introduced in the very early 1900s. Here big-going bird dogs can do their thing, roaming far and wide as you walk the endless-seeming, rolling land beneath the big sky. In some places, the Hun's range is shared by sharptail grouse, and a mixed bag is possible. To top things off, you might even just some ducks from a prairie pothole and have some swing your way.

742. Out to Get Some Chickens

The Greater Prairie Chicken, the pinnated grouse, or "squaretail" as hunters familiar with sharptail grouse call it, is hunted in North Dakota, South Dakota, Nebraska, and Kansas. The "chickens" once thrived in the weedy areas of the western prairies in such numbers that hunter like Theodore Roosevelt commonly had fifty-bird days. You won't find any such numbers today, due to the loss of habitat—not the shooting—but in areas when the chickens are still present in huntable numbers, you'll find a gamebird worthy of pursuit and great on the table.

743. Out for Revenge

Writer Rafe Nielsen got the title of his great chukar story on the Cabela's Web site from his observation, "There's an old hunting adage that claims the first time you hunt chukars, it's for sport. After that, it's for revenge."

744. Find the Water, You'll Find the Chukars

Water is scarce in the desert country where chukars live, Find the water, you'll find the birds—open springs, river and creek bottoms, even guzzlers built by state wildlife agencies are home to chukars.

745. Are You Ready for Chukars?

In a wonderful article on the Cabela's Web site, www.cabelas.com, Rafe Nielson writes: "By far, chukars are the most challenging and difficult North American gamebird. . . . What makes the chukka a difficult gamebird to hunt is the country they inhabit. The steep, rocky slopes of barren deserts are preferred habitat. . . . This most resembles the native land they come from [Afghanistan and India, introduced in the early 1900s] and provides excellent cover when the birds are pressured. Vegetation is also important, and the birds favor the round mountain brushes and grasses such as sagebrush, saltgrass and especially cheatgrass."

—Rafe Nielsen, "Chukar Hunting—This Time Is for Revenge,"
Field Guide Story, www.cabelas.com

746. With Ted Trueblood to Back up the Grouse Claims

Whenever someone challenges me on my Alaska ruffed grouse experiences, as they often do, claiming I was not hunting real ruffed grouse, I put their criticism to the sword by a column late Ted Trueblood devoted in *Field & Stream* to the exact same hunting I had been doing above Fairbanks. As I did, he found the Ruffed Grouse shooting, on the same hunts as the spruce grouse, to be amazing.

747. After the Covey Flush: Time to Start Scoring

When a covey of western quail has been busted, and the singles are scattered, you can reasonably expect these birds to sit tight and flush close to the gun. Hunting down the singles after the covey flush is what it's all about it western quail hunting.

748. The Snap Shot on Hun Coveys

Some hunters claim more success on Huns by taking a fast snap shot at the entire covey just as the birds jump. They follow up this "shoot and hope" blast at the covey en masse with a fast swing on one bird.

749. The "Easier" Chukar Hunting

The steep high-country hills and mountain draws that have chukar hunters gasping for breath and frustrated by the up-and-down escape routes of the birds aren't a factor in a lot of chukar hunting today. The chukar has become a favorite for preserve hunting, providing a hefty great-tasting bird to bag and holding well for pointing dogs on preserves. Many preserve hunters and managers favor stocking chukars over pheasants.

750. What to Expect on Hungarian Partridge

They're twice as large as bobwhites, and the coveys usually jump much farther from the gun and dogs than Bob does. When Huns jump 30 yards or more from the gun, they seem unbelievably fast, sure to be out of range in just an instant. Feeling somewhat panicky, the gunner may throw two fast snap shots at the birds, and will probably miss. A fast swing on a certain bird works better. The kind of swing and shot duck hunters are used to—not the quick snap of the bobwhite hunter.

751. Focusing on Mountain Quail

Mountain quail are larger than bobwhites, weighing about nine or ten ounces to bob's seven. Their daily range is larger than the bobwhite's also, as they move between food, water, and sheltered brush that protects them from their enemies. They particularly like canyons with streams in the bottoms, and their strong legs carry them on wide patrols for seeds and berries on the adjacent hillsides.

752. How We Hunted Ptarmigan with Spruce Hens

Driving along the gravel Steese "highway" we hunted these spruce grouse and ruffed grouse by parking the truck and working into the cover about 50 yards and paralleling the road. Even without a dog, we flushed spruce hens and ruffed grouse with such regularity that we actually had to pace ourselves on bagging a hefty limit. (Ten birds, as I recall, but don't quote me. The time was 1952–'54.) We always wanted to save some action for the pinnacle of the trip—a place called Eagle Summit where the hills rose above the tree line and flocks of ptarmigan could be found in almost every direction. The snow came early up here, and sometimes we were able to walk close enough to kick up flocks of twenty-thirty birds, trying for a double on the flush, then hunting down the singles, just as in quail hunting.

753. Why Mearns's Quail Are Special

The Mearns's quail lives in gentler, kinder terrain than his cousin desert quail. I've hunted them in the grassland canyons near Tucson, Arizona, in country once frequented by Apaches like Cochise. Found in smaller coveys than other western quail, the Mearns's is a hefty bird, great on the table, which feeds on seeds and tubers found in certain types of terrain. My hunts were in January from a motor home with the late Pete Brown, guns editor of *Sports Afield* for many years. During the day the air had a slight chill that made hunting a pleasure, and at night you felt you could grab a handful of stars, and one fell asleep listening to the sounds of coyotes. Great country, great hunting!

754. When It's Sharptails You're After

Sharptail grouse, a prime gamebird hunted in the prairies of Canada and several western states, can be bagged with pointing dogs, retrieving and flushing dogs, and plain old walking them up.

755. Tighter Chokes Take More Huns

Your wide-open favorite bobwhite quail gun may not get the job done on Huns. They jump so far out that you need modified and full tubes, rather than improved cylinder and modified.

756. "Cast-and-Blast" Chukar Hunting

On many western rivers, fishing can be combined with hunting, and chukars are the game. While floating trout and smallmouth rivers, anglers can spot chukar groups on the hillsides between casts, then off they go, scrambling up the mountain. They're guaranteed to be breathing hard when they return, with or without birds in their game vests.

757. Midday Sharptails: It's "Pick-and-Shovel" Work

Sharptails will spend most of the day dusting, loafing and staying out of sight in everything from brushy tangles to the deeper woods. Digging them out, even with a dog, is slow going compared to the action you can expect to get in the morning or late afternoon.

758. The Joy of Sage Hen Hunting

"When I lived in the East, I hunted grouse and woodcock in New England. The birds were grand and the country was beautiful, but I could never escape the feeling that I was cramped for room. Everything seemed small and pinched together. I can show you places in the West where you can stand on a hill and see nothing but sagebrush, clear to the horizon in every direction. Not a house nor a tree is in sight, and you know there isn't another living person within twenty miles except, perhaps, for a stray sheepherder or cow puncher . . . There is something in the air that is mighty good. It's sharp, clean, dry, almost brittle, and always there is the faint undertone of sage. It is exhilarating. You're high, so it often freezes at night in September, but the days are warm and you hunt in shirt sleeves. It's grand country for a man who likes a bit of room."

—Ted Trueblood, "Bird of the Wide Open Spaces,"
True Magazine Hunting Yearbook, 1951

759. Gravel Roads: Where the Game Wardens Stay Busy

When I lived in Alaska, I took note that the Fairbanks paper sometimes wrote about game law offenders. Constantly leading the list were people busted for shooting spruce grouse and ruffed grouse on the few gravel roads through the wilderness. Since grouse like gravel roads to pick up grit, the wardens kept busy, as certain individuals saw the birds standing in the roads, stopped their trucks, got out, and blazed away, collecting some grouse for the table. Today, the practice of shooting birds in the road is no doubt a leading cause of the demise of many ruffed grouse in the Maine and Canadian bush country, where dirt roads and logging lanes and skidding trails cut through some wild country and grouse come out to get grit on them.

CHAPTER 17

Dove Hunting

760. Those "Power Line" Doves

When you see doves sitting on power lines, you're not going to stop your truck and start blazing away. The sight is, however, a true indicator that doves are using fields in the area. Keep a close watch as the afternoon progresses and see if you can spot the fields they are using and the routes to and from resting areas and waterholes.

761. White-Wings Like It Hot

The white-winged dove of the southwest is larger than the mourner and prefers much, much hotter weather. In fact, the birds along the Texas, Arizona, and New Mexico borders shove off for Mexico when the weather turns the slightest bit down from sizzling. I gunned white-wings along the Arizona border on an annual basis back in the '70s, and found them to be strong fliers and great on the table. White-wings seem to bore ahead in a steady, more-determined nature than mourners, which twist and jink around a lot. Bag limits have declined steadily since that time.

762. The Perfect Dove Gun

You can shoot doves with any kind of smoothbore you have—from tight-shooting 12-gauge duck guns to wide-open 20-bore quail doubles. But let's say you really want to enjoy the experience to the ultimate, and that includes using the ultimate shotgun. So . . . what is it? And what do you feed it? What follows is a personal opinion, based on considerable experience. First, I want a side-by-side or over-and-under double. Pumps and autos throw their shells, which, in my opinion, must be retrieved and not left lying in the stubble. Next, the gauge. The 20-bore seems perfect to me, although the 28 will certainly do the job in the right hands.(In case you didn't know, 28-gauge guns throw a highly-effective pattern.) Even though some good shooters use the .410, I don't see it as a good dove gun. I've seen just too many cripples and missed birds with the .410, which has a pattern I don't trust. For chokes, I like improved cylinder and modified for my double, but if you can find—or order—one with improved cylinder and full, you might be better off. Number 8 shot seem right for most shooting, but in second seasons, colder weather, 7½ might bring down more long-range birds.

763. Marker Trees: Where Doves Fly Most

Doves often use prominent, single trees as a sort of intersection guidepost when crossing large expanses of fields. They fly past these positions frequently before fanning out for other sections of the fields. Sometimes these "markers" can be a low clump of small trees at an intersection of fence rows. If you can pick out one of these sites in your scouting, you should have great shooting.

764. The Pleasure of Small Hunts

Although most dove "shoots" are a big community affairs, with many shooters spreading out over the fields, there's still a place for smaller hunts, the kind two friends can take. Careful scouting over land you have permission to hunt can reveal excellent sites along flyways to set out your shooting stool and get consistent pass shooting. These two- and three-man hunts are especially fun and effective during the winter portions of the dove season, when the birds are bigger and faster.

765. Doves Like Clear-ground Walking

Wherever they feed, water or pick up grit for their craws, doves like walking over spots of clear ground. They may be flying over thick, tangled brush a lot of the time, but they do not favor walking around in the thick bushes. For watering places, look for open, sandy ramps along the water's edge. In fields, they will be landing in clearings or in the open ground between the rows of feed like sunflower seeds or millet.

766. Low Birds Spell Danger!

At every well-run dove shoot, you'll hear the person in charge point out the danger of shooting at low-flying birds with good reason: Low-flying birds are dangerous in the extreme. I personally will not even raise my gun to track a bird unless I have about a 45-degree angle.

767. Those Tough Overhead Shots

One of the toughest shots in dove hunting occurs on a bird flying straight overhead. It's hard to get your gun barrel ahead of one of these speedsters and keep it moving—and still be able to see the bird. Most of the people who are good at making this kind of shot preach the gospel of having the barrel overtake the bird in a rapid swing, then pulling the trigger just as the barrel blots out the bird. Of course, you have to keep that barrel moving (rapidly!), even after the trigger pull. Whatever you do, it's a tough shot.

768. A Box of Shells, a Limit of Birds

Wherever you go, you'll hear it said that shooting a limit of doves (usually twelve birds) with a box of twenty-five shells is the mark of a really good shooter. In my view, it all depends. If a lot of birds are flying, and you're a cherry-picker, taking only the easiest shots, bagging a limit of birds with a box of shells is no big deal. If a lot of the shots you're getting are long, high and far out and on strong, fast birds—the kind you get in the later half of the dove seasons—you might even consider yourself lucky to bag a limit of birds with two boxes.

769. Wear Camo for Dove Hunting

Yes, when there's a heavy flight of birds in the area, with plenty of chances to get some shots, you can bag your share of doves wearing just about any kind of shirt—as long as it's not white or solid black. But in normal conditions—and especially in tough conditions when not many birds are coming your way—you'll do a lot better by wearing at least a camo shirt and hat, and even better with camo trousers. Especially after opening day, and especially during the second seasons, doves can be skittish, veering off at the sight of a crouching figure in the bushes.

770. Dove Hunting's Finest Moment

For this old hunter, the finest moments—with images I can replay in my thoughts with great clarity—are those when five or more doves come slanting in from a side angle, then fly directly across my position. If you're ever going to bag a double, this is the moment. You usually settle for one, of course. And the sight of those sleek, beautiful birds in full flight over the field will come back to you often.

771. The Sunset Fliers

There's a moment in the dove fields when time after time I wish I could paint. It occurs in the slanting sunset light, when we've finished shooting and the birds are still flying. The setting sun gives them a sort of rosy tint makes the scene unforgettable, while filling one with confidence that there will be plenty of birds around for our next hunt.

772. Be Alert for Killdeer

Killdeer—those swooping, swerving, and constantly screaming dark-grey birds with pointed wings—are usually very much a part of the terrain where doves are found. If you mistake one for a dove and shoot it, you may face a fine. Be alert and learn to recognize these birds that can look remarkably like doves at times.

773. Eye Protection Is a Must in Dove Hunting

When dove season opens, chances are the sun will be bright, and seeds and all kinds of dry bits of trash will be blowing around. You'll be looking skyward constantly, and there's always a possibility of a stay shot pellet dropping on your stand—and into your eye. You need protection! Yes, sunglasses are a must. You might need two pair, one with lenses for cloudy days, another for the more-typical bright days.

774. Bad News Dogs in Dove Fields

Seems innocent enough: a guy wants to bring his retriever along on a dove hunt. He figures to get some good action for his lab, or whatever. Trouble is, the dog isn't trained properly. From the moment the guy gets in the field with his dog, bedlam ensues. The dog runs through all the fields, past everybody's stand, ignoring the master's screams and commands. The afternoon is spent trying to bring the dog under control, to no avail. If you—or a pro!—hasn't had the time to properly train your dog, leave Old Jake at home. And hope that everybody else does the same.

775. How NOT to Take a Tumble

Your favorite dove-hunting stool—Kool-Stool or whatever—is a great place to perch while waiting for birds to come your way. When you're presented with one of those high, fast birds heading straight for you, passing dead overhead, you ought to be aware of leaning back too far. You'll tumble over backwards, for sure. It's a bad, dangerous deal with a loaded gun, and your back isn't going to enjoy it either. If it happens to you, remember to keep the gun pointed skyward, no matter how embarrassed you are, and get the safety back on as soon as possible, definitely before you start trying to get up.

776. Late Can be Great in Dove Hunting

The second dove seasons—where and when they are scheduled—usually take place during days that seem more like real hunting season than the steamy, hot days of September. In the second seasons, the birds are now all (in September, some are not) full-grown, full-feathered, and in general fly faster than their September kin. The days can be blustery, the birds skittish, and your shooting ability will be challenged to the fullest. You may have bagged a limit of birds with a box of shells in September, but November or December will be a different story. Try it!

777. New Jersey Hunters: Cross over the River

Years ago, in a display of legislative weakness, anti-hunters managed to get mourning doves placed on the songbird list in New Jersey and dove hunting was banned. Still, all is not lost for enterprising hunters. Just across the Delaware River in Pennsylvania and Delaware, hunting is allowed and there are plenty of doves in places. Yes, you'll have to buy a non-resident license, yes you'll have to do lots of scouting, and perhaps you'll even take a lease. But if you're serious about doves, you'll find good hunting.

778. Light Loads, Better Shooting

At the tail end of the good old summertime, when dove shooting in your camo T-shirt, you don't want high loads banging your shoulders into a pulp—and bringing on an acute case of flinching. Doves don't take a lot of killing power. Use the lightest loads possible for the gauge you're shooting.

779. The Ultimate Dove Seat?

Over the years, I've watched dove-hunting (shooting!) seats evolve from canvas lawn chairs to Kool-Stools and beyond. Now perhaps the ultimate has come along. Cabela's, www.cabelas.com, has the Action Products Deluxe Super Seat, which is a padded seat with comfortable back, on top of a box that is a cooler with lift-out trays for gear. There's also a pouch on the side of the box for more stuff, all for $50. If you want less, that costs less and weighs less, you can opt for Ameristep's High-Back Chair for $19.99.

780. White-wings Are Down Mexico Way

For good white-winged dove shooting today, you'll be looking to book your hunt for one of the many outfitters in Mexico. Type in "White-winged Dove Hunting in Mexico" on your favorite search engine, and you'll see a lot of listings to choose from.

781. Flying the "Gauntlet"

Some of the most thrilling moments in dove hunting take place at a shoot that's going strong and a dove flies over the woods into the field and immediately meets a barrage of gunfire. Instead of turning back over the woods, the bird bores straight on across the field, unwavering, with more and more shots booming out until it passes out of sight at the other end. It's really something to see—and hear!

782. Dove Hunting in Mexico: A Look Back

Although this account by Tom Hennessey describes dove hunting in the Yucatan Peninsula of Mexico in the 1980s, you can find much the same kind of shooting today, in an area where there are so many doves they're actually considered to be pests: "You use an overused expression, 'You had to be there.' Far to our right, an immense undulating flock of doves moved across the horizon, like a wind-driven cloud. Like swarms of bees, more flocks arrived. Within seconds they reached the field and were greeted with snappy statements from 20-guage guns, punctuated by belching blasts from the heavier 12s. A fusillade followed, and few birds fell. Wheeling and flaring, the flocks scattered. Doves in every direction."

—Tom Hennessey, *Feathers 'n Fins*, The Amwell Press, 1989

783. The Toughest Shot of Them All

Perhaps the toughest shot in all upland gunning occurs when a dove, riding a tailwind, flying high, whips across your stand. Some of these birds actually rock their bodies from side-to-side, seemingly sensing your column of shot whistling past. This is prime-time, great shooting.

784. Doves Are Hard to Hit

More ammunition is expended shooting at doves than any other gamebird. Get the picture?

785. What to Expect from White-wings

"Coming into a field, white-winged doves are using at cruising speed—which ain't exactly slow. At the first shot, however, they switch on their afterburners and accelerate to a speed that is sickening—to the shooter, this is."

—Tom Hennessey, *Feathers 'n Fins,* The Amwell Press, 1989

786. Shoot Lighter-kicking Loads

Dove hunters should know that the 1-ounce "Dove and Quail" loads you see for $3 a box at the marts in August are loaded to almost 1,300 fps to ensure that they'll cycle in autoloaders. Spend a few more dollars and shoot light trap loads instead. When you're wearing no more padding than a camo T-shirt, 1-ounce target loads at 1,180 fps deliver excellent patterns and less bang for the buck, which is what we're after. If you want speed, try International target loads, which are quite fast at 1,325 fps, but low-recoil thanks to their $\frac{7}{8}$-ounce payload.

—Philip Bourjaily, "Reducing Recoil, Part I," www.fieldandstream.com

CHAPTER 18

Wingshooting

787. Don't Mix That Ammo

Mixing 12-, 20-, and 28-gauge shells—and even other gauges—in your gunning coat or shell box is a bad idea. The 20 and 28 can drop into the chamber and lodge in the barrel. Bam! Very bad things happen, like losing your hand or your life. We know of one prominent lady shooter who lost a thumb in just such a way during the excitement of crow hunting.

788. A Cheap Alternative to Clay Pigeons

"A cheap target for shotgun shooting is a Frisbee. . . . About 9 inches in diameter, it's larger than a clay target, and tougher. The Frisbee will still fly flawlessly at the end of the day with light streaming through countless shot hoes, and it's considerably easier to hit than conventional clay targets . . . a blessing for the beginning shooter."

—Bob Gilsvik, *The Guide to Good Cheap Hunting,* Stein & Day, 1978

789. Gauges, Chokes, and Pattern Density

The misconception that gauge-size determines shotgun pattern size should have been put to bed long ago. A full-choke pattern, or improved cylinder, or modified . . . whatever . . . is the same diameter and circumference regardless of gauge. It is the gauge that determines the density (the number) of shot within the pattern. Got it? The 12-gauge has more shot than the 20, the 20 more than the 28, and so on.

790. Steel Shot in Full Choke

There's a myth out there that steel shot won't perform properly in a full-choke gun. *Field & Stream* writer Philip Bourjaily takes it on as part of a wonderful article he did in 2004, "Shotgun Myths Explained," posted on the *Field & Stream* Web site, www.field-andstream.com. Bourjaily writes, "Manufacturers discouraged the use of Full chokes in the early days of steel for fear of barrel damage. However, almost any load of BB or smaller steel with shoot tight, deadly patterns through a Full choke and won't harm choke tubes, either."

791. The Straight-stock Bird Gun Preference

According to grouse and shotgun expert Nick Sisley, the straight-stock preference on classic upland bird doubles, and others being made today, is not simply for the racy, clean lines. The increased angle in the wrist of the shooter as the gun comes up results in the face achieving a tighter cheeking on the stock. In addition, the straight stock makes twin-trigger doubles easier to operate.

792. An Alternate Technique to the "Sustained Lead"

In many schools for serious shooters in the United Kingdom and even in the United States, a different technique than the "Sustained Lead" is taught. Instead of starting the swing with the gun ahead of the bird, the shooter is urged to start the gun barrel behind the bird, catch up with the bird, swing on past the bird, then pull the trigger while the gun keeps swinging. These shooters report that with this technique, the shooter is forced to swing the gun fast and keep it swinging fast throughout the shot. The fact that the gun has to catch up with the bird by a fast swing creates a swing that won't break down or pause as the gun whips on past the bird.

793. The Truth about the "Sustained Lead"

Whether they're aware of it or not, many shooters—most in fact—learn to shoot with what's called the "Sustained Lead." The gun comes up ahead of the bird and stays there swinging and tracking, even after the shot. Many serious shooters who put a lot of time and practice (skeet, trap, sporting clays) into their skills come to realize that the "Sustained Lead" is tough to sustain. Something causes the gun barrel to stop swinging fast enough, and the shot is missed. Sometimes, anyway.

794. The Deadliest Shooting Technique

In an article he wrote for me in the magazine *Waterfowl Hunter*, outdoor writer Tom Huggler described the swing technique favored by many shooters who don't like the so-called "Sustained Lead." In this technique, described in the "Alternative Technique" tip above, the gun starts behind the bird and comes on through. But Tom has a better way to describe it, a way to remember it in the field. As he swings the gun, he's thinking, "Butt . . . belly . . . beak . . . bang!"

795. Fast Fliers Take a Fast Reaction

On the kind of explosive flushes you're apt to be getting on birds like quail and grouse, getting the gun on your shoulder then swinging the muzzle toward the bird won't get the job done. The muzzle should be moving toward the bird as the gun is moving toward your shoulder and cheek.

796. Heavy Guns for Practice, Light for Hunting

You can't shoot round after round of sporting clays, skeet, or trap with a shotgun so light you can trudge through grouse, woodcock, and quail country all day carrying it in one hand. The light, fast-pointing guns can be used for a round or two to give you a "feel" for mounting and swinging them, but for serious clay-target shooting, a heavier gun is needed.

797. Clay-target Practice, and Real Birds

"Any shooting helps us become better, but a 100-straight in trap or skeet or gaining Master Class in sporting clays, using a pretty heavy gun, is not grouse or woodcock shooting—no semblance of it. There's no calling, 'Pull' and here comes the real bird. Instead, it's tramping mile after mile—and maybe you'll get a shot. If you do it's almost bound to be unexpected, even sometimes behind a good dog. Call 'Pull' all you want, but the bird is going to fly when it wants to."

—Nick Sisley, in an article for the Ruffed Grouse Society

798. Sorting out the Light Gun Debate

Although it's most unanimous among upland bird hunters that a light gun is needed in the field, the question of "Just How Light?" stirs some debate. Shotgun expert and writer Nick Sisley sheds considerable light on the subject: "The don't-go-too-light camp claims that light shotguns bob around too much, and are hard to control in making a steady smooth swing . . . The go-light-shotgun camp says that a heavier gun does not permit them to carry the gun in a ready-to-shoot manner for hours on end. . . . I've been in the go-light camp for decades. . . . I still can't carry a 7-pound shotgun for hours on end—just can't. So I don't try. Don't have to when carrying a grouse gun of about 6 pounds."

—Nick Sisley, in an article for the Ruffed Grouse Society

799. Ain't No Such Thing as "Straightaways"

"How can I possibly miss that shot?" a hunter exclaims. "It was dead straightway." We've heard that one many, many times and will keep on hearing it. But the truth is this: A real straight-away doesn't exist. The shift may be subtle, but your bird is either rising, dipping down, or moving from one side to the other. Dead straightaway, he's not!

800. Fine-tuning Your Skeet Practice

Skeet shooting is not only fun while improving your smoothbore prowess, it offers certain stations that really resemble the angles you get in all forms of wings-hooting. For the best practice on flushing upland birds like, quail, grouse, pheasant, and woodcock have someone pull for you while you concentrate on stations Low Five, Low Six, and Low Seven. Don't mount the gun. Have it in your bird-shooting carry when you call, "Pull!"

801. Picking out a Lighter Bird Gun

"Back in 1964 there weren't a lot of light-gun choices. This is not true today. There are a myriad of light ones available from Orvis, Browning, Caesar Guerini, Franchi, Benelli, Remington, Krieghoff (yes, Krieghoff), Kimber, Perazzi, Smith & Wesson, Cortona, Winchester, Connecticut Shotgun Manufacturing Company (Winchester Model 21 reproductions), Beretta, CZ-USA, Ruger, and others. Obviously, some of these makers also offer heavier shotguns. Don't forget the used market—for treasures like small-gauge Parkers, Fox, L. C. Smith, Browning (Superposed), Ithaca, and certainly small-gauge English doubles. (Editor's note: A tip for those who don't know their computers well, just type in the names of these makers on Google and you'll get the home Web site. Say you're interested in a Kimber shotgun. Type "Kimber Shotguns." You'll get the link to go right to Kimber.)

—Nick Sisley, in an article for the Ruffed Grouse Society

802. Just One More

"I've come to recognize collecting as a form of undiagnosed disease. Like the alcoholic who thinks he can just have one and he'll be fine, the gun collector kids himself. . . . The world's greatest easy mark is no longer the pushover he used to be. . . . But if you know of where I could get my hands on an old Model 21 in 16 gauge, bored about improved and modified with a straight-hand stock and checkered butt, at the right price, of course, you know where you can reach me. Just don't call me at home, if you can manage it—and if a lady answers, hang up."

—Gene Hill, "Shotgunners Anonymous," *Hill Country,* E. P. Dutton, 1978

803. How Far Was That Bird? You Don't Want to Know

Shotgunners, waterfowl hunters in particular, sometimes talk about making 60-yard shots, even 65. OK, I'll believe you. But sometimes before you go much further with such boasts, do yourself a favor and visit you local school's football field. Stand on the goal line and put a

box or marker on the 60-yard line. Was the duck you shot that far out? Thank you, I thought not. For you bird hunters, put the box at 35 yards. Does that range feel familiar? I thought it would.

804. A Short Course in Spanish Shotguns

"Most of the shotguns made in Spain did not have a great reputation until some time in the 1960s, when a few of the top Spanish side-by-sides were discovered by outdoor writers Jack O'Connor of *Outdoor Life* and Colonel Charles Askins. One of the outstanding Spanish makers they discovered was AyA, acronym for Aguirre y Aranzabal. The 'y' in Spanish is the same as 'and' in English. Since then many excellent Spanish double gunmakers have emerged or were already in production, like Arrizabalaga, Grulla, Arietta, Ugartechea, Garbi, and others. All of these makers are in and around Eibar in the Basque country of northern Spain, and they all concentrate on make side-by-sides in the finest English quality."

—Nick Sisley, in an article for the Ruffed Grouse Society

805. Checking out a New Spanish Double

"The shotgun the Ruffed Grouse Society and the Spanish maker AyA have collaborated on is the Model 4/53 in 20 and 28 gauge. The test gun I've been shooting is the 28-bore and it wears 29-inch barrels . . . There has not been one hiccup in the gun's performance, although the back trigger is a bit squishy. The trigger can no doubt be easily remedied by a gunsmith. This little 29 has ejectors, and it tosses spent empties with real authority. I say little 28 because the gun is so light. I assume this one is built on a true 28-gauge frame because it only weighs 5 pounds, 11.5 ounces."

—www.ruffedgrousesociety.org and www.aya-fineguns.com.

806. Want a Light Double? Check This Out

"The Dea Duetto is a new side-by-side from Stefano Fausti in Italy. The model designation means something like 'twin goddesses' in Italian, no doubt the 'twin' referring to this model always coming as a two-barrel set . . . one set of barrels is in 28 gauge, the other in .410, and both sets fit to a very tiny frame. The single trigger is non-selective. The right barrel will always fire first. It's going to be right at home when you are hunting the thickest of brambles, when you constantly have one one-hand the double to ward off briars, tiny saplings, aspen whips and alder branches with the other hand. With a so-called 'swing' seldom involved, its shoulder the Dea Duetto in lightning-fast action, point and shoot—all of the latter done in less than a heartbeat. The overall weight gets one's attention. With the 28-gauge set of barrels attached, this one sent my digital postal scale to 4 pounds, 15 ounces. With the .410 barrels the weight was 5 pounds, 1.5 ounces. The .410 set is 2.5 ounces heavier, no doubt, due to the slightly increased mass of metal at the monobloc—the part of the barrels next to the receiver. Ejectors. Screw-in chokes. $4999. Web site: www.faustiusa.com"

—Nick Sisley, in an article for *Sporting Clays*

807. "Patternmaster": A Choice Aftermarket Choke Tube

If you're happy with the patterns you're getting from the choke tubes that came with your latest shotgun acquisition, fine. But a lot of hunters keep looking for absolute perfection, and that's what makes the aftermarket choke tube offerings so hot today. There are several out there, but one we're hearing a lot about is Patternmaster, www.patternmaster.com. Philip Bourjaily, on the *Field & Stream* Web site, writes, "The Patternmaster, popular among waterfowlers, actually contains little studs near the end of the choke that grab the wad and slow it, producing extremely tight patters with little to no constriction."

808. "Hey, Dude, You Missed!"

In a column on the *Field & Stream* Web site, www.fieldandstream.com, expert shooter Philip Bourjaily says many shooters just can't admit it when they've made a bad miss: "The first thing he'll do is to look down at the ground." Pro shooting instructor Gil Ash told Bourjaily, "Look up at the spot where you missed the bird, replay what happened, and figure out why. Make a change and move on."

809. Try Straightening out Your Left Arm

In his classic *New England Grouse Shooting*, William Harden Foster makes a strong recommendation for right-handed shooters to hold the left hand far out on the forearm. If you're not used to this position, try it for repeated practice sessions and then on clay targets, and you might find your shooting greatly improved. Foster felt that the extended hand position made the gun steadier.

CHAPTER 19

Gun Dog Handling and Training

810. Love Me, Love My Dog!

No matter how much self-restraint it takes, you just cannot criticize another man's dog and dog-handling. Especially if he's a good friend, a friend you don't want to lose. Whatever terrible antics your friend's dog is up to during your hunt, you've got to find a careful, considerate way to get your friend on the right track.

811. Make a No-spill Drinking Dish

You can make a cheap drinking dish for your dog that won't leave water all over the back of your truck out of a medium-sized Tupperware container. Cut a hole out of the container's lid large enough to let your dog drink comfortably, but leave a wide strip of the lid in place all the way around the dish to serve as a baffle to prevent spilling.

812. Dog Not Trained? Don't Bring Him!

Whenever you take a gun dog that is not trained on a hunt, or to a hunting camp, you are being an inconsiderate jerk to your friends. You can think about it. But don't do it!

813. Working Your Retriever near Salt Water

Years ago, outdoor writer Tom Hennessey of the *Bangor Daily News* nearly lost his beloved lab Coke after the dog drank too much salt water while hunting coastal marshes. Today, when hunting the coast Tom carries a big plastic jug of water and a plastic bowl for the dog to drink from.

814. Your Retriever's Safety: Job One!

"A dog is not aware of death, nor does it realize that its strength and stamina are limited. Therefore, a hunter much know the capabilities of his dog, making judgments and decisions that will ensure the animal's safety. Remember, running a dog ragged to make yourself look good doesn't impress anyone. A dog will hunt its heart out for you. It's up to you to keep his or her best interests at heart."

—Tom Hennessey, *Feathers 'n Fins,* The Amwell Press, 1989

815. Five "Vest Pocket" Bird Hunting Dogs

In an article on the *Field & Stream* Web site, www.fieldandstream.com, writer Tom Davis, in an article called "5 Good Small-Breed Hunting Dogs," discusses the dogs the late *F&S* Gun Dog writer Bill Tarrant called "vest-pocket dogs." Davis says Tarrant admired their "lively spirit and work ethic." The dogs are: English Cocker Spaniel, Boykin Spaniel, American Water Spaniel, French Brittany, and Jack Russell Terrier. Read all about them and their individual distinctions in Davis's article.

816. Your Pointing Dog's Proper Range

"What I have in mind is simply for a dog to go where the birds are, not missing any he ought to have found on the way. The kind of dog I like to see will adjust himself to the territory and the game. In cover he will go a bit more carefully and work more closely. In the open we like to see him reach out to the cover that looks good. That's all there is to it."

—Horace Lytle, *Bird Dog Days,* D. Appleton and Co., 1926

817. Retriever Training That Works

Water-based training sessions are the best for sporting dogs in warm weather. Keep the sessions short to avoid stressing the dog, and, if possible, limit outings to early or late in the day.

818. Teaching a Pup to Back

"Keep the check cord on the youngster. When the older dog makes a find, try to wait until the pup sees him. There's a chance he'll back naturally, at least for a short period. This is the time to speak cautious and soothing 'whoas,' and try to get your hands on the check cord as quickly as possible. Hold the dog steady when the bird is flushed."

—Nick Sisley, *Grouse Magic,* self-published, 1981

819. When Your Dog's Caught in a Fence

When your dog's paw becomes entangled in a fence or wire left lying in the field, remember this as you move to help him or her: The dog will likely try to bite you when you grab the hung-up limb.

820. Richard Wolters: The Gun Dog Man

The late Richard Wolters was a good friend whose works I published in magazines from time to time, and whose company I always enjoyed—especially when he was showing off his wonderful labs. The Wolters dog-training phenomenon started with the publication of *Gun Dog* by E. P. Dutton in 1961. The book is so revolutionary, so good, with its detailed show-and-tell style of presenting the training material, that it has been reprinted many times. Dick Wolters followed up *Gun Dog* with *Water Dog* and several others, including the definitive book on labs, *The Labrador Retriever,* which, like *Gun Dog,* has been published in many editions. Look for his books, and videos, on www.amazon.com and many other sites.

821. Field Care for Foot Wear and Tear

If your bird dog somehow tears up his pads on a hunt, a little cellophane and a few wraps of duct tape will provide rapid and rugged protection from further injury.

822. How the Gun Dog Phenom Started

With so many printings, Richard Wolters' *Gun Dog* is obviously a book that has delivered the goods for its readers. In my opinion, one of the reasons why is the blending of the instruction text with good photographs and presenting the material in a sort of show-and-tell style. Until *Gun Dog*, most books only "told," they never "showed." Also, contributing to the book's success, Dick Wolters delivers on the promise he makes in the first pages of the book: "Don't think for a moment that this book is just a rehash of the same material that good men have written on this subject in the last *fifty years* . . . [Wolter's italics] *Gun Dog* is a revolutionary rapid training method. It's new. It's never been presented before, and we will explain new scientific findings about the learning habits of dogs that will startle the old-time trainers."

823. Using the "Wing-on-a-String" Trick

Trainer John Cameron of Cameron's Quail Preserve and Bird Dog Training School in Panola, Alabama, has a cautionary note about the very popular "wing-on-a-string" training trick: "One disadvantage to hunting a wing on a string is that the puppy quickly learns to look for the wing and starts pointing when he sees the wing rather than when he smells the wing. If you use the wing-on-a-string for more than a week, you're teaching your dog to rely on his eyesight rather than his nose . . ."

—John E. Phillips, "John's Journal," Night Hawk Publications

824. Starting the Year-old Pointing Dog

Trainer John Cameron (see previous tip) does not like the idea recommended by some trainers that you wait until a dog is one year, or a year and a half, before you start training. He told outdoor writer John Phillips, "If you wait until the dog's one to one and a half years old, the learning process takes longer. Often one-and-a-half-year-old dogs don't know the difference between a butterfly and a quail. When you start training a pup at six to seven weeks, he learns from an early age what a quail is, what a quail smells like, why quail are more fun to hunt that any other game and that quail are what he's been bred to hunt." Contact John Cameron at Cameron's Quail Preserve.

825. When a Puppy Just Doesn't Have the Stuff

Sometimes a puppy comes along that's just not going to make it: no game sense, poor nose, no "smarts," not much zest for the hunt, or, on the other hand, too much uncontrollable zest. If a professional trainer can't handle or train the dog, you may have to place it elsewhere with someone who wants a "pet" while you start over.

826. Starting a Pointing Dog Pup

Heaven for a bird dog has be growing up surrounded by quail. That's exactly what happens to the dogs of top trainer John Cameron of Cameron's Hunting Preserve and Bird Dog Training School in Panola, Alabama. "I start puppy training when a dog's six to seven weeks of age. As soon as the puppy's weaned and can eat dog food," Cameron told outdoor writer John Phillips, who reported the interview on his "John's Journal" on the Night Hawk Publications Web site, www.nighthawkpublications.com.

827. The Labrador Retriever on Upland Game

In case you ever needed some convincing on just how good Labrador retrievers can be on upland game, consider this testimony from writer John Barsness in his magnificent book, *Western Skies*, from Lyons and Burford, 1994: "My canine partner for the first decade of my bird-chasing career was a lean and energetic black Labrador named Gillis, who was raised on sharptailed grouse, pheasants, and Huns on the plains of eastern Montana, with occasional side forays involving jump-shooting mallards, hot sage grouse walks, and chukars in Wyoming."

828. That First Point on Real Game: Don't Miss!

Growing up as I did in Georgia, I remember always hearing a lot of talk about striving to make sure you kill the bird during your puppy's first point on real birds in the field. I always believed it, and I still do. Bring that bird down in a shower of feathers, try to get your dog to retrieve it, and whether he or she does or not your pup will at least taste the bird and learn the rewards of the point and the shot. Very important, I think.

829. Be Patient on Downed Birds

When your dog doesn't pick up a downed bird immediately, don't despair. Be patient, remembering that the air-washed down bird may not be giving off much scent. Avoid walking about the area where the bird is and give your dog a decent chance.

830. "Gatorade" for Gun Dogs?

The canine hydration supplements on the market can be helpful in maintaining your bird dog's vitality in the field. However, try out different products during train sessions. You'll find your dog will react to each supplement differently. Figure out which supports him best before you hunt.

831. Emergency Help Numbers for Your Dog

Before you make a bird-hunting trip to a new area or distant state, use the Internet to find contact numbers for vets where you're headed. Then, if your pooch has a medical emergency, you won't be in a panic to contact help.

832. A "Must" for Your Dog's ID Tags

Add your cell phone number to your bird dog's ID tag. That way, even if your dog gets lost on a hunt in strange territory, you'll get him back more quickly if his finder can call you directly.

833. Keep the Windows Up

As much as he or she seems to love it, refrain from letting your bird dog stick its head out the window as you drive to a bird hunt. The speed-induced wind will quickly dry out his nasal passages and impair his ability to smell game.

834. Use Pigeons for Training

Live bird work is the best of dog training, but pheasants can get pricey. Pigeons work almost as well, and you can often buy them for a buck or two apiece.

835. When Your Dog Is Lost . . .

If your bird dog turns up missing, leave a dog bed and one of your jackets or other garment at the last spot your saw the dog working—and another at or near your parking spot. If the dog returns while you're off looking for him, chances are he'll stay with the familiar-smelling gear.

836. Running Cool on Hot Days

When it's hot out, keep canine training session short and sweet. Maybe a brief session in the morning and another late that evening. And make sure the dog gets plenty of water.

837. Hunting Dog for Seniors

Let's face it: When you become a senior citizen you just may not be up to the big-hunting tramps you used to make with wide-going pointing dogs. It might be time to consider a lab for your upland hunting, or a flushing dog like a Springer spaniel. Remember this about Springers: Many of them are not bred from pure hunting lines. Go to a quality breeder to get a Springer for great hunting and enjoy slower, more-careful upland bird hunting. And you'll have a great friend in the house to boot.

838. Room to Stretch Out

When a long hard hunt is over, your dog needs room to stretch out. A cramped dog box may lead to his "stiffing up." He or she would be better off on the back seat. And they deserve it.

839. Remember This about Gun Dogs

"Each dog is an individual, as truly as is each person, and I suspect many sportsmen would enjoy their dogs more if they paused occasionally to consider this. A dog isn't a machine to find birds or retrieve ducks or follow a trail."

—Ted Trueblood, "How Not to Train Hunting Dogs," *Field & Stream,* December, 1961

CHAPTER 20

Squirrel Hunting

840. Staying Put on Your Stand

When you've selected a good spot to sit and wait for squirrels to show themselves, don't be in a hurry to walk over and pick up the first two or three you down—with shotgun or rifle. Mark them carefully and keep sitting tight and watch for another target to show.

841. The "Trunk-hugger" Squirrel

When a squirrel hugs the trunk, high in the tree and not moving, it usually is facing up the tree. By hugging the trunk yourself, you can outlast the squirrel into thinking the coast is clear. It will make a move, giving you a shot.

842. A Squirrel Hunt Can Make Your Day Great

Many hunters get so caught up in the pursuit of deer and "glamour" upland birds like grouse, quail, and pheasant that they forget the simple pleasures of a great day out squirrel hunting. Take a golden autumn day, a small pack with sandwiches and a thermos, a scope-sighted .22 rifle, and local knowledge of an area and you can walk for miles—that is, walk when you wish to. A lot of your day will be spent sitting quietly at the basses of trees, watching the canopy overhead. One caveat: You can't do this hunt when and where firearm deer hunting is in progress.

843. The Trophy Squirrel

The big, dark fox squirrel is not considered as good on the table as the smaller and more-plentiful gray, but many hunters find ways to enjoy them on the table. They also lend themselves to becoming a beautiful trophy mount. Famed Georgia outdoor writer, the late Charlie Elliott, keep a mounted fox squirrel that drew more comments from visitors than any of the trophy big game heads he had on his walls.

844. Important Deep-winter Hunting Tactic

The most important tactic to remember about deep-winter squirrel hunting (other than the places to find the squirrels!) is to hunt with your eyes scanning the trees far in the distance. You'll see your quarry at much longer distance in the winter. Once you've spotting a squirrel, make your quiet stalk and try to get into position for a shot with your .22.

845. Can You Keep Still?

Just as in deer hunting or in a duck blind, staying still—really still—pays off in squirrel hunting from a stand. Some hunters are just too fidgety.

846. Playing "Hide-and-Seek" with Squirrels

When a squirrel is on the opposite side of a tree, and keeps going around and around as you circle, trying to get a shot, try throwing something noisy over to the squirrel's side. A heavy fallen stick or something. You can often move him to your side this way.

847. Squirrel for Supper

Don't sell the squirrel short as table fare. I love them fried, in flour and hot fat. Tastes as good as sweet nuts to me. The hell with the Cholesterol Police!

848. Squirrel Recipe

Among the many ways of cooking squirrel meat add this to your recipes: Cook the squirrel with the same recipe you use for Buffalo Wings.

849. Those Wonderful Squirrel Dogs

They'll never have the glamour and appeal of labs and pointers and setters, but good squirrel dogs are worth their weight in gold. What kind are they? All kinds! Feists, curs, whatever. A good nose and desire to hunt are the credentials, and the best way to take advantage of them is to have your squirrel dog puppy hunt with an accomplished squirrel dog. The really good squirrel dogs hunt close to the gun and use their nose, eyes, and ears to find squirrels. Easing slowly through the squirrel woods with one of these dogs is a wonderful way to go hunting. In many areas, you'll have a bonus: You'll flush coveys of quail, and send rabbits bouncing away.

850. Crock Pot Squirrel

Frying your squirrel meat isn't the only way to enjoy it. Try cooking your squirrel meat in a crock pot with sauerkraut. About six hours should be right to have the meat tender and falling off the bone.

851. Cutting-edge Squirrel Loads

In a comprehensive article called "Cutting-Edge Squirrel Loads" on the *Game & Fish* magazine Web site, www.gameandfishmag.com, writer Mike Bleech gives today's squirrel hunters the latest details on shotgun and rifle loads that do the best job in bringing home a limit of bushytails. Bleech examines the important differences in magnum versus standard shot loads, with emphasis on the all-important velocity considerations. He brings the .22 hunter right up to date with test-firing comparing the venerable .22 Long Rifle against the scorching hot newcomer the .17 Hornady Magnum Rimfire and the newer, but slower, Hornady .17M2. The .17M2 gets Bleech's nod as the best way to go because, as he says, "The light crack of the .17M2 is barely noticed by the squirrels."

852. Deep-winter Squirrel Hunting

Even when Old Man Winter has a solid, white grip on the woodlands, good squirrel hunting with a scoped .22 rifle can be found. Local knowledge of harvest crop fields like corn, and groves of oaks, hickories, walnuts, pecans, and other foods are essential. Look for the woodland areas with squirrel nests adjacent to areas with food.

853. Listen Up!

Are the trees too thick to see the squirrels? Perhaps you can hear them "cutting," opening nuts and letting shells drop to the forest floor. You won't be the first to find and bag a squirrel which has tipped off his position in such a way.

854. Call Squirrels with Fifty Cents

A cheap and easy way to call to a squirrel in order to get it to give away its location is to strike two quarters together, edge to edge. Done right, this will sound enough like a squirrel barking to get the real thing to bark back.

855. Mast Crop Low, yet Hunting Great

When the crop of acorns on the white and red oaks is low, look for squirrels to be concentrated in areas where some trees have bucked the trend. Whatever good spots for acorns are available, the squirrels will find them—particularly the white oak acorns. White-tailed deer do the same.

856. The Pecan Tree Bonanza

The shady, fruit-bearing groves of pecan trees planted throughout the southeast and on into Texas are squirrel magnets. Forested edges of the groves will hold good populations of squirrels. With the landowners' permissions, you'll be set for good hunting.

857. Shoot Squirrels with Erasers

When hunting squirrels with a recurve or longbow you can keep your arrows from sticking into tree limbs too high for you to retrieve them by using a rubber pencil eraser in place of a metal field point. You can buy these erasers at any art supply shop. Look for the large, arrowhead-shaped kind that slips over the top of a pencil's normal eraser.

858. The Nests Are Off-limits!

Sometimes when squirrel hunting, the thought may cross your mind that firing at one of the lofty nests you're seeing might be a good idea—get the squirrels out and moving. It's a bad idea, and illegal. Your shot into the nest could kill or wound a squirrel you could never retrieve. Don't do it!

859. You Need the Optics for Just Plain Fun

People have been bagging limits of squirrels for a long, long time without using optics, but that doesn't mean you should. By taking along binoculars and using a scoped rifle, the fun you'll have during the time you spend in the squirrel woods will be greatly magnified (pun intended!).

860. Midwinter Fox Squirrels

When there's a crust of snow on the ground and the temperatures have dipped into the 20s, don't expect fox squirrels to be on the prowl in early morning. You'll find the best hunting doesn't get started until around ten o'clock. Although like gray squirrels, fox squirrels like acorns and other nuts, in midwinter they will always head for corn if it's nearby. Fox squirrels prefer belts of trees near croplands instead of dense forests, more so than grays.

861. Wait until Later to Pick up Your Squirrels

"Don't pick up a downed squirrel immediately. Moving from a stand to recover downed game will end the hunting temporarily."

—Bob Gilsvik, *The Guide to Good Cheap Hunting,* Stein & Day, 1978

862. Try More-aggressive Squirrel Tactics

Successful squirrel hunters today have come as many calls and calling techniques as duck hunters. Consider these two examples: On the Hunter Specialties Web site, www.hunterspec.com, pro Alex Rutledge shows how to use the H.S. Squirrel Call to do the "Barking," "Chattering," and the "Young Squirrel Distress Call." All are effective, but "Barking" is one known to set off a chorus of squirrel answering calls and tip off their locations in woods you're hunting for the first time. Outdoor writer John E. Phillips, in his "John's Journal," on his Night Hawk Publications site, www.nighthawkpublications.com, also likes "Barking," along with some other calls he describes in his article, "How to Hunt Squirrels Aggressively."

CHAPTER 21

Rabbit Hunting

863. The Hunter's "Rabbit's Foot" Luck

Rabbits are the Number One game for hunters everywhere—and with good reason. They breed like crazy, which is great since few of them survive the predators they face for even one year. There are still plenty to go around for hunters, who prize delicious rabbit on their tables and like the way rabbits can be hunted with a variety of methods and a minimum of expensive gear.

864. After the Shot

Even when you think you've missed a rabbit, check around in a circular area of about 20 feet. When wounded, a rabbit may run a little distance and then stop and sit tight.

865. Watching for the Rabbit You've Jumped

When your dog is running a rabbit, don't keep your eyes locked on the path the dog is taking. Keep looking in other directions, and you may spot rabbits that are trying to slip past all the action, or others that are just sitting tight waiting for you to go past.

866. Top Tips for Late Season Rabbits

Late season is a great time to hunt rabbits because deer hunters have ceased activities. Hunting can be tough, though. According to writer Ed Harp on the Indiana state site of *Game & Fish* magazine, www.indianagameandfish.com, the most important four considerations in finding late season rabbits are to find the clover, find blackberry and raspberry bushes, find the pine sapling stands where rabbits have chewed the bark in a circle, and find deer hunter food plots. Harp has six more top tips to help you get your limit in the article, "Ten Tips for Taking Winter Rabbits."

867. Use a Stick to Beat the Brush

When hunting rabbits without a dog, use a brush stick, like a wading staff, to beat on the edges of thick cover where they may be hiding.

868. Cold and Windy Mornings

On a windy morning, after a very cold night, look for rabbits to be on the sunny and lee sides of ridges, forests, and brush rows.

869. Hunting the "Slabfoot" Rabbits

He's not called the "Varying Hare" for nothing, possessing two coats of fur to wear as needed. With the fall sun starts riding lower and lower in the sky, the days becoming shorter and shorter, the Snowshoe rabbit starts putting on its white coat whether needed or not by snowfall. Even with nary a flake on the ground, the big hares begin to change color—a dangerous situation for them since they stand out in the forest so starkly. In Alaska, where I spent two teenage winters, Snowshoe rabbit hunting became a big part of my life. I loved hunting them and eating them.

870. Snowshoes in Winter: The Going Gets Tough

The hunting in the hills not far from Fairbanks, where we lived, was easy until the snows came, then became more difficult with each passing day. The Snowshoe is mostly a nocturnal animal. During the day the rabbits hole up under the endless spruces and don't move until after dark. Kicking them out is tough work without a dog. When we were lucky enough to get one bounding away through the snow, they were remarkably fast and hard to hit in their great leaps over the snow. Old "Slabfoot." I loved them.

871. The Snowshoes' Survival Plan

When winter grips the great North woods, the icy winds moaning through bare limbs without a scrap of vegetation, the snow piling on the endless spruce forests, the Snowshoe rabbit makes out just fine. Gone are the succulent plants of spring and summer, but the "Varying Hares" do just fine on a diet of willow, poplar, and other saplings of tender green bark. The Snowshoe has four big front teeth perfect for gnawing a bellyful of bark every night. Days are spent in cozy holes back under the spruces. No matter how cold, they make out just fine.

872. Tactic for Snowshoes: Leave the Feeding Grounds Behind

The area where you find the great crisscrossing webs of Snowshoe tracks may not be the best place to make your hunt. They were there last night feeding; now they're dead certain to be in the thickest cover of the nearest swamps. That's where you want to make your hunt, moving slowly past the beaver dams, humps of brush, fallen trees, and limbs—the places where Snowshoes spend their days, not their nights.

873. Your Best Rabbit "Scouts"

The best rabbit scout you can find will be the farmer who owns the land you hunt on. Next will be the deer hunters who've been working the area. Many of them aren't interested in rabbit hunting, but they will have seen the spots where rabbits thrive.

CHAPTER 22

Varmint and Predator Hunting

874. How to Get Cattle Ranch Hunting Permission

Cattle ranchers are rarely fans of coyotes, so about all you need to do to get access to hunt them is ask. Best of all, weeding out a few 'yotes may lead to an invitation to come back for antelope, deer, or elk next fall.

875. The Western "Varmint" Advantage

Hunting gophers and prairie dogs will quickly turn you from a shooter into a marksman. When you reach a point where you're popping tiny varmints at 400 yards consistently, sniping an antelope or deer at that same range is no sweat.

876. Where to Count on Coyotes and Foxes

It's a sure bet that a spot that's loaded with pheasants is also a prime spot to call coyotes and foxes.

877. Your "Coyote Rifle" Is Ready to Go

You don't need to invest in a special rifle to hunt coyotes. There's no bigger confidence builder than whacking a few varmints from hundreds of yards out with the same rifle you use for elk and deer.

878. Doubling Your Varmint Rifle's Effectiveness

Take a page from the tactical shooters' book when you set up your varmint rifle. A bunch of scope mount makers now offer tactical rings that allow a shooter to mount a red-dot-type sight over the standard rifle scope. Set your scope up to zapping coyotes in the next zip code; dial in the red dot for varmints that come up close and personal.

879. The Endless Hunting on Coyote Grounds

It's nearly impossible to "shoot out" prime coyote grounds. While coyotes establish territories, busting one puts his stomping ground up for grabs. Activity from other varmints will likely increase until a new top dog is established.

880. Hunt Coyotes Where You Hunt Geese

Coyotes wise up to the fact that there are easy meals on the perimeters of large decoy spreads. At times, hunters barely have time to retrieve wounded birds that drop out of shotgun range. After the goose hunters have departed for the day, set up with a pair of binoculars and your varmint rifle for a sure shot at a hungry 'yote.

881. When Your Rifle Needs a Bipod

Buy a good-quality bipod—preferably on that attaches to rifle—before you head out to hunt varmints or predators. You'll rarely have the luxury of a conveniently placed log or boulder to steady your rifle. A stock-mounted bipod guarantees a solid rest where and when you need it.

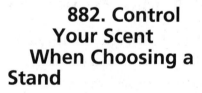

882. Control Your Scent When Choosing a Stand

Foxes and coyotes have extremely sensitive noses. Put as much care into scouting out the best places to locate a predator blind as you would when selecting a stand site for whitetails, paying special attention to prevailing winds. Also make sure to use cover scents to hide your activities. Wear gloves and make sure your hunting clothes are stored where they won't pick up human scent—you'll spread much less sign of your presence when scouting for and hunting from your stand or blind.

883. Don't Call as Soon as You Sit Down

It's vital to always approach your predator stand or blind quietly, but it's also often impossible to be as stealthy as you should. You don't want any nearby predators associating the noise you made when approaching your stand with your calling; once you're settled in, don't immediately start squalling like a dead rabbit. First wait for at least a half hour, enough time for the woods and fields around you to settle down and for you to pick up on the natural rhythms of the area.

884. Set Up in Comfort So You Don't Have to Move

Coyotes, foxes, and bobcats are excellent hunters with acute senses. If they detect something unnatural about a setup they will melt away, often before you ever have a chance to spot them. The easiest way for you to give yourself away is to move. Scratching your nose, shifting your seat, even turning your head can be all it takes to spook a wary predator. Make sure you set up your stand or blind so that you'll be as comfortable as possible. Use cushions, stools, backrests, and bipods or shooting sticks to help you remain motionless but alert and ready to fire quickly. You should be able to sit for at least 45 minutes without shifting position.

885. Call to the Close Ones First

The first calls you make after you've settled into your stand and let the woods calm down should be quiet ones. If you've approached your stand properly, there may still be predators quite close, and a subtle squeaking can be all it takes to bring them running.

886. Make Your Calling Paint a Picture

A good caller becomes the animal he or she is imitating. If you're imitating a rabbit, imagine that you are that rabbit, then imagine yourself in various distressing situations. If you've practiced using your calls you'll be able to string together a sequence of sounds that paint the picture you've visualized in the mind of a hungry fox, coyote, or bobcat.

887. Practice Calling in Your Car

One of the best places to practice calling is when you're alone in your car. Simply pop in an instructional CD and play along until you can't tell the difference between your calling and the sounds coming from your car's speakers. You won't bother anyone with the horrible sounds you're making (though you may get some odd looks from other drivers).

888. Save Ammo by Competing

"An interesting way to cut down on the waste of ammunition and to put a premium on accurate shooting is to introduce competition into prairie dog shooting. . . . The shooters flip a coin for first shot and the winner gets to continue firing as long as he maintains a 100-percent string of kills. When he misses, the shooting goes to the next in order on the same basis."

—Bob Gilsvik, *The Guide to Good Cheap Hunting,* Stein & Day, 1978

889. Two Requirements for Proper Calling Practice

Predator calls are musical instruments, and any musician will tell you that the most important skill required to play an instrument is the patience to practice it. To practice properly you will need two things: first is a place to practice. Make sure that you choose a location far from anyone who might be bothered by the noises you're going to make. There are few things more grating to family members than the sound of a squalling rabbit, so avoid making the living room your new sound studio. Second is an example to imitate. There are many CDs, DVDs, and online audio and/or video tutorials available that serve this purpose. Pick a good one and play along with your own calls until you're confident in your skills.

890. Form a Habit during Your Commute

One of the benefits of practicing your calling in your car is that you'll generally be sitting in it every day, especially if you drive to work. To grow truly skilled with any instrument you must make your practice a habit; you'll form this habit faster if you can piggyback it on your regular commuting schedule.

891. Practice Makes Permanent

That old saw "practice makes perfect" is incorrect. Practice doesn't make perfect, practice makes permanent. Make sure you understand the proper ways to hold and blow your calls before beginning a repetitive practice session, or you could develop bad habits that will handicap your calling for a long time.

892. Put Real Fear in Your Prey Calls

"Don't forget to put as much emotion into your predator calling as you possibly can. Imagine a jackrabbit being caught by a fox and fighting for its life. The more emotion you put in your calling, the more confidence you will have that something is going to come and investigate the sound. The more confidence you have, the more patience you will have. The more patience you have, the more dogs you will kill."

—TheDogSlayer, www.nodakoutdoors.com

893. Make Your Loud Calls Short

Don't get carried away. If you're imitating the sounds of a small animal in distress you don't want it to sound as if it has human-sized lungs. A long, drawn-out squall at maximum volume is not a sound a rabbit is capable of producing. Loud wails are often required to reach predators in the distance, but you should keep them short.

894. Learn to Call with Your Hands

Reproducing the sound of an animal's voice is only the first step toward becoming a good caller. A truly skilled predator hunter knows how to make that voice behave like a live animal, not just sound like one. Once you can imitate an animal using only your mouth, lungs, tongue, and call, start practicing how to throw the sound in different directions, as well as how to muffle it naturally, with your hands. If you're imitating a coyote, you should be able to simulate the sound of an animal in motion. If you're imitating a dying rabbit, make it sound as if the animal is twisting and turning in the grip of a hawk or fox, one second squalling into the air, the next with its face pressed against the dirt.

895. Whistle at Woodchucks to Make Them Stand Up

If you're hunting woodchucks and want one to stand up at the mouth of his hole or pop his head higher above a stand of long grass long enough for you to shoot him, blow a blast on a loud, shrill coaches whistle.

896. Don't Give up if You Miss

If you shoot (or miss) a coyote from your stand, don't assume that you've burned the area for the day. Keep calling. Gunfire is a hard sound for an animal to pinpoint. You can often shoot multiple predators from the same spot before they wise up to your presence.

897. Clean Yourself up before Asking Permission to Hunt

Most landowners, especially those in agricultural areas, are happy to have hunters help them control predator populations on their property. All you have to do is ask. But don't do so when dressed in full camouflage regalia. You'll up your chances of securing permission if you don't walk up looking like the Swamp Thing in a ghillie suit, especially if any non-hunters in a household open the door.

898. Hunt over Natural Shooting Lanes

One of the best places to set up when calling coyotes, foxes, and bobcats in dry, open country is on a high point overlooking a brush-lined wash or gully. The open washes serve as shooting lanes while the brush lining them provides the cover predators need to feel secure when investigating your calls.

899. Hunt Coyotes to Shoot More Deer

Coyote hunting is a great way to keep yourself sharp during the off season. You'll stay in shape hiking through the brush. You'll maintain that mental connection to the rhythms of the land you hunt. You'll also stay in practice with your rifle. Consider chasing predators with the rifle you use hunt bigger game. You'll be much more accurate once it's time to take it out for deer or elk.

900. Break up Your Downwind Silhouette

Predators generally approach the sounds of a distressed prey animal from downwind. Set up against a backdrop of thick brush and make sure you have a clear view of the route you think they'll take to investigate your calls. Make sure you're positioned so that the cover you've chosen breaks up your outline when viewed from this approach. The spot you choose should also ideally create shade that will hide the motions you make when calling.

901. A Good Emergency Cover Scent

The next time you forget to bring a cover scent with you on a western hunt, try crushing a handful of juniper berries or sage leaves and rubbing them on your hands and boots. The strong natural scent of these plants will mask your own odors and could help prevent a blown stalk or stand setup when an animal you're hunting works downwind.

902. Unzip Tails to Preserve a Pelt

Coyote pelts are luxurious furs you can use for many purposes, but only if you preserve them properly. If you plan to skin them in the field, bring along a choke chain, skinning knife, and don't forget a tail zipper. You can use the chain to hang the dog from a tree, skin it with your knife, and unzip the tail to prevent it from rotting and eventually losing its hair.

903. When Crow Calls Work on Coyotes

You can use a crow or magpie call to convince call-shy coyotes to approach your setup. These birds often follow predators through the brush, waiting for a chance to grab scraps of any animals killed or carcasses scavenged. They also act as extra sets of eyes and ears, and coyotes, foxes, and bobcats will watch their behavior to see if danger is present. By imitating the sound of one you can put the animals you're hunting more at ease with your other calls. Make sure you know the difference between the birds' alarm calls and their normal vocalizations.

904. Howling Range vs. Hunting Range

If you're howling for coyotes and get one to respond from far away, chances are the animal is not going to come in to your setup. It may be in a different pack's area, or it may be too lazy to work in your direction. It's a good idea to work closer to where you heard the animal respond before calling again. Once you cross into an animal's territory you'll be much more likely to get it to investigate, especially if you're hunting in February and March, when the animals are establishing their breeding sites.

905. Don't Let a Fence Ruin Your Hunt

Here's a great tip from a hunter going by the handle of "Plainsman" on the great nodakoutdoors.com Web site: "Be careful when crossing fences," he says. "Remember the tin can and wire you used as a telephone when you were a kid? Wire will carry the noise much further than you think when it squeaks while you shove it half way to the ground to get over."

906. Rig Your Truck for Silent Running

Unlike many ungulates, coyotes, foxes, and bobcats often spook at the sound of an ATV, truck, or other hunting vehicle. Make sure yours is equipped with the quietest muffler you can find. Secure any tools or other items that might bounce or rattle in beds and cargo boxes. Oil your door's hinges, and never slam it shut. And always walk far from where you park it before setting up to call.

907. Jump out of a Moving Truck

Here's another tip from "Plainsman," this one for reaching your setup from a vehicle without spooking any animals in a pressured area: "If you have a hunting buddy, play drop and roll. Slow down enough to let him out, and then keep on going. Stop a mile away so he can signal you to return. Using this method 300 yards off the road will get you coyotes in some areas. I guess it goes without saying take turns."

—www.nodakoutdoors.com

908. Observe Coyotes Year Round

Coyote packs often have large territories. Just because you hear a bunch howling in a certain area one night doesn't mean you'll find the animals there the next day. To pattern them properly you need to be constantly looking for tracks, listening for calls, and understanding how their behaviors change depending on the season in which you're hunting them.

909. The Best Spring Calls for Coyotes

Spring coyotes are focused on giving birth to their litters and defending their breeding territories from competitors. If you can imitate the calls of a lone, transient dog, they will see this as a threat to their pups. Augment your calling with the sound of a pup squealing and they will run right to your setup.

910. The Best Summer Calls for Coyotes

Summer is the best time of the year to imitate the sounds of distressed rabbits, mice, birds, fawns, and other prey species to attract coyotes. Breeding coyotes will be hunting overtime to feed their litters and will be anxious to take advantage of any opportunities to capture easy meals.

911. The Best Fall Calls for Coyotes

These tips come from commercial coyote call manufacturer Knight & Hale, who say on their Web site (knightandhale.com) that ". . . the predator call type you use during the fall depends a lot on the amount of predator hunting pressure the area is receiving. Early in the fall when many hunters are focusing on other species, the prey-in-distress calls continue to work very well. Plus, there are plenty of young, stupid pups roaming around learning the ropes who are willing to run right into a prey-in-distress sound. Sometime late October or so, a coyote howler may be your better predator call, especially if there's been some hunting pressure."

912. The Best Winter Calls for Coyotes

Howling and barking are traditionally the best calls to use on winter coyotes, but you can also use prey-in-distress calls this time of the year. The best time to do so is right after a bad winter storm leaves the area. Coyotes will have been hunkered down waiting out the rough weather and will be actively searching for food as soon as it clears up.

913. Don't Shoot Too Early

"Wait for the coyote to get close enough. If you can see him at 400 yards, but think you can call him to 200 or even 100, go for it. I've had partners get too excited and blow shots at animals that are still running in towards the call. That means an educated coyote and one less fur on the stretcher."

—price403, www.nodakoutdoors.com

914. Why You Need a Hunting Buddy

"Probably tougher to find and just as important to put fur in the truck is to find a good hunting partner. One that has good ethics, ambition, loves the sport at least as much as you do. It's much more effective working the wind with a partner and being able to cover more area. It's also more enjoyable to not hunt alone all the time along with scouting and gathering permission. If he can shoot well and pitch in for gas/driving /food etc., you're well on the way to a more successful and enjoyable season."

—FurGittr, www.nodakoutdoors.com

915. Hunt Downwind of the Barn

One of the best places to look for a good coyote-calling setup is downwind of a farmer's calving barn. Coyotes view these as food sources and will stay downwind of them, often a mile or more, in order to keep track of when new calves are born.

916. Don't Call in the Herd

It's a good idea to avoid calling for coyotes from too close to livestock. Horses, mules, and even cattle can grow aggressive when they hear what they think is a threat to their herd, and while this is generally not dangerous to the hunter, a bunch of horses running into your setup isn't going to do much for your chances at a song dog.

917. The Most Accurate Over-the-Counter Rifle You Can Buy

This review of the Savage Model 12 Long Range Precision Varminter Dual Port comes from renowned rifles columnist and gun blogger David E. Petzal, by way of the *Field & Stream* Web site. "In designing this rifle," Petzal says, "Savage went to cutting-edge custom gun builders for their input. From the dual-port loading and ejection, to its super-heavy barrel and ultralight trigger, to its three-screw bedding system, it is total state of the art—a custom gun at one-fifth the price of a custom gun. It is also probably the most accurate rifle you can buy over the counter. To take full advantage, you had better be a very good shot."

—www.fieldandstream.com

918. The Best Places to Shoot Varmints in the U.S.A.

Outdoor Life magazine recently listed their picks for the top five varmint-shooting sites in the United States. They are, in order: 1. Phillips County, Montana (prairie dogs); 2. Thunder Basin National Grassland, Wyoming (prairie dogs); 3. Central Oregon (ground squirrels); 4. Carrizo Plain National Monument, California (rock squirrels); 5. Magic Valley, Idaho (Paiute ground squirrels). Visit outdoorlife.com for full descriptions of each location.

919. Keep Your Ammo in a Bib

"A good day in the prairie-dog field is measured by the amount of brass you have to shovel out of the truck at sundown. To keep ammo handy, I use an old-style carpenter's bib. Fill it with cartridges instead of nails. Ammo is always at your fingertips for loading and you never have to take your face off the stock."

—Jim Carmichael, Dial-a-Dog, www.outdoorlife.com

920. A Varmint-sized Varmint Dog

Dachshunds bred for the field—"standard-size" hounds as well as the diminutive "miniatures," which weigh less than 11 pounds—have no fear, owners say. Their German name means "badger hound," and in Europe dachshunds were bred to go to ground to root out and kill badgers (no easy task). Dachshunds will also dive unhesitant into the dirt to take on foxes, raccoons, rats, muskrats, and woodchucks.

—Tom Meade, "Varmints Beware," www.outdoorlife.com

921. Jim Carmichael's Standard Varmint Handloads

There are so many excellent propellants and bullets available today that it would be impossible to claim that any particular combination is more accurate than any other. However, these "standard" bullet/cartridge combinations have produced outstanding accuracy and downrange varmint performance in a variety of rifles:

- .22 Hornet PROPELLANT: Hodgdon Lil' Gun CHARGE*: 13 gr. BULLET WT.: 45 gr.

- .222 Rem. PROPELLANT: Alliant ReLoader 7 CHARGE*: 21 gr. BULLET WT.: 50 gr.

- .223 Rem. PROPELLANT: Vihta Vuori N133 CHARGE*: 25 gr. BULLET WT.: 52 gr.

- .22-250 Rem. PROPELLANT: Hodgdon Varget CHARGE*: 37 gr. BULLET WT.: 52 gr.

- .220 Swift PROPELLANT: IMR 4064 CHARGE*: 38 gr. BULLET WT.: 52 gr.

- .243 Win. PROPELLANT: IMR 4350 CHARGE*: 44 gr. BULLET WT.: 75 gr.

- 6mm Rem. PROPELLANT: IMR 4350 CHARGE*: 45 gr. BULLET WT.: 85 gr.

*None of these loads are max.

—Jim Carmichael, "My Favorite Loads," www.outdoorlife.com

CHAPTER 23

Beyond the Basics: Advanced Tips on Hunting and Getting Ready to Hunt

922. Big Game Hunt Planning: Think Months, Not Weeks

For planning a big game hunt to remember in the high country of the West, or in Canada or Alaska, your planning and thinking must begin months ahead, even a year ahead. Seasons, licenses, and even lotteries for permits are complicated and take long-range attention.

923. "Still-hunting"—The Most Confusing Words

The most confusing expression in all hunting is "still-hunting." It actually doesn't mean sitting still at all. Instead, the expression has come to describe sneaking slowly through the woods, pausing every now and then to look and listen more carefully.

924. Hunting a Place to Hunt: A Bad Deal

Once the season opens on upland birds, your hunting time is precious—too precious to spend driving around the countryside looking for a place to hunt. To enjoy good hunting, you absolutely must have your places to hunt well scouted, permissions obtained, maps studied, and your mind made up on the best areas to try.

925. Up with Suspenders!

If you're built like most of us and do not have the body of a professional athlete or Greek god, you probably will find that your hunting trousers are more comfortable when you use suspenders—upland trousers, waterfowl, whatever. Suspenders will make you more comfortable, and you can stuff more stuff in your pockets without weighing yourself down.

926. Shorten up Those Upland Trousers

OK, you've got a great pair of upland hunting boots and good trousers with brier protection built into the fronts of the legs. What you need to do now is have those trousers hemmed about two inches shorter than normal. You'll find much better walking when your trousers aren't touching the mud, leaves, or sticks under your feet.

927. When Guides Give You a Bonus

The money you invest in a hunting trip with a good guide isn't just paying for the trip to his favorite hot spots. If he's any good, he knows stuff, lots of stuff. Watch him and learn his techniques. Ask questions. Consider him your "hunting professor."

928. Snoring Is Serious

Sharing a room with a loud snorer can wreck your trip—no matter how expensive it is and no matter how carefully you've checked the outfitter. A night or two in camp without sleep is a terrible ordeal. Carry earplugs, they'll help. Demand another room. Trips are too expensive and too short to have to put up with this malady. For a private hunting club of buddies . . . well, you'll just have to sort things out regarding who sleeps where.

929. What the Writers Say

People who write articles and take photographs for outdoor magazines and Web sites are generally dependable and take their reputations seriously. When they write glowingly about a place they've hunted—with a free ride from the owners, of course—you can bet they're telling the truth about what they saw and experienced. When most writers visit a place and it turns out to be a bummer, they don't write pieces knocking it. They just don't write anything at all. Some writers, however, may feel indebted to a place where they've had lavish treatment, and even though the hunting wasn't what they expected, they'll make it sound like heaven. Knowing that the writers got the trip they're writing about for free, before plunking down your hard-earned money for a big trip, you owe it to yourself to check out everything about the place—from other articles, if they're available; references; and Web sites. Check it out. If the place is really good, it will stand up to your inquiries.

930. The Rangefinder Can Make a Difference

Invest in an accurate rangefinder. It may seem silly, but a great many hunters spend hours working up accurate long-range rifle loads and then all summer practicing at the range, only to guesstimate the ranges of game they see in the field. Practice using the rangefinder, learning to use it quickly and accurately.

931. Guns on Planes: How to Get It Done Today

No one can blame you for wanting to take your favorite rifle or shotgun on a long-planned hunting trip, and there's really no reason for you to dread doing it. Here's what you need to know. First, if you live in a state such as New Jersey, which requires a permit even for long guns, be sure you're legal and have it with you. If you were at Newark Airport, let's say, and intended to check a gun and did not have a New Jersey gun permit, you would probably be arrested. Next, you need a good gun case *that locks* or *takes a lock*. *Do not* carry ammo in the gun case! It's better not to carry ammo at all—it's so heavy—but if you do, it must be in the *original manufacturer's box* and must be in your other bags, not in the gun case! Next, at the check-in counter, tell the attendant, "I have a firearm. It's *not loaded,* and I have *no ammunition.*" Those words are important. The attendant may ask to look inside, and then will have you fill out a form and place the form in the case. Then you will be asked to lock the case. Next, you probably will be sent to TSA or another portal. Just go where you're told. Upon reaching there, you may have to open the case again for inspection. That should be it.

932. A Pair of Hunting Trip Aces

Two hunting (and fishing!) trip outfitters most highly recommended are Detail Company and Trek Safaris. Argentina for ducks and doves, big game wherever it can be found—you name it, they've got it. Check them out:

- Jeri Booth, Detail Company Adventures, 3220 Audley, Houston, TX; (800) 292-2213; www.detailcompany.com
- Trek Safaris, PO Box 1305, Ponte Vedra Beach, FL 32004; (800) 654-9915; www .treksafaris.com

933. Russell Annabel: The Alaska Legend

The legendary Russell Annabel wrote about Alaska hunting as few writers ever have, and few writers have enthralled reading audiences as he did during his reign as the "king" of hunting adventure stories for *Sports Afield* and *Field & Stream.* Some readers wondered if he was for real, and not a fictitious person. In fact, he was very much for real. During my years as editor of *Sports Afield,* I had the opportunity to publish several Annabel stories but never had the chance to meet him, for he had moved into virtual exile in the far reaches of Mexico, where he passed away in 1979. My predecessor, Ted Kesting, however, knew him well and had stories about "Rusty," as did Annabel's agent, Lurton Blassingame, and his book editor at Knopf, Angus Cameron. Look for Annabel's stories in books such as *Hunting and Fishing in Alaska* (Knopf, 1948), and many others at sites such as Amazon, www.amazon.com.

934. Computer Search Engines Make Life Easier

For those who do not work with computers, a tip about home computers might be useful. Today, search engines such as Google are absolutely invaluable in getting information quickly on both where you want to go and how to do the things you want to do. The trick is to ask Google (or any of the other search engines you prefer) very specific questions. Let's say you want black bear hunting, but you'd like to hunt in Manitoba. You don't just type in "bear hunting." You type "bear hunting in Manitoba." Or, to start getting creative and even more specific, search: "Manitoba bear hunting guides and outfitters." Give it a try on any subject under the sun. If you don't work around computers all day, you'll find a good search engine to be a great friend you never knew you had. Learn how to talk to your "friend" and you'll be rewarded by getting everything you wanted to know.

935. The Gordon MacQuarrie Storytelling Legacy

When my friend Zack Taylor, who was boats editor at *Sports Afield,* put together the first Gordon MacQuarrie anthology, *Stories of the Old Duck Hunters and Other Drivel,* he did the book as a personal labor of love so that the MacQuarrie stories would not be lost over time. Readers embraced the collection eagerly, particularly those in the Upper Midwest, where MacQuarrie's stories of waterfowl, grouse, and trout were well known. MacQuarrie worked for Milwaukee newspapers and hunted mostly in Wisconsin, Michigan, and Minnesota. He centers most of his tales around what he calls, "The Old Duck Hunters Association, Inc." The tales are timeless classics, and the treasury that Zack started with the first book at Stackpole has now been expanded into several volumes containing all the stories MacQuarrie produced. Willow Creek Press is now the main publisher. It's a real tragedy that MacQuarrie's life and tales were cut short at age fifty-nine due to a heart attack. Today, you can find all the MacQuarrie story collections on sites such as www.amazon.com.

936. Cabela's: A True "Superstore" for Hunters

If Cabela's doesn't have what you're after, it may not have been invented yet. This is a true "superstore" for all outdoorsmen, especially those who hunt and fish. Visit them at www.cabelas.com to find the gear you need and help yourself to an amazing inventory of helpful articles and information from pros who've been doing the things you want to do. If you can, visit one of their premier stores for an experience you and your family will enjoy.

937. The Bass Pro Shops Aren't Just for Fishing

Don't let the name Bass Pro put you off in your search for good hunting gear. The Bass Pro Shops Web site, www.basspro.com, and their premier stores make hunters right at home, and you ought to order their catalogs and check them out (there are lots of articles and information, too).

938. Herter's Knows Hunters

The name Herter's has been around a long time and is an esteemed one with hunters. Check them for all kinds of hunting gear at www.herters.com.

939. Hunter's Specialties: Like the Name Says

They're run by hunters, they understand hunters, and they've got what hunters need and want. Just go to www.hunterspec.com.

940. How to Double-check Guides and Outfitters

While you should always check references from a guide you might book, also check with state and provincial wildlife departments for complaints. It's not likely the guide will refer you to an unhappy client. Getting the real scoop will take some digging.

941. Your Prospective Guide's Repeat Customers

A key question to ask a prospective guide: How much of his clientele is repeat business? If it's less than 50 percent, something smells funny. (During the current economic recession, many guides' repeat business has suffered due to client cancellations. Consider that fact when checking out the repeat business.)

942. Is Your Guide Handing You to "Someone Else"?

The outfitter you're thinking about booking may have a great reputation, but be sure to ask how involved he'll personally be in your hunt. He may have built his rep on great sheep hunts, but his elk hunts are subcontracted to someone else. If that's the case, you want to know the facts—and know who the "someone else" is going to be.

943. What Have You Done for Us Lately?

His brochure might be nice and slick, but ask a prospective guide to see images of trophies he's guided hunters to in the last two years. If he built his business around a single good year during the Carter administration, his response can be telling. You want a guide who produces for his clients every year.

944. Say "Thank You" to Farmers, Ranchers, and Landowners

Give gift memberships to a conservation group like Pheasants Forever, Delta Waterfowl, Ruffed Grouse Society, Ducks Unlimited, Quail Unlimited, Rocky Mountain Elk Foundation, and others to the owners of the properties you hunt. Such a membership acknowledges their stewardship of the land, and the accompanying magazine subscriptions serves as a frequent and repeated "thank you" throughout the year.

945. Don't Start a Kid Too Soon

"When you introduce a youth to hunting, let the youth decide when he or she is ready. Don't force them to hunt or you'll turn them off. Teach your kids to shoot an air rifle and a .22 rifle first. Don't let them shoot a big-bore deer rifle until they're ready."

— Jackie Bushman,
Jackie Bushman's Big Buck Strategies, 2002

946. Search for Hunting Land from a Canoe

"The outdoorsman who is 'up a creek' is probably having the time of his life, at least if he's in a canoe. Small creeks can lead to hidden hunting spots even within the shadow of city and town. You may discover packets of wildlife rarely reached by others."

—Bob Gilsvik, *The Guide to Good Cheap Hunting,* Stein & Day, 1978

947. *The Hunting Report*: Here's the Real Stuff!

The Hunting Report newsletter, like its associated *The Fishing Report,* is a monthly newsletter and Web site specializing in reports on outfitters, guides, and lodges written by people who have been to them. These include outdoor writers sometimes, but most come from everyday folks—from surgeons to hardhat workers—people who spend more than $500 per year on hunting trips. The Web site is a treasury of archives and reports spanning the globe over many years. A one-year subscription costs $60. An extra $3 per month will give you access to the archives and special bulletins. Check it all out at www.huntingreport.com.

948. *Hunting from Home*: A Book to Remember

Christopher Camuto's book *Hunting from Home: A Year Afield in the Blue Ridge Mountains,* in our opinion, is destined to become a classic in hunting and fishing literature. The prose sweeps the reader into the mountains with Camuto throughout the seasons—hunting deer and grouse, fishing for trout, observing nature in a superb setting. I guarantee you that when you read this book, you'll be back for a second helping of Camuto's prose—even a third!

949. Vacuum Sealers: How Can You Live without One?

You have to love modern inventions like this one. If you're a serious hunter and angler who brings home lots of game and fish, you'll find the vacuum sealer devices on the market today to be a godsend for keeping your game fresh. They're not only easy to use and keep game fresh for what seems forever, the sealed packages end up saving tons of space. Check them out at www.basspro.com or www.cabelas.com, or many other Internet sites.

950. Great Way to "Survey" Your Hunting Area

Check out your presently used or new hunting spots via Google Earth on the Internet at earth.google.com. The basic setup version is free, and once in it you'll be viewing your hunting area as if you're hovering over it in a helicopter. At a glance, you'll get a feel for where things like choke points in cover, fields, buildings, and roads can be found. A topo map of the same area will provide an accurate preview of topography. The combined sources give you a surprisingly good working knowledge once you're on the ground.

951. You Need Extra Felt Liners

Invest in an extra pair or two of felt liners for your pack boots. They are relatively inexpensive, and they are a small price to pay for dry feet every day of a hunting trip.

952. Glassing the Big Sky Country

The ideal setup for glassing the wide-open spaces of the West is a pair of binoculars and a spotting scope. Use an 8X or 10X to scan broad areas of terrain, then use the spotting scope—minimum of 20X—to evaluate bucks you've located with the binocs. In addition to producing more game, optics are just plain fun.

953. Going by the Book

Keeping a journal of your hunts may seem a bit old school, but eventually you'll realize how much valuable information they'll yield in the future. (You'll be amazed by how much detail you forgot!) Include GPS coordinates to feed your need for twenty-first-century data.

CHAPTER 24

The Hunting Spirit: Lore Worth Remembering

954. Walt Whitman on Hunting

Alone far in the wilds and mountains, I hunt,
Wandering amazed at my own lightness and glee,
In the late afternoon choosing a safe spot to pass the night,
Kindling a fire and broiling the fresh-kill'd game,
Falling asleep on the gather'd leaves with my dog and gun by my side.

—Walt Whitman, *Song of Myself*

955. Hunting with TR

"I rode into a great bend, with a grove of trees on its right and containing excellent feed. Manitou was loosed, with the lariat round his neck, to feed where he wished until I went to bed, when he was to be taken to a place where the grass was thick and succulent, and tethered out for the night. There was any amount of wood with which a fire was started for cheerfulness, and some of the coals were soon raked off apart to cook over. The horse blanket was spread on the ground, with the oil-skin over it as a bed, underneath a spreading cotton-wood tree, while the regular blanket served as covering. The metal cup was soon filled with water and simmering over the coals to make tea, while an antelope steak was roasting on a forked stick. It is wonderful how cozy a camp, in clear weather, becomes if there is a good fire and enough to eat, and how sound the sleep is afterwards in the cool air, with the brilliant stars glimmering through the branches overhead."

—Theodore Roosevelt, *The Wilderness Hunter*, 1893

956. A Dream of Wings

Some kids grow up worshiping idols whose faces appeared on baseball cards or scoring touch-downs in the sports pages. My heroes wore waders and blew duck calls, and wrote articles about their experiences. They had names like Nash Buckingham, Gordon MacQuarrie, and Jimmy Robinson. Their experiences fed my dreams of someday being like them, going where the ducks were and pulling them from the sky. And because I live in a nation where dreams can come true, I did exactly that.

957. Lure of the Wilderness

"Wilderness is that odd feeling that comes over us, every once in a while, in some quiet spot: a sensation of sureness, of strength, of an almost-forgotten feeling that we could really cope—we could have made it—anytime, anyplace. We could have walked right along with Boone or Clark. We could have stalked the buffalo and then slept in the robe around the same fire with Bridger or Carson—because we can feel and understand the very same things they did."
—Gene Hill, "What Is Wilderness?" from *Hill Country*, E. P. Dutton, 1978

958. A Patch of Wildness

"Wilderness can be truly the 'back of beyond.' Or it can be where church bells are still faintly heard. Working with an ax in my woodlot is a little, momentary brushing with it—the sound of my blade thunking is just as comforting to me as an early Dakota Territory homesteader's was to him. . . . We must have our little wildernesses, no matter what size they are, no matter where they would in reality sit on a map."
—Gene Hill, "What Is Wilderness?" from *Hill Country*, E. P. Dutton, 1978

959. Hunting Expectations

"I hunt for the keyed-up conversation, for the laying of plans and the devising of strategies, for the way memory and experience spark imagination and expectation as we drive into the low-angled sunshine on an autumn morning, for the coffee we sip from a dented old Thermos, and the for the way the dogs whine and pace on the way to the day's first cover."
—William G. Tapply, *Upland Autumn: Birds, Dogs, and Shotgun Shells*, Skyhorse Publishing, 2009

960. Children of the Hunter

"If the sentimentalist were right, hunting would develop in men a cruelty of character. But I have found that it inculcates patience, demands discipline and iron nerve, and develops a serenity of spirit that makes for long life and long love of life. And it is my fixed conviction that if a parent can give his children a passionate and wholesome devotion to the outdoors, the fact that he cannot leave each of them a fortune does not really matter so much. They will always enjoy life in its nobler aspects without money and without price. They will worship the Creator in his mighty works. And because they know and love the natural world, they will always feel at home in the wide, sweet habitations of the Ancient Mother."

—Archibald Rutledge, "Why I Taught My Boys to be Hunters,"
from *An American Hunter,* Lippincott, 1937

961. The Friends You Make

Sing me the old songs.
Tell me the stories of times gone by.
I want to spend an evening or so with you to hear about your dogs.
I want to see your guns.
I want to read your favorite books.
I want to warm my hands in front of your fire and try your pipe tobacco and taste your-
    whisky.
Do you remember all the names?
Tell me them.
Talk to me about the horses.
Talk to me about the dogs.
And the L. C. Smith, The Parker, the Baker, the Lefever and the
    Ansley H. Fox.
Tell me about the cold and the wind and the sea and the river and the kettle pond.
Fill my mind with pictures of your prairies, your swamps, your sedge fields, your mountains
    and your endless plains.

—Gene Hill, "The Old Songs," from *A Hunter's Fireside Book,*
Winchester Press, 1972, now offered by Skyhorse Publishing

962. On Safari

"Our camp was cuddled in the crook of a low mountain's arm, but behind was plain, a brilliant yellow plain dotted with blue-and-white primrosy sorts of flowers. Wherever you looked there was life. Five thousand wildebeest there. Five thousand zebras yonder. Two hundred impala here . . . If you grew grass in Times Square and cleaned up the air and made it suddenly quiet and filled it with animals instead of people you might approach some likely approximation of what I saw that morning, with the sky blue and the hills green and the plain yellow and blue and white."

—Robert C. Ruark, *Horn of the Hunter,* Doubleday, 1952

963. Hemingway's Shot on Pronghorn

Here's Hemingway describing a shot at pronghorn antelope from a hunt with his friend Taylor Williams in the Sun Valley, Idaho, area. He has jumped a bunch of antelope feeding in a draw, and is off his horse with a trusty .30-06 in hand. He runs to the spot where he sees he will have a clear shot at the antelope passing, about 250 yards away: "I picked the biggest buck when they came streaming over the edge of the hump and swung ahead of him and squeezed gently and the bullet broke his neck. It was a lucky shot. . . . Taylor said, . . . 'I'm going to pace it.' I didn't care, because nobody ever believes shooting stories ever, and the pleasure had been in the run and trying to hold your heart in when you swing and hold your breath, sweet and clean, and swing ahead and squeeze off lightly with the swing."

—Ernest Hemingway, "The Shot," from *True* magazine, April, 1951; reprinted in *By-Line: Ernest Hemingway,* edited by William White, Scribner's, 1967

964. The Never-ending Story

"Thousands of years ago, men crouched at the edge of ponds to fling their stones and arrows at ducks and geese lured by crude facsimiles of themselves. So long as waterfowl and men exist, we will hunt the wings of dawn."

—George Reiger, *The Wings of Dawn,* Stein & Day, 1980

965. The Season of the Big Buck

"A twelve-point buck flushes our of the brush at the head of the deer track woodlot one September afternoon, its bowl-shaped antlers carrying sunlight into the shadows of dry hollow. Blinded by the trophy, you hunt it hard all season. You see it, too far off when you are bow hunting in October, and too late when you are carrying a rifle in November. You see it when it is not there. . . . The big buck that sounded so heavy running with its antlers in full sunlight takes the whole season away with it."

—Christopher Camuto, *Hunting from Home: A Year Afield in the Blue Ridge Mountains,* Norton, 2003

966. With Time Running Out: A Whitetail Hunter's Lament

"Deer may be numerous, but they don't walk in the back door. You take an animal as wary as white-tailed deer for granted, or hunt distracted, as I had hunted, and you will be sitting on a log in the cold on the last day of the season in a state of deeply rueful attention. At that point you are depending on dumb luck, patron saint of hunters having a bad year, to bail you out."

—Christopher Camuto, *Hunting from Home: A Year Afield in the Blue Ridge Mountains,* Norton, 2003

967. When You're Running the Show

"I think on the whole the host gets more fun out of a shooting party. Although the worries are trebled for him, the corresponding delights of strategy and tactics amply make up for them. Just as it is a real tragedy to see a covey go sideways out of a drive, so is it a real delight to see one's plans work out . . . One is being a general, on the humaner scale: pitting one's wits against the animal kingdom; balancing wind, weather, season, habit and experience against one another."

—T. H. White, *England Have My Bones,* Macmillan, 1936

968. The Frightening Misfire

"The most terrifying sound in nature is not the roar of a charging lion, nor the whistle of a descending bomb; rather it is a click when you expect a bang."

—Peter Hathaway Capstick

969. Stay Hidden from Geese

"The first rule of goose hunting is simple: If the geese can see you, you're freezing your butt off for nothing."

—Jim Zumbo

970. Why Hunters Kill

"One does not hunt in order to kill; one kills in order to have hunted."

—José Ortega y Gasset, *Meditations on Hunting*

971. A One-shot Proposition

"Part of the drama of [big game hunting] lies in the fact that it is literally a one-shot proposition. It is not unusual for someone who is serious about big game hunting to spend thousands of dollars, travel thousands of miles, and invest weeks of backbreaking effort toward an end that will hinge on one squeeze of the trigger."

—David E. Petzal, *The Experts' Book of Big-Game Hunting in North America,* Simon & Schuster, 1976

CHAPTER 25

The Safe Hunter:
Recognizing and Avoiding Tragic Possibilities

972. The "No-brainer" Accident Waiting to Happen

A loaded gun placed in a vehicle is going to kill somebody—sooner or later—even if it is in a case. As the gun is shoved into the vehicle, or as it is being pulled out, the barrel probably will be pointing right at somebody, and the motion will set off the blast. Terrible way to die, for no good reason!

973. Tragedy at Dawn's Early Light

A deer hunter was taking his stand when he saw a shadowy shape outlined in the dawn's early light in a nearby tree. He evidently thought, "Roosting turkey." The fact that turkey season was closed didn't matter. He fired away, killing another deer hunter sitting in the tree.

974. Whitetail Disaster

A deer hunter saw white, flickering shapes through the brush. Thinking he was looking at a whitetail, he fired a shot. He killed a woman wearing white gloves who was hanging clothes on a clothesline in her backyard.

975. The Lee Wulff Argument

The late Lee Wulff was a close friend who was never reticent about his views on important subjects. He told me many times that he was dead set against requirements for hunters to wear blaze orange. The reason: He felt the rule increased the margin for error by having some hunters, stupidly, assuming that if they didn't see blaze orange, they were seeing game. "The real question," Wulff used to say, "is this: Do I look anything like a deer? Hell no! If you're really looking at what you're shooting at, really seeing it, you can see I'm not a deer!"

976. An Elk, a Bear, and a Guide

Time after time, no matter where the hunt is taking place, tragedy occurs when the hunter does not completely identify his target. It doesn't only happen in the thick whitetail woods. Here's the gist of one that occurred in the wide-open high country. With his guide, an elk hunter downed a bull. The guide suggested that while he was dressing out the elk, the hunter should work up the nearby hillside and back around through a small valley off to the side. A large black bear had been reported to be using the area. The hunter did just that, and as he eventually got back to where he could see the elk-kill site in the distance, he paused. A bear was working on his elk. The guide wasn't to be seen. You can guess the rest. The "bear" he thought he saw was the guide, dressing the elk, with his coat off. Unfortunately, the shot at the "bear" was on target. The guide died.

977. A Simple Squirrel Hunting Mistake

Whenever you're holding a loaded gun in your hands with the safety off, if for any reason the barrel comes to point at a person or a dog, a tragedy can take place. When a hunter takes his safety off because he thinks he's about to get a shot, then fails to put the safety back on when the shot doesn't develop, look out! (Author's note: That's exactly the reason I never take my safety off until the gun is actually coming to my shoulder to make the shot.) In one noteworthy case, a squirrel hunter and his buddy saw a squirrel scamper up a tree as they walked down a woods lane. One hunter took his safety off to make the shot, while the other stood behind him, but the squirrel disappeared. The lead hunter turned around to tell his friend he couldn't see the squirrel. The gun turned with him, safety off. The inertia of the turning motion thrust the gun forward, setting off the trigger. Another hunting tragedy.

978. The Dick Cheney Accident

How did Vice President Dick Cheney shoot his friend? The facts, as I have read them, point to the classic kind of mistake that can happen in any upland bird hunting, but particularly in quail hunting. Out for quail with a friend, Cheney continued to walk and hunt while his friend was retrieving a couple of birds. Not good! Cheney should have waited for his friend. But on Cheney went, and when he kicked up a bird, it turned and flew back in the direction he had been walking from—the direction where his friend was. Unfortunately, at that very moment Cheney's friend was walking up to rejoin him. Cheney failed to see that the bird was flying toward his friend and fired. Despite the pellets in his face and upper body, Cheney's friend survived.

979. Waterfowl Gun Handling

A duck or goose blind is no place to become so excited that you don't even realize how close to the far side of the blind and other hunters your gun is swinging. Before the action starts, make sure you mentally assign yourself a quadrant, a certain area where you can shoot. Then don't let your gun wander out of it.

980. Clay Targets: The Most Dangerous Moment

The most dangerous moment in clay target shooting occurs when a shooter on the line has a malfunction and wheels around to tell the other shooters about his problem—wheels around with the gun loaded and the safety off! Inertia, the gun moving forward in his hands as he turns, causes a shot and a possible tragedy. Not putting the safety back on is a mistake, of course, but the real accident causer is, as in so many instances, allowing the barrel of the gun to point at people. The correct procedure when a malfunction occurs on the line is to keep the gun pointing downrange while you get the safety on and ask for assistance.

981. Test Borrowed Gear

Always check borrowed hunting equipment thoroughly, especially a firearm, before taking it into the field. Do this even if the person you're borrowing it from is an experienced and respected hunter. Most borrowed gear is old gear, and he or she may not be aware of any problems if it has deteriorated while in storage. Pay close attention to ensuring the integrity of critical gear such as tree stands and safety straps, as well as compasses and other survival equipment.

982. The Unbreakable Rule

The rule that saves lives in shooting and hunting is the one that experienced shooters never, ever break under any circumstances whatsoever. It's simply this: Never aim the barrel of your gun to point at people or dogs. Never mind that it's unloaded, never mind that you're taking it apart to put in its case. The rule holds: That barrel never points where it can do harm.

983. Permanent Stands Can Be Dangerous

Be careful before climbing into a permanent tree stand you've never used before, especially one made of plywood or untreated lumber. Wet weather and exposure to the elements will weaken these stands over time, as will the motion of the trees they are attached to. The surfaces of the wood used can also grow quite slick, making it hard to keep your footing.

984. Wear That Safety Harness

This tip is a no-brainer, but one surprisingly few hunters follow. Always wear your safety harness when hunting from a tree stand. If you're not wearing one and slip while standing up, or fall asleep while sitting down (something all deer hunters will be guilty of if they hunt as often as they should) you run the risk of dying or becoming paralyzed for life.

985. Loaded Guns and Fences

Never carry a loaded rifle or shotgun across a fence. Instead, carefully lay it down on the ground on the other side before climbing over or crawling beneath the barrier, then retrieve it once you're through. Even if the safety is on, the sudden impact of the gun hitting the ground could cause it to fire if you trip and fall awkwardly while attempting to cross.

986. Let Them Know Where You're Going

Always leave a friend or relative with an itinerary showing where you plan to hunt and when you plan to return before heading out into the woods, especially if you're hunting far from where people normally travel. You'll be evacuated much more quickly if the rescue team knows where to look should you become trapped, fall unconscious, or are too injured to hike out under your own power.

987. Stay Safe in Your Own Home

"In the interest of post-hunting safety at home, after being gone for days on a hunting trip, when arriving back home be sure to greet your wife with a big smile and a dozen red roses."
    —Gail Dennis, *Workings* magazine (the news magazine for Jim Walter Resources, Inc.)

CHAPTER 26

Rifle Shooting

988. Know Your Equipment

"Becoming a good field shot is simply a culmination of using good equipment, developing skill, and understanding limitations. Money and good sense will outfit you with the proper equipment, but it takes diligence on your part to feed the monster called practice that most of us ignore."

—Richard Mann, www.shootingtimes.com

989. Where to Balance Your Rifle

"A rifle that balances behind the front of the action will handle smoothly, and a rifle that balances forward of the action will hang on target better. A compromise is a rifle that balances very near the front of the action, provides good handling characteristics, and a reasonable steadiness on target. The balance point can be adjusted by adding weight to the front or rear of the stock or by shortening the barrel. A rifle's balance is critical for good offhand shooting."

—Richard Mann, www.shootingtimes.com

990. Breathe Right to Shoot Straight

The best time to squeeze the trigger is at the end of a natural exhale, when you've expelled all the breath from your lungs. The U.S. Army's manual on basic rifle marksmanship describes this as follows: "There is a moment of natural respiratory pause while breathing when most of the air has been exhaled from the lungs and before inhaling. Breathing should stop after most of the air has been exhaled during the normal breathing cycle. The shot must be fired before the soldier [or in this case, the hunter] feels any discomfort."

991. Where to Squeeze a Trigger

According to the U.S. Army's manual on basic rifle marksmanship, "The trigger finger (index finger on the firing hand) [should be] placed on the trigger between the first joint and the tip of the finger (not the extreme end) and adjusted depending on hand size, grip, and so on. The trigger finger must squeeze the trigger to the rear so the hammer falls without disturbing the lay of the rifle."

992. Make Scope Covers out of Inner Tubes

"You can cut your own scope covers from used inner tubes. The fit of a pickup-truck tube is about right for most big game scopes. For small scopes, use a smaller tube."

—Bob Gilsvik, *The Guide to Good Cheap Hunting*, Stein & Day, 1978

993. Quickly Inspect Your Rifle Barrel in the Field

"Insert a Q-Tip into your barrel . . . and it will reflect enough light so that you can get a real good look at the last half inch of rifling and the crown of your barrel. In most cases you'll find that this works much better than a flashlight. This is a good way to judge approximately how well you are cleaning your barrel when you're at the range. It's also the best way to examine your barrel when you're in the field."

—Larry Willis, www.larrywillis.com

994. When Your Barrel Heats Up

"How hot is too hot? Rifles vary in their tolerance for heat, but as a rule of thumb, if you can't grasp your barrel in a manly handshake and hold on, you've gone too far."

—David E. Petzal, "When You're Hot, You're Hot," www.fieldandstream.com

995. Practice on a Moving Target

You can practice shooting at moving targets by sticking a sheet of cardboard into the center of an old car or truck tire, tacking a target to the cardboard, then asking a partner let it go at the top of a hill so that it rolls and bounces its way down to the bottom. Make sure your partner is sheltered behind cover adequate to stop a stray bullet, however. If such cover is not available, do not use this method.

996. Is Your Rifle Accurate?

". . . A big-game rifle is perfectly fine if it puts three shots in an inch and a half at 100 yards. If it's a brush gun that will never be used past 100 yards, two inches is okay."

—David E. Petzal, "How to Diagnose What's Wrong with Your Inaccurate Rifle,"
www.fieldandstream.com

997. Why You Missed That Off-hand Shot

"Jerking the trigger is a major cause of missing. Don't do it! Train your finger with dry-firing exercises so that the pad of the finger presses straight back until the rifle fires at the optimum instant. This is called 'thinking' the trigger off."

—Jim Carmichael, "Make the Shot: Off-Hand," www.outdoorlife.com

998. The Proper Way to Grip a Rifle When Shooting Off-hand

"Hold the rifle firmly for good control but don't strangle it. The left hand should also hold the rifle firmly, but not so tightly that 'death grip tremors' are transferred through the stock. Crook your trigger finger so it touches no part of the rifle except the trigger."

—Jim Carmichael, "Make the Shot: Off-Hand," www.outdoorlife.com

999. Store Your Guns near Your Furnace

"If you plan to build a gun cabinet or gun rack in [your] basement . . . a good location is close to a gas furnace. The flow of warm air in winter will help keep your firearms from rusting. In summer the slight heat from the pilot light will help keep the weapons dry in what might otherwise be a damp environment."

—Bob Gilsvik, *The Guide to Good Cheap Hunting,* Stein and Day, 1978

1,000. The Problem with Muzzle Blast

Many hunters think recoil is the reason they flinch when shooting their rifles, and spend lots of time and money figuring out ways to reduce it. But muzzle blast—the sound a rifle makes when it is fired—is the primary cause of most misses, especially for hunters using smaller calibers. You can handle the kick if you conquer the noise. Save your money and wear good ear protection while shooting your rifle at the range, and you'll become a more confident and accurate shooter.

1,001. Zero Your Rifle in the Field after Traveling

Always check the accuracy of your rifle if you've had to travel any distance before hunting with it. Changes in temperature and humidity can cause your stock to swell and your cartridges to behave differently than they did at the range before you left. Spend the time to zero it at the place you'll be hunting and you'll eliminate these problems.